SLAVE LAWS
IN VIRGINIA

STUDIES IN THE LEGAL HISTORY OF THE SOUTH

Edited by Paul Finkelman and Kermit L. Hall

This series explores the ways in which law has affected the development of the southern United States and in turn the ways the history of the South has affected the development of American law. Volumes in the series focus on a specific aspect of the law, such as slave law or civil rights legislation, or on a broader topic of historical significance to the development of the legal system in the region, such as issues of constitutional history and of law and society, comparative analyses with other legal systems, and biographical studies of influential southern jurists and lawyers.

SLAVE LAWS
IN VIRGINIA

PHILIP J. SCHWARZ

THE UNIVERSITY OF GEORGIA PRESS

ATHENS AND LONDON

© 1996 by the University of Georgia Press

Athens, Georgia 30602

All rights reserved

Designed by Betty P. McDaniel

Set in 11/14 Walbaum

by Books International, Inc.

Printed and bound by Braun-Brumfield, Inc.

The paper in this book meets the guidelines for permanence and durability of the Committee on Production Guidelines for Book Longevity of the Council on Library Resources.

Printed in the United States of America

00 99 98 97 96   C   5 4 3 2 1

Library of Congress Cataloging in Publication Data

Schwarz, Philip J., 1940–

Slave laws in Virginia / Philip J. Schwarz.

p.   cm. — (Studies in the legal history of the South)

Includes bibliographical references and index.

ISBN 0-8203-1831-0 (alk. paper)

1. Slavery—Law and legislation—Virginia—History.   2. Slaves—

Legal status, laws, etc.—United States—History.   I. Title.

II. Series.

KFV2801.6.S55S386   1996

342.755'087—dc20

[347.550287]   96-1010

British Library Cataloging in Publication Data available

To the memory of my father,
Hamilton D. Schwarz,
1905–1992

7E.

CONTENTS

TABLES

PREFACE

My thinking about slavery has an identifiable genealogy. Uneasy with the faceless, nameless, and lifeless abstractions of some historical scholarship, yet aware of the analytic weakness of traditional narrative history, I was open to a new theoretical approach. In the foreword to Elizabeth Fox-Genovese and Eugene D. Genovese's *Fruits of Merchant Capital,* Harold Woodman comments that much of the "so-called 'new history' . . . ignores the larger political and social context in which these ['inarticulate'] people lived." He also remarks that "it is one of the ironies of modern historical scholarship that historians in rejecting as impossible the notion that they simply tell things as they happened and in recognizing instead the need for an organizing theory to give meaning to their work, so often turn to static theories from the social sciences."

A year's reading in selected works of anthropology sharpened my understanding that cultural interaction is at the heart of human history. However, growing up in the nuclear age, living in Virginia in an era of sometimes dramatic political change, prodded by articles such as Fox-Genovese and Genovese's "The Political Crisis of Social History" in *Fruits of Merchant Capital,* and spending more than a decade in research concerning the profoundly political relationship of master and slave, I remained convinced that the political dimension of slavery was as important as the cultural interaction experienced by owners and bondspeople. The heart of human history has at least two chambers, one cultural and one political. And those chambers are connected.

A discussion of the law of slavery thus must concentrate on the cultural and political interaction of African Virginians and European Virginians to paint a picture of the inner workings of slave societies. It must also pay close attention to the development, whether positive or negative, of slave laws as products of that cultural and political interaction. Virginia is but one such society, yet an excellent one to study because of the longevity of the institution there and the numbers of people involved in it. Valuable comparative studies of slavery have begun to appear; still more are needed. I regard it as equally important to capture the interactive or integrationist aspect of the history of slavery, however, and so I have chosen to confine myself here to "internal historical migration." My next project, a study of people who left Virginia to avoid slavery, will concentrate on "external historical migration."

These essays make my theoretical base clear. It is simple but hardly simplistic. Historical change derives from human interaction as much as from the cycles of human life. The Introduction sketches my general theme of the development of the law of slavery. Chapter 1, "'Lawlessness,'" argues that because people bring their experience of former interactions to new settings, Africans probably carried their understanding of various African judicial institutions into their interaction and confrontation with Virginian slaveholders.

Once we have comprehended the broad outlines of the role the law of slavery played in the interaction of masters and slaves in Virginia, we can look at the impact of the developing law on human beings. Chapter 2, "Thomas Jefferson and the Law of Slavery," considers the experience of one human being—and an extraordinary human being at that—with slave laws, which affected his relationship with several hundred people of African descent whose destinies were bound up with his. More than one thousand people are the focus of chapter 3, "Slaves and Capital Punishment in Virginia," an examination of a legal response to the behavior of slaves and to the changing white perception of that behavior. A similar process figures in chapter 4, "The Transportation of Slaves from Virginia, 1800–1865," which is complementary to chapter 3. In chapter 5, "'The Full and Perfect Enforcement of Our Rights': Fugitive Slaves and the Laws of Virginia," I try to show that even those black Virginians who took the obvious route away from slavery—that is, escaping from the state—still helped to provoke extensive development of the law even after they were long gone. Using the history of one particularly large and extended family of former slaves, the Conclusion suggests what aspects of the legal relationship between former slaves and former masters shaped their interaction after Appomattox and the apparent death of the law of slavery.

Anyone who has read my previous study, *Twice Condemned: Slaves and the Criminal Laws of Virginia, 1705–1865* (1988), recognizes another genealogical line of this book. Most of the essays are by-products of research for *Twice Condemned.* Chapters 1–3 and 5 are in print for the first time, however. I have found research possibilities in the history of bondage in Virginia to be extraordinarily rich. Since I began work on *Twice Condemned* in the mid-1970s, more and more historians have learned just how seemingly inexhaustible are the resources of the Library of Virginia (formerly the Virginia State Library and Archives), the Virginia Historical Society, and other repositories in the state. My debt to these institutions, to the many people who make them work, and to dozens of fellow historians has become so great that I cannot fit any suitable expression of it into the confines of even several pages. I hope, then, that this book will be accepted as one token of my gratitude for my association of great length with all of these people—even though I cannot mention each one of them.

I must specifically mention Norrece T. Jones Jr. and James T. Moore, my colleagues in the Department of History at Virginia Commonwealth University, because of our many conversations

about this book and their reading of parts of it. A. Gregg Roeber
offered valuable suggestions about a somewhat different version of
the Introduction; Daniel C. Littlefield and T. J. Davis commented
with insight on versions of chapter 1; and Lucia C. Stanton, Warren Billings, Michael McGiffert, and participants in the Institute
of Early American History and Culture Colloquium discussed
earlier drafts of chapter 2. I am also indebted to Edward L. Ayers
and Juliet E. K. Walker for their comments, criticisms, and suggestions concerning chapter 3, and to John B. Boles, Pauline Maier,
and Paul Keve for criticisms and suggestions concerning chapter 4.
Stanley Engerman generously read the entire manuscript and
made many worthwhile suggestions. Several anonymous review-
ers deserve my appreciation as well. Melvin I. Urofsky and Peter
Hoffer provided important encouragement and direction at a
crucial stage of this book's preparation; Peter also commented
helpfully on the conference paper that contributed to the Introduction. Paul Finkelman and Kermit Hall have been excellent editors
of this new series, Studies in the Legal History of the South. Mal-
colm Call, Kelly Caudle, Angela Ray, and Cisley Owen at the University of Georgia Press have been mountain goats to this sheep's
ascent of the crags and peaks of publication. While they and others
certainly influenced the development of this book, I take the
blame as sole perpetrator.

SLAVE LAWS
IN VIRGINIA

INTRODUCTION

Lawmakers wrote the laws of slavery; judges and juries enforced or applied them, the former mostly in criminal cases and the latter primarily in civil cases. Slave owners also enforced their own rules, or customary laws. Who can argue with the simplicity and validity of these statements? They tell only part of the story of the law of slavery, however. It is unimaginable to write about labor law in the 1930s and 1940s without studying such figures as John L. Lewis, A. Philip Randolph, and Walter Reuther and with no treatment of the United Mine Workers, the CIO, the Brotherhood of Sleeping Car Porters, and the UAW. When did lawmakers and law enforcers react to nothing outside themselves? Lawmaking and law enforcement are both deductive and inductive. Any discussion of laws that leaves out those people whom laws are meant to benefit, control, or regulate is incomplete.

Yet how easy it once was to leave enslaved and free African Americans out of analyses of the laws of slavery. This denial of part of the history of slavery makes it possible to ignore many choices and decisions that perpetuated or transformed the institution and to obliterate from memory many changes in Virginia that strongly affected the nature of slave laws. Paying close attention to slaves is one of the hallmarks of the late twentieth-century upsurge of histories that deal with slavery. Building on the foundation of these pathbreaking studies, as well as on the superstructure of diverse histories of the law of slavery, I wish to explore several aspects of the process by which lawmakers and law enforcers in Virginia *responded* to slaves' behavior and to whites' perceptions of and assumptions about that behavior. Legalized lifetime bondage

1

was in force in Virginia for two centuries. So were the laws of slavery. Only a discussion of the context of legal choices concerning slavery, as well as of decisions made about slavery in light of the law, will adequately illuminate developments in the law of human bondage.

Once the entire era of slavery becomes the unit of study, nothing is more obvious than that the most important characteristic of the law of bondage—other than its unyielding support and defense of slavery—was change, the grist of the historian's mill. Throughout this book I seek to analyze the importance of diverse changes in the laws that upheld slavery in Virginia and changes in the context of lawmaking concerning slavery. If the laws of slavery could be changed, they could be adapted to changing circumstances. Change frequently resulted from the interaction of slaves and owners. By their customary as well as changing behavior, African Americans could have some influence on lawmaking; in their habits of rule and their responses to slaves' behavior, white Virginians played a crucial role in white legislators' crafting of statutes. This pattern of interactive change and adaptation began in the 1660s and continued for two centuries.

The age-old connection of force and violence with bondage was very real. Threatened or actual force and violence were the constants. Yet there still was room for laws to change. How could law alter an institution based on such elemental factors as force and violence? Close attention to the development of the law of slavery changes our perspective on the peculiar institution because it reveals the strong tension between often rational and predictable laws and irrational and unpredictable human emotions, motives, and behavior. Evidence concerning white brutality and black resistance leaves no doubt about the force and violence at the heart of bondage. Yet neither African Americans nor European Americans wanted to rely exclusively on coercion. Coercion was simply too dangerous and often self-defeating to be constant, even though it was often feared by both groups. The only solution to the dilemma of enforcing slavery without using "too much" force was to turn to the law. Reliance on the law could sometimes benefit slaves—at least temporarily. But economic behavior was as much involved in slavery as was personal action. Lawmakers also had to incorporate the law of human property into the law of property. Hence slave societies depended as much on law as on force and terror to perpetuate bondage. Similarly, enslaved Virginians could hardly rely exclusively on violence to protect themselves. So they changed their modes of coping, of resistance, and of attack. New laws were often efforts to respond to changes in slaves' behavior.

There was no ready-made blueprint for the development of the law of slavery. True, new slave societies could borrow from older ones, as when New World colonies borrowed from Roman law and when South Carolina drew on the experience of Barbados.[1] But South Carolina's evolution into a rice colony encouraged patterns of labor organization and property control that demanded variations on the slave law of the sugar colony of Barbados, just as Virginia's transformation into a tobacco colony and later its turn to mostly grain and cereal crop production changed its approach to indentured servitude and slavery. And economic change was by no means the only external force to shape the law of bondage.

Perhaps nothing more effectively evokes the tension at the heart of a slave society based on law than the phrase "a slave commonwealth." This expression yokes the reality of Virginia's social system, slavery, with the highest ideal of the Old Dominion's leaders, republican freedom. Edmund S. Morgan and Orlando Patterson have told us how those leaders held the opposites of slavery and freedom together in their brave new world.[2] One depended on the other to some degree, in the same way that the European aristocracy and rentier classes "fed" each other, or the way that English bishops and kings, at least before 1642, needed each other. "No bishops, no king," cried the royalists. "No slavery, no freedom" might have been the cry of the slaveholder. And nothing made this paradoxical social system, based on slavery and freedom, more palatable and supportable to its leaders than the law, which conferred political and social legitimacy on the only people—free whites—in a slave society who were allowed to lay claim to that valued attribute of freedom.

Concentration on statutes can make it rather easy to ignore the fact that lawgivers were by no means the only people who influenced the development of the law of bondage. Even though human interaction is the focus of historical studies, the history of slavery has too often been somewhat unifocal. The earliest writings concentrated on slave owners' thinking or behavior; by the 1940s and 1950s the most innovative work shifted attention to enslaved people as victims; and more recently, historians have tried to understand "the world the slaves made." As David Levering Lewis has remarked, "Now that the specialty has come of age," it may be time to promote "a racial integration conception" of the history of slavery. "Without comparison and integration," Lewis continues, "historians must inevitably stray into byways of interpretation." Lewis cites Mechal Sobel's *The World They Made Together* as an example of the integrationist conception that he advocates.[3]

Sobel's book is an exciting but troubling attempt to explore the influence of African American thought and behavior on European Americans. It is exciting because it breaks new ground; it is troubling because Sobel's evidence is sometimes thin and circumstantial. While most of the chapters in this book are based, I hope, on a combination of extensive and strong evidence, some, such as chapter 1, occasionally share with Sobel's *World They Made Together* a reliance on sketchy evidence and speculative interpretation. I have included the latter kind of work because I share with Lewis, Sobel, and other scholars the wish to change our perspective as historians on the interaction involved in the history of slavery. Bondage was an institution to be sure, but it was also a relationship among people, however unequal, distorted, exploitative, corrupting, and destructive of the best human qualities it often was. We need to know more about all of the people involved in this relationship.

I cannot confine myself to "history from the bottom up," like a cave explorer who looks down at the stalagmites and ignores the stalactites. I must investigate both "history from the top down" and "history from the bottom up." It is therefore most useful to analyze the intersection or interaction of the behavior of owners and of the enslaved. Among the many ways to analyze this interaction is to focus on the manner in which white and black Virginians influenced developments in the law of slavery.

The customary law of slavery is useful as the basis for constructing a model of the interrelationship between masters' and slaves' behavior and the changing law of slavery. Most of James Curtis Ballagh's nearly forgotten 147-page *History of Slavery in Virginia* (1902) is a chapter entitled "The Development of Slavery," which begins with Ballagh's discussion of theoretical matters.[4] First comes the creation of legal legitimacy: "The creation of legal status is dependent locally upon either customary or statutory law, and in the case of organized society usually upon both. It is the result of development rather than of a single specific act." Even more essential to a model for the interrelationship between masters' and slaves' behavior and the law of slavery is Ballagh's later statement that the "addition or modification of some essential incident . . . may at any time involve such important consequences and differences in legal relations as to justify the creation in terms of law of a new status marking the rise of a new institution which, historically, is but a part of a previous institutional growth."[5] Ballagh's scientistic, legalistic language reveals his institutional bias: once passed, laws possessed an immutable character, independent of the biases and ideologies of those who wrote them. Yet Ballagh still understood the developmental relationship between custom and laws.

More recent writers on the subject of customary law, like writers on statutory law, point out that laws result from what people in particular social and historical contexts think about human behavior.[6] The history of law is not, they insist, the analysis of concrete, immutable laws that exist independent of time and space. Ballagh's theoretical construct reveals that he thought quite the opposite—that laws live unto themselves. Even his explanation of the laws and conditions of slavery demonstrates his time-bound ideology.[7] Remembering this weakness in his analysis, we can still employ his model's emphasis on the development of laws. This book concentrates on the developmental relationship between slave laws and all the people who influenced their nature.

The most satisfactory method of placing the slave laws into what Jeffrey Crow has called "the social, political, and economic context in which they were formulated, amended, and revised," and of showing the role both masters and enslaved people played in this process, is to follow the causal chain that connected customs, behavior, and statutes.[8] Some writers on the law of slavery have already paid attention to "the social, political, and economic context." Thomas D. Morris, for example, is well aware of the impact of the circumstances of slave labor on lawmaking concerning mortgages. His article on slave torts also reflects his understanding of context. He is certainly not alone. The writings of Andrew Fede, A. Leon Higginbotham Jr., Michael Stephen Hindus, A. E. Keir Nash, Mark V. Tushnet, and others all follow the emphasis of late twentieth-century historiography on social, economic, and political factors in the making and administration of legal codes.[9]

The criminal law shows well the special social, political, and economic factors involved in the law of slavery. I have discussed elsewhere the cycle of slaves' behavior, slave owners' lawmaking, and criminal court action.[10] Between 1705 and 1865 the broad outlines of the cycle show some African Americans' search for weapons to use against certain white authorities. For example, 1748 legislation concerning poisoning reflected black behavior as well as white fear. Between 1740 and 1784 poisoning and the illegal administration of medicine were prosecuted in the Old Dominion's slave courts more often than any other offense except burglary. Yet between 1785 and 1831 prosecutions for violent murder and conspiracy and insurrection predominated. The decisions of the judiciary were harsh. During those nearly fifty years, more than seventy black Virginians met their deaths on the gallows because of conspiracy and insurrection convictions. The making or revision, and perhaps the impact, of statutes concerning conspiracy and insurrection during those years were significant. An abrupt drop in insurrection convictions followed during the antebellum period. Instead, arson started to spread, becoming, appropriately enough, the most feared and suspected response of nearby blacks to John Brown's Harpers Ferry Raid of 1859. Once again, lawmakers and judges worked to keep pace with perceived behavior.

How do we connect Ballagh's method of analyzing developments in the law of slavery to cycles of slaves' actual or suspected behavior and court decisions or statutes? An essential component of my model is the influence of customary law on statutory law. Such factors as emergencies, public opinion, prejudices, fears, preconceptions, special agendas, ideology, and even mental limitations affect lawmakers' work. But most lawmakers also have an eye to what it is possible or practical to do. A supposedly pure law of slavery would be absolute and immutable. The actual law of slavery was flexible and changed constantly. Once again, we already know that customs are inherently evolutionary and that the writing of statutes often, although certainly not always, follows custom. Historians of the peculiar institution must examine the customs of slaveholders as well as the customs of their human property when tracing influences on lawmaking in slave societies. My model is a hybrid or blend of Ballagh's theory of the temporal precedence of customary law, of Crow's and other authors' strictures concerning the socioeconomic and political context of lawmaking, and the suggestion that blacks in bondage, as well as slaveholders, influenced lawmaking.

Could slaves have any impact on civil law? This is admittedly a murky area. There is some reason to look for light, however. For example, Suzanne Lebsock maintains that the wills made by white women in Petersburg, Virginia, show they were "kinder to their slaves than were men" and "more likely to set their slaves free." Women were more alert than men to individuals and to special cases, she concludes.[11] The appropriate question to ask here is whether other documents show that individuals in bondage were active participants in the process of attracting white women's special attention. Similarly, how did black families bring pressure on owners concerning the planned division of estates? We also need to know how black family formation related to legal choices concerning whites' inheritance of slaves.

We must remain quite cautious about another missing component in the historical analysis of the law of slavery. We have only the most primitive notions of how African American slaves resolved disputes among themselves without the intervention of masters. It is quite possible that slave owners, like European colonial administrators in Africa and Asia, customarily accepted some methods of conflict resolution among slaves and rejected others, thus incorporating certain aspects of slaves' customary law into plantation customary law.[12] If slave owners were ignorant of or badly misunderstood some methods of conflict resolution on which slaves relied, they consequently denied themselves the economical reliance on slaves to manage their own disputes and instead intervened in a fundamentally disruptive fashion. Such intervention was based, as might be expected, on the owner's claim to absolute power, so there was little political incentive to question the disruptive method of settling arguments among slaves. Saving time and energy at the cost of sacrificing authority would appear to masters to be a poor and dangerous trade-off.[13]

Owners' claim of absolute authority is both a well-known and an inadequately understood aspect of the law of slavery. In the late twentieth century some are quite ready to argue that even though the form of slavery was absolute, the actual relationship between master and slave was paternalistic and based on a system of reciprocal obligations, albeit obligations understood in conflicting ways by owners and bondspeople.[14] But such interpretations of the master-slave relationship risk two errors. The first possible error is the notion that statutes fully control society and are therefore a valid historical guide to past societies. That error has often been exposed. The second possible error has enjoyed considerably greater support. It is the argument that because it was impossible to make a person into a thing, to force a human being to be chattel, and even to make a slave society work in conformity to the logic of slave codes, then the driving force in any slave society was therefore the customary manner in which the enslavers and the enslaved worked out their relationship to each other. Thus, according to Eugene D. Genovese, "The slaveholders did not intend to enforce their severe legislation strictly and considered it a device to be reserved for periods of disquiet and especially for periods of rumored insurrectionary plots."[15]

Several hard realities of the legal system for Virginian slaves weaken the force of this argument. The first hard reality is the fact that *several* levels of force stood behind each law: private action, local sanctions, and state power, as well as federal power in the case of post-1789 insurrections. The second hard reality is that even though there were regular acquittals, reduced sentences, reprieves, and even pardons of slaves accused of capital crimes, the severity of punishment of convicted slaves was invariably higher than for convicted whites. Finally, the claim of the legal system to supreme power over bondspeople was of a different order than the claim of legal systems over other people. Consider Bernard Bailyn's judgment that the claims of British royal governments over colonists represented unsupported excess.[16] The claim of slave codes to absolute power over human chattel was excessive to be sure, but nevertheless usually well supported. The claim of state statutes over free people was less secure.

These qualifications by no means negate the contradictions and complexities within slave codes, particularly as they were interpreted by state judges. But the unambiguous message of the slave codes was domination of African American slaves by whites. Ideally the white elite would use no more force than was necessary to maintain their control over bondspeople, but that self-limitation could not be guaranteed. And they would be fully armed and ready to use *all* the force necessary to achieve the same end. That could be guaranteed, as the responses to Gabriel's Plot and Nat Turner's Revolt revealed. So it was only within a circumscribed area of private interaction that the enslavers and the enslaved followed conflicting understandings of their relationship. Whatever recognition of slaves' humanity was implicit in the criminal code and courts for slaves, and no matter how much influence some changes in slave behavior might have on lawmakers, the law of slavery as enforced primarily by slaveholders ensured that in certain areas of interaction governmental power would buttress white, slaveholder supremacy.

It is this ultimate domination of slaves through the law—and through the use of force authorized by law—that explains how amelioration of the laws could be part of the developmental process of the slave codes. Had any development in the positive law of slavery threatened slaveholders' ultimate power over slaves, legislators could hardly have regarded that development as beneficial to owners. From the 1790s through 1865 Old Dominion lawmakers increasingly transported and decreasingly executed slaves convicted of the most serious offenses. This was possible because the reduction of hangings of free people made almost any execution of a slave a more severe penalty than that experienced by almost any free convict, and because only slaves—with the exception of two dozen free African Americans in the mid-1820s—could be transported. Supremacy was maintained. But not all developments in the law of slavery during the same period were ameliorative. Free black slaveholding and slaves' escapes both presented a growing threat to white hegemony by the late antebellum period. Legislators responded with prohibitive or harsher laws.

It was at the nexus of public and private power over bondspeople that the law of slavery showed the most inconsistency and sometimes weakness. This crack in the edifice of slave law elicited diverse and changing responses. The manner in which Thomas Jefferson exercised private, and occasionally called on the aid of public, power over bondspeople reveals the paradox he and other slaveholders had to face. In order to be supreme, government intervened in the master-slave relationship. In other words, the slave code sometimes required compliance from the slaveholder as well as the slave. This was the same government that allowed great autonomy to slaveholders in much of their interaction with slaves. It should be no surprise at all that slaveholders like Jefferson sometimes found ways to circumvent such laws, even as they regularly conformed to other laws and advocated the passage of new laws. Here Ballagh's theory of the temporal precedence of customary law holds true. Virginia's government regularly renewed laws against self-hiring by slaves; owners such as Jefferson just as regularly allowed or encouraged some bondspeople to hire themselves. When as powerful an economic entity as the Tredegar Iron Works of Richmond consciously encouraged self-hiring and other freedoms among skilled slaves they sought to employ, neither negative public opinion, white laborers' protest, nor concerned city lawmakers successfully changed these practices in any substantial way.[17]

These few examples of the law of slavery in action show that if we keep the limitations of Ballagh's historical analysis in mind, we can gainfully employ his implicit model. What that developmental model fosters is precisely the study of the impact of human customs and behavior on the law that I seek to pursue. In the following chapters I will apply this model to the development of the law of slavery in Virginia, with an eye to the influence of all Virginians, both whites and African Americans, on the making of the law.

1
"LAWLESSNESS"

We know some ways that European laws influenced slave laws in Virginia. African laws could not directly affect Virginia's legal development, but did Africans held to slavery in the Old Dominion perceive slave laws through the prism of their native societies' legal systems? It is difficult to find evidence of just how African-born slaves in the Old Dominion may have applied their own legal traditions to their new situation in North American slavery. Nonetheless, it is still demonstrable that some of the societies from which they came had traditions that could have influenced their perception of the legal systems they encountered in North American bondage. We can see in full the intersection of the law of slavery, human behavior, and society only if we are aware of this possible "Old World" African influence on African American perceptions. If African institutions, assumptions, and traditions influenced North American slaves' perception of their owners' legal and judicial systems, then the legal encounters and confrontations between African Americans and European Americans were more complicated and subtle than we have thought.

AFRICAN SOURCES

In the late eighteenth century, Venture Smith, son of an African prince, former slave to three wealthy New Englanders, and successful free black entrepreneur on Long Island and in Connecticut, fell victim to a prominent merchant who knew how to manipulate the civil courts in his own behalf. The businessman had relied on legal delays to prevent Smith from collecting payment for services he knew he had performed but that the merchant unreasonably claimed Smith had not. This was highway robbery, Smith angrily declared, for which the laws of his father's African tribe would have condemned a man. "But Captain Hart was a *white gentleman*, and I a *poor African*, therefore it was *all right, and good enough for the black dog.*"[1] In his published attack upon his legal tormentor, Smith described an experience he possibly shared with other eighteenth-century African Americans. These involuntary immigrants and their descendants commonly suffered from racist injustice. They could easily conclude, as did Smith, that the mistreatment of people of African descent in American courts made those judicial bodies inferior to African ones.

Africans who first experienced racial slavery in seventeenth-century Virginia held certain assumptions about the limits of legal behavior. So did the Europeans who forced slavery on them. Both groups also handed down to their descendants certain ways of thinking about what it meant to be a slave or a slave owner. If there were fewer and fewer men and women of African birth in Virginia by 1778 and almost none by 1865, there were still many thousands of their descendants. We do not know exactly how much of their African legal heritage slaves were able to pass on to their communities, but it is reasonable to infer that their legal heritage did have some influence on their perceptions.

I intend this chapter to be speculative. My purpose is to influence the questions historians ask about the law of slavery. I intend to offer a plausible explanation of how transplanted Africans could have understood the slave courts and the laws of Virginia from the vantage point of African judicial institutions. Any attempt to do more than that would badly overreach the evidence I have. My concern is to focus primarily on the existence of precolonial African laws and judicial systems and only secondarily on their diverse forms and rationales. I welcome the efforts of Africanists to study the latter.

In any analysis of the frequently tense, hostile, and often violent relationship between the enslaved and the enslavers, there
must be some effort to trace the sources of African as well as European assumptions. This chapter provides a sketch of the diverse
practices and rationales of several West African criminal justice
systems.[2] The nature of racial slavery in Virginia was the most
important of the factors that shaped the confrontation between
slaves and owners in the Old Dominion's criminal courts, but West
African assumptions about crime may also have been important.
Africans enslaved in Virginia *developed* an understanding of the
colony's judicial system by hearsay or direct experience. To do so,
they had to start the process of comprehension on the basis of
what they already knew. What they knew, of course, were various West African assumptions about crime. When preserved—or,
in Robert Farris Thompson's brilliant term, *reblended*—these assumptions may have provided a significant number of slaves with
a standard of comparison. Those bondspeople could judge slave
laws and courts not only on the basis of their inherent character-
istics but also in relation to the laws and courts of their homelands.
The behavior of slaves who possessed a reblended consciousness
could at least indirectly influence many other slaves, whether consciously or not.[3]

White Europeans based their decisions about how to treat
Africans in court partly on previously held assumptions. Europeans made a pervasive and pernicious connection between black
Africans' origins and various kinds of "darkness," sin, and evil.[4]
The expectation that black Africans would not be able to conform
voluntarily to European, Christian norms of behavior helped to
generate, and later to rationalize, the conviction that the laws that
governed them could not possibly be based on their informed consent. A distorted view of the history of Africa and some ethnocentric accounts of contacts with West Africans reinforced the
widespread opinion that Africans were by and large "lawless" sav-

ages. "Lawless" has long been a crucial connotation of the adjective *savage*.[5] Regarding Africans and their descendants as savages, Europeans and their American descendants persistently accused Africans and African Americans of inherent criminality.[6] Besides being a crude, racist, ethnocentric smear, this notion was also an integral part of the Europeans' ideology of domination with which they justified, not just excused, the denial of many English rights to slaves taken from Africa. Distorted though the image of Africans was, it was still one basis of slaveholders' ideology.[7]

Enslaved Africans were not the only early Americans who had to adjust to the Anglo-American judiciary. Many colonists found modified or novel versions of the judicial institutions they had known in their countries of origin.[8] But few colonists faced courts that categorized them separately and invidiously. The experience of African American slaves was somewhat unique—comparable, perhaps, only to that of Native Americans. (European servants were at least regarded as Christians.) Because of this, it has been all too easy for historians to see African Americans only as victims of a judiciary intentionally weighted against slaves, as slaves, or against free blacks, as more black than free.[9] Such a perception ignores the active role played by slaves in defining their "place." Slaves who did nothing to whites were still perceived as African and often also as not Christian. But slaves who acted against whites inevitably provoked a response. Their behavior influenced slave owners' creation and modification of the criminal code and courts for slaves. Many slaves aggressively refused to accept their legal status as beings without wills. A significant number acted on the basis of that refusal. Some of those who had lived in Africa or who knew of their former societies' customary laws and courts had the opportunity to confront such slave societies as Virginia armed with knowledge of legal systems they valued. Africans held to slavery in the Old Dominion were neither "lawless savages" nor tabulae rasae on whom slaveholders could easily impose their social and legal values because of the absence of any preexisting, conflicting values.

The slaves' African origin and the facts of slavery itself do make African Americans' memory of their homelands' laws and courts somewhat difficult to uncover. The people involved in the diverse judicial institutions of West Africa left only the most minimal record of their activities. As a result, it is necessary to rely almost exclusively on "white sources," and this creates a problem of method. Yet the available seventeenth- and eighteenth-century European observations of West African legal and judicial systems contain a historically useful bias.[10] Europeans were quick to comment on those aspects of Africans' criminal laws and procedures that they thought resembled or contrasted with European practices. Such implicit and explicit comparisons—especially those that appear in different times and places—provide some measure, albeit imperfect, of the nature of Africans' experience. The evidence that survives in European descriptions of West Africa, from which traders wrested most American slaves, allows only a general overview of many groups' different experiences of laws and courts.[11] Another problem of method is that West African societies, and consequently West Africans' laws and judicial procedures, were not of one type. West Africans may have shared certain fundamental values, but that sharing by no means resulted in similar institutions. So this chapter must confine itself to recorded European observations of diverse West African laws and courts.[12]

This attempt to survey diverse African precolonial legal systems faces another problem of method. Interpretations of how Africans understood the law have either changed significantly or have been hotly disputed, particularly during the last twenty years.[13] It is not my purpose to prove the validity of any point of view in these historiographical disputes. So it is possible for me only to suggest patterns so as to demonstrate that many West African societies had

well-developed judicial techniques, however conceived or administered, for resolving disputes or punishing offenses against individuals or society. While the shape of precolonial African legal
systems is worth arguing about, the long-term existence of those
institutions is the salient fact for my discussion of transplanted
Africans' cultural and intellectual assumptions about American
slave societies' slave laws and courts.

My reliance on European observers' bias toward recognition of
what they perceived as familiar or unusual in African judicial
practices may preclude accurate analysis of those practices. The
Europeans may have seen what they wished to see rather than
what was there. This problem is very real, but it can be controlled
to some extent by maintaining the same focus on the existence
of precolonial African legal institutions as discussed above. Europeans were most likely to misperceive the social context and
meanings of practices; they might easily misconstrue important
details. But it is rather unlikely that they would miss the fact that
some sort of judicial action was taking place. Because it is the
existence of such practices that I wish to discuss, I feel confident
about cautious use of the European sources. Because of the wish to
demonstrate the existence rather than to analyze the diverse char-
acteristics of West African courts and laws, I have also not paid
special attention to gender-related differences in African law.

There remains the very difficult problem of how to "track"
African legal assumptions in Virginia. I have managed to achieve
only inferential tracing of such influences. Given my argument
for the existence of laws and judicial institutions in West Africa, I
have inferred that Africans who were forcibly brought to the New
World took many African legal assumptions with them. It is thus a
fair inference that involuntary African migrants to America were
not legal tabulae rasae. It is my hope that this chapter will spur
some historians of Africa and of American slave societies to search
for ways to track African legal assumptions in America.

JUDICIAL PRACTICES AND INSTITUTIONS IN WEST AFRICA

Village, district, religious, or royal courts were an integral part of the West African landscape. It is doubtful that adult Africans could have avoided at least vicarious knowledge of judicial systems that sometimes involved entire networks of kinship or that relied for their effectiveness on community participation and support. Moreover, those slaves who came from Muslim groups had witnessed or experienced the administration of a well-developed, comprehensive, written criminal code. Even though it originally came from external sources, it was no less important a part of the groups that had accepted it for hundreds of years before 1700 and that still revere Muslim legal systems today. It held in common with some other West African judicial systems its grounding in religious beliefs that sometimes assumed the power of gods, spirits, ancestors, priests, conjurers, or "root men" to punish evil deeds, especially those of people who threatened communities. While these various agents of divine or spiritual power served as enforcers of duties, rituals, and customs, they also could give ethical force to the laws and judicial institutions of West African social organisms.[14]

If conscious or unconscious "reblended" memories of African judicial systems survived in the African Virginian community, they probably lacked unity. They apparently lacked unity in West Africa as well. Such judicial systems, of course, could hardly have been unified in the environment of racial slavery if they had not been unified in Africa. Instead, the African Virginian experience was likely to be eclectic and adaptive, drawing upon certain assumptions in order to deal with new institutions. Some legal anthropologists have posited a fundamental structural unity in African law, but they have not claimed coherence for the practical, institutional arrangements contingent upon the underlying structure.[15] Moreover, there was no published or otherwise promulgated

African jurisprudence as such. Yet West African societies from which the slavers snatched their involuntary products did often emphasize the primacy of reciprocal community obligations and the importance of solidarity among relatives. Variations in how each society applied these assumptions abounded, but the assumptions appear regularly in West Africa. When some West African governmental authorities defined criminal behavior, therefore, they gave special consideration to the impact that certain actions had on West African networks of kinship. At the same time they, like many courts around the world, allowed individuals to defend their own interests. Methods of conflict resolution as well as sentences for criminal offenders could involve the parties' or the defendants' immediate or extended families. Court procedure might be confined to the sponsorship of kinship arbitration, or it might be subjected to the review authority of local or even royal judges.

The memory of African judicial institutions did not have to be of static forms. While "immigrant" slaves had to experience rapid change from African to American legal and court systems, their experience with modifications of the African judiciary might have prepared them for their adaptive American experience. The international slave trade subjected certain West African societies to devastating cultural shocks that corrupted some leaders and destroyed the ordinary bonds of several societies.[16] Thus some slaves who came to Virginia had already suffered under legal systems that the slave trade had distorted. People from coastal areas or from regions recently dominated by slave traders or their African allies would have been more vulnerable to such corrupted systems. In addition, the judicial systems of those societies that operated under customary law also underwent dramatic transformations, occasionally as the result of warfare or natural disaster.[17]

Those people whom African judicial institutions treated unjustly found themselves in an ambivalent position. Scattered Africans may even have had bitter recollections of the judicial processes of their homelands, leaving them wary of any court. African criminal courts bore responsibility for the initial enslavement of a significant minority of Africans.[18] Before the European intrusion as well as afterward, tribunals enslaved Africans as the punishment for such offenses as adultery, murder, some kinds of theft, and even witchcraft.[19] Slavery in some African societies was sufficiently harsh to be met with resistance. But there were less harsh forms of African bondage. Some forms reduced the status of an African but might last for a only a short term and might not cause displacement, family separation, or suffering under severe physical conditions.[20] Moreover, even when slavery in Africa was based on ethnic and religious differences, it was never racial slavery. The growth of the slave market in the Western Hemisphere not only meant that condemnation to slavery as a punishment for criminal offenses would guarantee exile, division of families, wrenching cultural shock, and all the terrifying prospects of the Middle Passage, but it also increased the chance that some corrupt African judges would deliver more guilty verdicts and would sentence more offenders to slavery in order to profit. Those Africans whose polities' judicial processes had ultimately condemned them to American slavery may very well have been unable to fall back on their memory of West African institutions as a standard against which to measure the American judiciary.

In spite of damaging foreign intervention, corrupting internal factors, and local variations, some common features do appear in the customary laws with which many West Africans were familiar. The classification of major crimes shows the greatest unity. As might be expected, West Africans regarded murder as a heinous crime. Yet several important groups allowed private financial settlement of murder cases on the assumption that homicide violated reciprocal obligations. Some societies allowed authority figures within systems of kinship to settle homicide cases. There was a very good reason for letting private parties do what Europeans and their descendants might call society's work. Because society revolved around the structure of familial obligations and ancestral, patriarchal, or matriarchal society, intra- or interfamilial conflict resolution often worked best.

Some of the same societies that allowed private settlement of homicide cases required judicial disposition of others. Local, district, royal, or imperial authorities would intervene in these cases. The same kinds of leaders regularly heard and determined murder cases elsewhere, but even they might recognize the primacy of kinship by awarding compensation to the victim's family and by imposing sentences of one kind or another on the convicted murderer's near relations. Still other varieties of judicial officers would impose more direct punishments on persons convicted of homicide. As in many other societies, on the assumption that taking a life injured or offended society, the state, the king, or the emperor as much or more than it affected victims or their relations, authorities would fine, corporally punish, or execute such offenders.

West African leaders reacted to major property crimes in the same diverse ways they dealt with murder and other crimes against persons. Property assumed great importance in West African customary law; definitions of crime inevitably included offenses involving property. Theft could be a matter that the thief and victim would settle or that their relatives would arbitrate. In the more serious cases—however variably seriousness would be defined—judicial authorities could detect and punish the offender against property. Because the idea of compensation proved to be more germane to property crimes than to personal crimes, replacement and fines often resolved such criminal cases. Yet certain authorities regarded stealing as so reprehensible and so damaging to society that they regularly sentenced thieves to banishment, enslavement, or execution. Courts based on Muslim law could exact equally harsh penalties.

West African customary law uniformly recognized adultery as a serious crime; leaders resorted to a great variety of punishments to try to control it. It is no wonder that an offense against marriage, a most essential relationship in a society based on kinship solidarity, should have been so generally criminalized and yet handled with such diverse techniques. For adultery with royal or noble wives, those societies that organized themselves as states under chiefs, kings, or emperors decreed the harshest—indeed, sometimes the most brutal, by twentieth-century standards—of all West African punishments observed by Europeans. If the offending individuals did not suffer enslavement or quick execution for their insult to royalty or the allies of royalty, they reportedly would occasionally undergo gruesome tortures before being forced to die a slow death. Europeans probably understood this kind of punishment as easily as West Africans would have comprehended the terrifying manner in which Europeans executed regicides or traitors. In societies whose integrity depended on hierarchically arranged obligations of kinship, adultery with a royal or noble wife resembled regicide because of the offense it gave to royal authority.[21]

Similarly, because of adultery's grave implications for the viability and legitimacy of kinship, adulterers could be punished with enslavement. The offenders or their relatives could pay compensation to the victims or their kin, but the rate of compensation for adultery could be so high as to increase the chance of enslavement for this offense. Officers or even victims could always enslave convicted criminals who could not pay a fine or compensation. Moreover, some groups required enslavement as the regular punishment for adultery. One could, however, avoid slavery by supplying a substitute from one's family through purchase or by coercion. Naturally, members of elites had a much better chance of escaping enslavement as a sentence for adultery.

As West Africans dealt with the judicial institutions of their polities, they could enjoy some aspects of what European Americans call the due process of law. Besides fairness, mercy, and efficacy, among the key features of due process are clear definitions of crimes, regularized procedures for determining innocence or guilt, and a uniform set of punishments. The West African population could have had a fairly clear idea of the major criminal offenses in their societies. Oral tradition or the written Muslim code, regular prosecutions in numerous villages, and formal trials of offenders in higher courts could have assured widespread understanding of what constituted a crime. West Africans might have known from exactly the same sources that certain punishments resulted from conviction for certain crimes. It is, of course, equally true that West Africans could have experienced a complete denial of due process in spite of the judicial standards they held. Denials of justice resulted from the usual human weaknesses and evil motivations. The practice of selling West African criminals to European slave traders undoubtedly excited contempt when it did not provoke fear.

In traditional judicial processes, the seriousness of the offense could influence the formality and level of the court that dealt with the offender. On the village level of some societies, headmen extended their role as arbiters of "civil cases" to cover a wide variety of criminal cases. As locus of village authority, the headman could intervene in violent or otherwise injurious conflicts to protect the aggrieved, maintain peace, restore stolen property to its owner, provide compensation to the wronged party, and protect the community interest. Depending on village organization, responsibility for hearing testimony, weighing it in the balance, delivering a verdict, and ordering punishment or fines lay with an individual headman, a council of headmen, a headman with advisers, a court in dialogue with assembled residents, or some other combination of these.

West African criminal suspects could also stand trial before higher and more powerful courts. In some societies district or centralized tribunals oversaw prosecution of certain categories of crime. A person accused of a more serious crime, such as murder, might have to appear before a district court. District officers appropriately heard cases that involved people from separate villages. Treason against the state or offenses touching upon the polity's central authority fell within the province of royal or imperial courts. Some societies even allowed appeals from lower to higher courts. A powerful, yet most obscure, West African judicial body was the secret society, which conceivably strayed from due process. It is not clear just when the secret societies claimed jurisdiction, but some of them may have held great significance for those people destined to be slaves in North America. The meager descriptions of the courts held by a few of these organizations make them sound somewhat like the quasi-judicial activities of urban New England slaves during "Negro Election Day." The correspondence may be accidental, but "Negro Election Day" warrants investigation as a possible African American adaptation of a West African institution.[22]

Strict rules of behavior often governed public courts. Formality increased as the level of the court rose, yet procedure could be as sacred in a headman's village court as in a royal court. What Westerners would call professionalization, or professional specialization, existed in many tribunals but hardly figured in others. For instance, professional advocates did act in the name of clients in a minority of West African courts. Elsewhere, time-honored regulations were supposed to protect the right of the accused and of witnesses to present their best case. Some authorities even threatened execution for the mere interruption of testimony.[23] At times West African courts countenanced trial by ordeal when they could not determine guilt or innocence on the basis of available evidence. Such practices fell short of today's standards of due process, especially in the case of tests that could easily prove "guilt" in order to ensure revenue for authorities. For example, European observers sometimes disparaged those groups that subjected defendants to swimming as a means of deciding cases. People were often such good swimmers that they were bound to float and survive, forcing them to pay a fine. Other kinds of trial by ordeal abounded. Frequently the innocent would float, unlike Europeans suspected of being witches; the guilty would not survive doses of poison; and convincing rituals would expose previously hidden malefactors. Europeans also commented on one technique of settling arguments that looked very much like dueling.[24]

West African judicial punishments resembled those used around the world in the seventeenth and eighteenth centuries. Sources contain descriptions of several punishments that West Africans hoped would quell crime or secure retribution against offenders. They included fines, whipping, chaining, holding in irons, placing in "stocks," banishment, "bills of attainder," summary execution, burning to death, the equivalent of drawing and quartering, hanging in chains, the placing of heads on poles in public places, and combinations of or variations on all of these. Indeed, these particular penalties would stand out for Europeans because the courts of their home countries had applied them to criminals. The European experience of servitude as a criminal sanction made condemnation of Africans to slavery somewhat comprehensible. European tribunals sentenced fellow Europeans to servitude before the eighteenth century, as did British American courts into that century.[25]

West Africans in the Middle Passage carried knowledge of their societies' criminal law and judicial procedures. They ordinarily knew little or nothing about the legal and court systems of the European colonies to which they sailed. But those people who had lived in coastal African towns had already had some encounters with Europeans. A handful of West Africans in the areas under the jurisdiction of slave trading companies had already appeared in criminal cases before European factors or other officers.

Others had learned from long contact with transplanted, some-times rootless, and generally ethnocentric Europeans an unwrit-ten rule—"Us against them"—that would assume the greatest importance for many African American slaves. Even those Afri-cans who chose to deal with Europeans could suffer from cultural confusion when they found themselves as the degraded objects of the European assumption of cultural and racial superiority. How much worse it could be for the great majority of West Africans who interacted with Europeans unwillingly.[26]

At least it was possible in the West African setting for Afri-cans as well as Europeans to express openly their suspicion of each other based on ethnic pride as well as on a history of unsatisfac-tory encounters. Hostile Europeans almost unanimously accused West Africans of addiction to stealing, lying, and other "perfidy," many of them unwittingly revealing that Africans had singled out Europeans as targets for attacks rather than members of their own societies.[27] In the trading of insults, some Africans managed to show that their anti-European sentiments competed equally with the anti-African attitudes of resident whites. The testimony of the Reverend John Newton, a famous abolitionist who had commanded a slaver in the 1750s, illustrates how anti-European suspicion could influence Africans' attitudes toward European jus-tice. According to Newton, when he charged Africans with some kind of misbehavior, those who cleared themselves would ask him "with an air of disdain, 'What! Do you think I am a white man?'" To say the least, Europeans' successful capture, or "manstealing," of West Africans for the Atlantic slave trade could only have rein-forced hostility toward European injustice.[28]

ADAPTATION TO VIRGINIA

In Virginia, assertive "new Negroes," as whites called recent ar-rivals, could quickly come into contact with the hierarchy of slave

27

control that the Old Dominion's leaders had developed level by level in the seventeenth and eighteenth centuries. Slaves who violated plantation rules learned that owners and overseers constituted a novel kind of local "headman" who acted on the basis of what we might call the unwritten, customary law of plantations.[29] The most threatening slaves would often end up in the European Virginian courts. African Virginians would then have to accustom themselves to a new set of symbols of judicial authority, but not to the idea that judges would rely on such symbols to buttress their position. Court sessions themselves could hardly have been significantly more mysterious to "new Negroes" than they were to many a white indentured servant who could not distinguish between a writ and a true bill. Because justices directed court sessions verbally and expected only spoken responses from defendants, the most important actions of a trial would not have been beyond the capacity of illiterate slaves to follow. Justices would have made certain of that; otherwise there was less justification for holding a public trial that took away a slave's work time from her or his master. Only the most recent arrivals suffered from the handicap of understanding no English.[30]

Trial by a jury of one's peers was not open to African Virginian slaves after 1692. That may only have constituted a deprivation rather than a loss, because a good many Virginians of diverse origins had never enjoyed trial by jury in the seventeenth century. But legislation of 1692 guaranteed that only white slave owners and their supporters judged slave defendants. Those African "immigrants" accustomed to judicial procedures based on communal values in their homelands could experience a significant loss of familiar procedures when subjected to the authority of slave courts. No longer could they expect to hear the judgments or openly expressed opinions of the groups of which they had been an integral part. Instead they had to submit to the censure of powerful individuals who forcibly held Africans in bondage and tried some of them in segregated courts.

It was racial slavery that required the biggest adjustment on the part of new slaves in Virginia. The sharpest discrepancy between West African customary law and the slave code of the Old Dominion painfully underscores this fact. The colony's slave code rested on a distorted, partial definition of community and perpetuated the violation of the integrity of the family. Whites defined community through white dominion, trying to render slaves subservient members of artificial families headed by white patriarchs.[31] The economic and legal exigencies of slavery ensured that Virginia's statutes could provide absolutely no protection for slaves' marriage or family ties. Nor would white governmental authorities proscribe or punish adultery between owners and slaves or among slaves as a crime. While some people, such as those beset by objectionable spouses, might benefit from the latitude that this lack of legal sanctions against adultery granted to them, others thereby suffered more vulnerability to becoming the "aggrieved party" in an adulterous situation.[32]

Could involuntarily transplanted West Africans have regarded the white criminal justice system for bondspeople as anything but a travesty, especially in comparison with the traditional West African judicial processes? Those West Africans whom corrupt African courts had falsely convicted in order to meet the colonial demand for slaves may have been at best confused and at the worst budding anarchists. On the other hand, they may have developed a cynicism about judicial institutions that would be a form of preparation for some slave courts. The situation was not always simple, however. Compare the cases of West Africans subjected to very harsh, even capital, punishments for property offenses and African Americans in the nineteenth century at least being subjected to less stringent punishments than Africans of the same era. Yet in some situations they had to regard the slave courts as a travesty of justice. Slaves who never had the African experience could reject white justice on the basis of their present experience, but that involved a learning process. Virginia's "new Negroes" often had a basis for denying the legitimacy of slave courts the moment they first stepped on British American soil.

Lacking testimony from those African Virginians in the best position to know exactly how West African legal and judicial assumptions and values influenced their many confrontations with European Virginians, we must settle for a conjectural model of the process of blending and confrontation that made the history of North America's earliest slave society. The first element in this speculative model is the blending of diverse West African values in the context of New World interaction of African Virginians with one another. The second element is the refraction of the blended West African legal and judicial values necessitated by the hard facts of slavery in Virginia.[33] A construct of Creole values may have resulted from the many confrontations, private and public, manageable or intolerable, in which African Virginians and European Virginians participated. Certain slaves may have been able to transmit these values both laterally within their communities and forward into future generations of slaves. Always influencing the process were the many social, economic, and political changes in both the slave and white communities.

This conjectural model derives in part from anthropological studies of the manner in which distinct national, ethnic, or racial groups define the boundaries that separate them. The formation of boundaries often begins in the way members of one group perceive members of another.[34] The classic instance of this is racial identification. The person who is regarded as white in one Caribbean society can be regarded as colored in another. Considerations of class, status, and power certainly influence the delineation of cultural barriers as well.[35]

Indeed, racial slavery as it developed in Virginia is an excellent example of how perceptions of one group by another—combined with ongoing delineation of class, status, and power—controlled the formation of cultural boundaries in that slave society. The process involved racist perceptions by whites of black Africans

and African Americans, the customary law of slavery by which
slave owners attempted to control their relationship with slaves on
the plantations, and the statutory law of race and slavery that the
white leaders of slave societies formulated in order to reinforce
their customary law and to create a final line of defense against
black slaves' encroachments against whites' boundaries. As more
and more historians have recognized, especially when they have
depended on anthropological models in designing their research
strategies, it was slaves' perceptions of whites as well as slaves' customary laws, grounded in their sense of their own communities
and related to considerations of class, status, and power within
both their communities and the larger slave societies of which
they were part, that determined the nature of cultural and political boundaries in slave societies.[36]

There is a window through which historians can view the
major dimensions of this process. Keeping in mind the assumptions of Africans as suggested by the legal and judicial history
of their homelands and the assumptions of European Virginians
as revealed in their history, it is possible to see slave and white
leaders trying either to impose their assumptions on each other
or else negotiating, reaching impasses, or fighting in open com-
bat. Some of these people knew better than others what was
happening; others merely reacted to a process that the more
knowledgeable had created and perpetuated. Either way, the result was the creation by white Virginians of slave codes and courts
in which they tried to control the behavior of those slaves who
chose to mount the greatest challenges to whites' authority or control. Each trial based on the slave code and held in the slave courts
is a window on this kind of interaction between some whites and
slaves that historians need. Important as were the African and
African Virginian assumptions, it was their interaction with the
conflicting assumptions of slave-owning authorities in the formal
environment of the courtroom that made the window available
to us.

Even though we cannot trace the exact genealogy of African Virginian ethical values, the foregoing discussion of West African experiences with and values concerning the law and the courts reinforces the view that slave resistance was more than a visceral reaction. Transplanted Africans could not re-create Africa in Virginia, but they could attempt to make the values they learned in or inherited from Africa prevail in Virginia. If that attempt forced them into conflict with white Virginians, then their behavior could not possibly be a mere reaction. Instead it was part of the ongoing interaction between African Americans and European Americans from the seventeenth century onward.[37]

CUSTOMARY LAW

African Americans held to slavery in Virginia obviously could not transfer the laws and judicial institutions of their homelands to the New World. But the story of their effort to follow their own values may go beyond their arrival at Virginia plantations and their early years in the Old Dominion. That is because of the possibility that slaves developed their own *customary* law. Verbally transmitted, "customary" laws had the greatest probability of gaining operative acceptance within the slave community. The customary laws of the slave community were those rules to which slaves commonly attempted to bind themselves, as opposed to those regulations to which masters tried to force slaves' conformity. Legal anthropologists and historians have recognized the primacy of customary law in preliterate or largely illiterate societies. The ancestors of the Africans and Europeans who lived in North America relied almost exclusively on customary law because of their common need to sustain their social systems. If communities were to form, survive, and develop, then they needed binding rules that their members devised, to which they consented, and which they enforced by various means.[38]

The evidence that slaves formulated and enforced customary law is only suggestive. This evidence is implicit in slaves' nearly omnipresent—in the nineteenth century—distinction between "taking" and "stealing," in the moral authority exercised by slave preachers, conjurers, and other authorities in the slave community, in such reports as that by antebellum South Carolinian Jacob Stroyer that his fellow slaves tested the guilt or innocence of slaves accused of theft, in the call of some slave insurrectionaries for equal justice, in the explanation by some observers of the reasons why an insurrectionary spared some whites while single-mindedly killing others, and in the decision of various bondspeople to reject insurrection and even to inform on plotters. By inference, one can see the ethical distinction inherent in the motivation of slaves convicted of stealing goods from whites other than their owners. Indeed, they were prosecuted predominantly for theft of necessities such as food and clothing. Crimes of violence showed the prevalence of another kind of ethical distinction. A large number of slaves convicted of killing white people had reacted to various kinds of mistreatment by white authorities. In less supervised circumstances, slaves convicted of killing other slaves were certainly no more numerous than slaves convicted of killing whites. Even if we double or triple the number of mortal conflicts between slaves to allow for unreported incidents, the aggregate figure is decidedly lower than circumstances permitted, suggesting that slaves' self-restraint and values limited such killing.[39]

The problem of evidence remains, however: To what extent did transplanted or "reblended" African legal values actually influence African American slaves' customary laws? The evidence I have discussed does not tell us clearly. I hope that other scholars will find the evidence needed. That leaves me with the task of investigating the manner in which the well-documented legal assumptions and institutions of white Virginians affected the lives of the many thousands of African Americans who lived in Virginia. Lamentably, this tends to steer attention away from the African American bondspeople who acted on the basis of motives that still need to be understood. Yet I attempted to deal with the motives of enslaved African Americans in *Twice Condemned*. In this book I wish to focus more on the other part of the social equation that generated the legal relationships experienced by slaves. White leaders developed a legal and judicial system for the usual reasons: order, security, and economic development. But they paid special attention to the legal control of the African Americans in their midst in order to perpetuate slavery and to secure white supremacy. Focusing on this aspect of the equation certainly tells us something about white Virginians, but it also helps us understand the system that African Americans had to face.

2

THOMAS JEFFERSON AND THE
LAW OF SLAVERY

Slaveholding American revolutionaries so revered the rule of law that they relied on the law to help rule their slaves. An apostle of republicanism in the United States, Thomas Jefferson is no exception to this generalization. He faced the same dilemma as did other slaveholding American revolutionaries. How could the defenders of liberty simultaneously deny liberty to the African Americans whom they held to slavery? How could they be slaveholders without denying liberty itself? Louis Masur commented in 1989, "In the late [nineteen] sixties and early seventies, when historians examined the dilemma of slavery in a land of liberty, no one seemed to have more to answer for than the enlightened slaveholder of Monticello."[1] Some revolutionaries answered these questions or avoided these charges by freeing their slaves, but Jefferson chose not to do this.[2] Instead he believed that the law helped to justify his ownership of human beings. Thomas Jefferson's legal transactions concerning his bondspeople reveal that part of his answer to the problem of slavery in a revolutionary, republican society was to make certain of the legality of his behavior as a master. He believed that conformity to the law of slavery constituted a civic duty, protected him from some of the dangers inherent in slavery, preserved his liberty to hold humans in bondage, and even, secondarily, gave some personal security to the enslaved.

This chapter explores the nature of Jefferson's relationship to the law of slavery in Virginia. I analyze the extent to which

Jefferson used the law to control his bondspeople and also the degree to which he had to answer *to* the law of slavery as long as he lived under the statutes of the Old Dominion. He bound human beings with the help of the law, but the law bound him, albeit to a lesser extent, to societal needs as well. And that obligation to live by the law of slavery created a dilemma. Was it enough for Jefferson to follow the law of slavery? Did compliance with the law of slavery make him an enlightened slave owner?

In the same famous letter of 1820 in which he referred to a "fire bell in the night," Thomas Jefferson described a dilemma: "But as it is, we have the wolf by the ear, and we can neither hold him, nor safely let him go. Justice is in one scale and self-preservation in the other."[3] Jefferson used this image of danger to explain the difficulty—to him an insuperable one—inherent in governmental sanctions against slavery, as in the Missouri Compromise. While Jefferson probably did not intend it to have other meanings, his dramatic depiction of the wolf can be borrowed to aid understanding of how he perceived the law of slavery. Lawmakers like him faced a dilemma—the seemingly impossible choice between giving up the benefits of the law of slavery and eliminating that law's self-evidently unjust consequences. Besides reflecting pain and ambivalence, this articulation of the dilemma of the republican slaveholder effectively characterizes the relationship between the purportedly enlightened lawgiver and the unenlightened institution of slavery. Few people were so conscious of and articulate about this dilemma as Jefferson, and few left us a more voluminous record of their thoughts and actions in relationship to the dilemma than did this owner of nearly two hundred human beings.

"I write on the human skin," Catherine the Great wrote to Diderot in the 1770s, to dramatize the direct practical impact she had as ruler on the lives of her subjects.[4] Thomas Jefferson also wrote on the human skin of his enslaved "subjects." Just how he did so has been the topic of little study until recently. The many discussions of Jefferson the slaveholder and the major biographies have generally only touched on Jefferson's relationship with specific African Americans.[5] Historians of the last twenty years have begun the needed thorough study of black Monticello.[6] Herein I wish to contribute to this scholarship a focus on Jefferson's legal oversight of African Americans at Monticello and elsewhere as revealed in his transactions concerning his human property.

This legal oversight, which spanned more than half a century, created a unique, rich, and unrivaled record of the relationship between written laws and human behavior in a representative, developed slave society. This chapter focuses on the meaning of Jefferson's translation of statutory law into practice and of his development of the customary law of the plantation. The statutory law of slavery must be understood as it was applied, not just as it was published. Comprehension of the customary law of bondage—rules adopted and enforced by plantation owners with the tacit approval of governmental lawmakers and the knowledge, but obviously not necessarily the approval, of slaves—depends completely on analysis of the application of such law. Thanks to Jefferson's careful retention of his papers, we can obtain a more complete picture of his legal—statutory and customary—relationship to the bondspeople under his dominion than that in almost any other case. The advantages and limitations of each form of law—statutes could work only to the extent that they were enforced, and customary law depended upon the maintenance of private rule—are particularly apparent in the record of Jefferson's long-term efforts to protect his investment in and maintain control over human chattel. Jefferson publicly displayed some ambivalence about the existence of that "species of property," but he rarely wavered about its legal status.

Jefferson helped to make the statutory law of slavery. He served in the Virginia House of Burgesses and as state governor. He was instrumental in the Commonwealth's revisal of laws. While president, he influenced passage of the Old Dominion's transportation law of 1801; he also led the effort to secure passage in 1807 of the national law to prohibit the slave trade from Africa.[7] However much power and authority he enjoyed because of his public role in the creation and revision of laws of slavery, Jefferson as slave owner had to live with all of Virginia's statutes concerning bondage. His brief practice as a lawyer, his familiarity with statutes, and his experience made him well aware of this. Analysis of the manner in which Jefferson lived with the law of bondage makes possible an interpretation of the interrelationship between slave law and slave owners' practice.[8]

To anyone who has studied slavery in any society, day-to-day legal transactions concerning bondspeople are notable for their routine, prosaic quality. One can find similar transactions in the records of slave societies throughout the Western Hemisphere. In other words, such laws were supposed to provide some predictability, consistency, and security for those whom they affected, three essential aspects of good laws. Property laws, other civil laws, and criminal laws also constrained slave owners—whether they held two or two hundred people. Thomas Jefferson's legal transactions concerning slaves show how the law of slavery placed him and other slave owners within the confines of a prescribed system that was supposed to command their obedience just as it was meant to help them command the obedience of their slaves. Other circumstances certainly influenced or circumscribed Jefferson's choices concerning slavery. For example, Jefferson believed that his deep attachment to the mores of his society, his "conspicuous consumption," and his chronic debt problem held him captive to bondage.[9] Overpowered by his defense of slavery, his Enlightenment ideas about bondage nevertheless had some impact on his behavior toward bondspeople. In his public role as a leader of the Enlightenment in America, as "Citizen of the World," as statesman, and as the "Sage of Monticello," he occasionally professed antislavery ideas that moved many people. But those statements against the evils of slavery never kept him from acting as a legalized inheritor, manager, giver, capturer, purchaser, hirer, and seller of human beings.[10]

Rather than arguing, as has Orlando Patterson, that the devotion to freedom of Founding Fathers like Jefferson arose directly from their experience of slaveholding and from their knowledge of the degraded status of bondspeople, I wish to emphasize the tension between Jefferson's devotion to the rule of law and his adherence to the proslavery behavior of the slave society of Virginia.[11] Like a monarch, Jefferson the slave owner inherited an assumed and apparently unimpeachable prerogative to rule his enslaved subjects; at the same time, however, he ruled in accordance with the law and was ordinarily subject to the law. Yet, even if he would, he could not escape the role of master by subjecting himself completely to the rule of law, the sine qua non of a republican leader. He was not a slave to slavery; he chose to remain a slave owner. By freely subjecting himself to the law of slavery, he committed himself to an unjust institution. "The slave holder can never be a Democrat," declared a "gentleman" in a newspaper letter in 1800.[12] Jefferson could not make it a rule to govern with the consent of his slaves; he could not accept any such thing as a *vox servi.* What then was a leader of a republican revolution and of the Democratic-Republican Party to do if he also wished to keep his slaves? He could not truly propound antislavery. He could only act like an enlightened, limited monarch whom laws restricted as well as empowered, and who reserved the right to make some laws of his own.

JEFFERSON'S POSSESSION AND PRESERVATION
OF HUMAN PROPERTY

Like a monarch or aristocrat, Jefferson was born into the ranks of slaveholders. His direct ancestors owned slaves at least as early as 1697 and undoubtedly earlier.[13] Thomas received his share of the descendants of those people as well as others on the deaths of his father in 1757 and of his mother in 1776.[14] The Hemings family, most famous among Jefferson's bondspeople, descended through the Eppes and Wayles lines and came under Jefferson's supervision—because of his marriage to Martha Wayles Skelton—after the division of her father's estate in 1774. On her death in 1782, they came into his ownership along with numerous other purchased slaves.[15] Owning about two hundred slaves at any given time thereafter, Jefferson thus became a slaveholder of major proportions. He would remain one until his death in 1826.

One key to the perpetuation of this kind of power over other human beings was the manner in which slaves' increase advanced the prosperity of the owner and of his descendants. The law of slavery had long been able to guarantee that the children of female slaves would belong to those slaves' owners. *Partus sequitur ventrem*, the doctrine of Roman slave law assimilated to the slave codes of the Western Hemisphere, ensured that the condition and ownership of children would follow the condition and ownership of their slave mothers.[16] Slave-owner procreation was thus bundled with slaves' procreation: slaves must procreate to raise the income of their owners and their owners' children.[17] Ensuring that biology would help his descendants as well, Jefferson made certain to settle slaves on his daughters and sons-in-law at their marriages. "Come then, my dear Sir, and let us place them in security before their marriage," he wrote to Thomas Mann Randolph as they were negotiating the marriage settlement for Martha Jefferson and Thomas Mann Randolph Jr. And this they did, settling the couple with no fewer than twenty-seven Jefferson slaves and forty Randolph slaves, making them more than secure as long as they managed well. With this legal settlement, both fathers conferred great responsibility on their affianced children, but the law would uphold the security of the settlement transaction itself.[18] Years before, a special settlement for Martha Wayles Skelton had made a great deal of difference in her inheritance of chattel from her father; a similar settlement would be made upon the marriage of Maria Jefferson to John Wayles Eppes in 1797.[19]

Taking, keeping, and relinquishing possession of bondspeople required close legal attention. Hence the legal aspects of purchase, retention, and sale of slaves are familiar to students of slavery. So much were these transactions taken for granted in the slave society of Virginia that the colony's and state's laws rarely required a public record of any purchase or sale of a slave. Some of Jefferson's acquisitions and sales were recorded, but usually only in connection with another kind of transaction. Thus Jefferson's financial accounts contain a train of slave conveyances, while his legal records contain relatively few. "Negroes alienated from 1784. to 1794. inclusive," apparently once part of Jefferson's "Farm Book," lists 161 people, 94 of whom he had sold within those eleven years alone.[20]

Jefferson was well aware of the risks involved in the purchase and sale of bondspeople. In 1817 he exercised the option to annul the sale of a five-year-old slave to someone else when the arrangement stipulated in the bill of sale of 1815 could not be fulfilled. Jefferson paid interest and some maintenance costs as well as the sale price.[21] He frequently urged agents to demand bonds, even two bonds in some cases, for credit purchases.[22] Jefferson also took a risk every time he entrusted the power of purchase or sale to someone else, whether for convenience or to conceal such conveyances from the public while he was in office. He never had to correct or sue a representative in such instances, but danger still existed. His financial suffering from a once-wealthy friend's default in 1819 on a large debt for which Jefferson provided security was but one reminder that the "best" people could fail and that such failures could jeopardize the future of slave owners and slaves. No fewer than eighty-two slaves of Wilson Cary Nicholas were in danger of being sold because of this default.[23]

Even when Jefferson hired or hired out bondspeople, he had to protect himself and simultaneously to take into account the generally understood legal responsibilities and liabilities connected with slave hiring. No statutes made clear all of these responsibilities and liabilities. Instead the common law of slavery, established by court decisions and shared assumptions, stipulated how hiring was to work.[24] Because economic, seasonal, and crop variations forced Jefferson to rely on hired slave labor quite regularly, especially between 1797 and 1813, he often found himself in the position of the obligated party—that is, the hirer.[25] Slave hiring was widespread and regularized, in that agreements were settled annually; Jefferson also was generally on good terms with the slaves' owners. Yet the practice required him to petition and pay the owners, and in the event of the slaves' illness, resistance, or death, it made him liable to the owners in certain respects.[26] Jefferson also confronted the legal dimensions of this practice from the opposite perspective, as one who allowed others to hire his slaves. Besides wondering in 1786 whether he could simultaneously make as much profit from hiring out his slaves as from working his land and still see to "the comfort of my slaves," he also declared in 1788 that certain people—Great George, Ursula, Betty Hemings, Martin, and Bob—were never to be hired out.[27] Otherwise he hoped to hold hirers to their agreements and successfully did so without ever having to resort to legal action.[28] For his part, it was necessary for him on only one occasion to submit to arbitration a disputed bill for medical care of a slave he had hired.[29]

The statutory and common law of slavery conferred on Jefferson and other owners the power to use their human chattel as collateral or as security against a debt or mortgage, like any other kind of movable property. But Jefferson rarely availed himself of this practice. Land was usually quite adequate as collateral. Yet in 1796 he used more than fifty of his slaves, most of whom lived at Poplar Forest, to secure his long-standing debt to British creditors.

Listed in family groups, the named people were all equally subject to Jefferson's fluctuating ability to pay his debt, while Jefferson's future solvency was at stake should he lose all these pro-
ducers of work and children. Jefferson hated debt, so it should not
be surprising that he rarely offered his slaves as security for debts;
however, given his constant indebtedness, he had learned much
about how to avoid such mortgages. He had, after all, sold ninety-
four slaves between 1784 and 1794 to clear the inherited Wayles
debt as well as his own. "In this, as in all other cases, providence
has made our interests & our duties coincide perfectly," Jefferson wrote at another time.[30] If Jefferson regarded the general exclusion of slaves from security for mortgages as a matter of duty,
then his perceptions of his duty to protect his chattel and his interest in keeping them certainly could coincide—but by no means
always.[31]

The laws of slavery unmistakably protected the Monticello
master's many sales of numerous slaves. Jefferson's detailed record
of the ninety-four slaves he sold between 1784 and 1794 leaves
no doubt about that. These sales financed lavish living, the payment of his prerevolutionary debts, and the attempted retirement
of the Wayles estate debt. They also reduced the size of his labor
force when great numbers of slaves were no longer needed because of sales of Wayles land and other tracts in the 1780s. Uncertain transfer of title would have frustrated Jefferson's attainment
of his financial and managerial objectives for selling slaves. The
many civil cases concerning titles to slaves could not have evaded
Jefferson's attention: he had reported some of them. So he knew
better than to take a sale for granted.[32]

JEFFERSON'S EFFORTS TO CONTROL HIS HUMAN PROPERTY

The law of slavery helped people like Jefferson to control the wills
of their human chattel. Uncontrolled, the wills of chattel could

become wholly the wills of human beings, which would weaken or destroy slavery in addition to endangering property or people. But laws could do only so much to control behavior, especially when slave resistance could as easily arise from hatred of bondage as from other motives. Consider the constant worry of slave owners about fugitives, as reflected in Jefferson's often-cited *Virginia Gazette* advertisement of 1769 for Sandy, a thirty-five-year-old shoemaker, carpenter, and jockey who allegedly had run away from Monticello. The statutory law of slavery gave owners of "slaves who stole themselves" some help in finding runaways, and it ensured that once they did, there were legal means of establishing their ownership.[33] It is questionable, however, how much good the law did Jefferson: virtually every person who escaped from him was initially retrieved, but almost every one of those returned people ultimately proved to be uncontrollable and often ran away again, sometimes permanently.[34]

The chief executive strongly agreed with an agent who was searching for one of Jefferson's runaways. All enslaved people should be "kept in proper subjection," the agent wrote to Jefferson. Before Jefferson's first presidential term had ended, he had sold Kit, who had run away. Jefferson attempted to handle a runaway tactfully in 1805. James Hemings, Critta's son and Betty Hemings's grandson, had gone to Richmond. Jefferson had no intention of bringing the law to bear on James; he attributed his flight to "the follies of a boy." (James was about eighteen at the time.) This approach did not work: James slipped away from Jefferson's agent in Richmond and never reappeared in Jefferson's records.[35]

In September 1805 Jefferson had to pay the Fairfax County jailer thirty-five dollars to get Jamey Hubbard back. Jail and recapture were no more effective than "mercy." By 1812 Jamey had escaped and was recaptured still one more time. Jefferson, "the enlightened monarch," now exercised his prerogative to rule in accordance with the customary law of slavery. "I had him severely flogged in the presence of his old companions, and committed to jail," Jefferson wrote. "The course he has been in, and all circumstances convince me he will never again serve any man as a slave. The moment he is out of jail and irons off he will be off himself." Although the flogging was the most severe physical punishment of one of his slaves ever recorded by Jefferson, it was no more successful than earlier measures. Jefferson's prediction was correct: Jamey Hubbard had "absconded" again by late 1812.[36]

Jefferson underscored his choice of weapons when he disciplined Hercules, a member of the workforce at Poplar Forest. Having been confined in the Buckingham County jail as a runaway during July 1813, Hercules went directly to Monticello, where Jefferson assured him that he left the choice of further punishment to Jeremiah Goodman, his overseer at Poplar Forest. Jefferson then wrote to Goodman that he should pardon Hercules on his own authority, "and not by my interference, for this is what I would have none of them to suppose." In other words, Jefferson believed he could not afford to be perceived as responding to the voice of a slave, especially when his response might eclipse the day-to-day rule of a steward or overseer. Jefferson's discretionary power was only reinforced when Joel Yancey, a later Poplar Forest overseer, reported Hannah's Billy as a runaway who was apt to return to Poplar Forest from Monticello. Yancey asked Jefferson to "dispose of him." Billy was soon in jail in Charlottesville and later had "again disappeared." By 1821 he was "still out" and had "joind. a gang of Runaways" whom it had been impossible to capture.[37] The legal paradox was difficult and perhaps disturbing to Jefferson. Had Hannah's Billy been a hiree, Jefferson could have relieved himself of the problem slave much more quickly, by simply refusing to rehire the laborer. Even though both statutory and customary law gave Jefferson nearly absolute powers of discipline over his slaves, use of some of those powers—jailing and the threat of sale—had been unavailing, and Jefferson faced the loss of capital and labor because of a runaway's success.

The same rationale for slave owners' absolute power governed statutes and the customary laws of slavery, on the basis of which Jefferson was ordinarily supposed to control his slaves: bondspeople must be extensions of the will of their owner. Yet this assumption that the owner's will should operate through a slave paradoxically allowed Jefferson to delegate to African Americans powers ordinarily reserved to whites. Thus Jefferson did sometimes entrust contractual responsibility to a slave. For example, when confined to Philadelphia in 1798, Jefferson allowed his slave George to purchase some plow horses on credit for Monticello.[38] In 1803 he even asked Thomas Mann Randolph Jr. to send one of his or another relative's slaves to pick up a pistol he had left in Orange County on his way back to Washington.[39] He also regularly paid slaves for goods or services, especially for what he regarded as extra services.[40] Still, such actions constituted ad hoc concessions to practicality rather than a concession of legal rights, whether derived from customary or statutory law.

Yet Jefferson did go beyond ad hoc concessions when he acknowledged the existence of the customary law of the *peculium*, property allowed to slaves by owners as if that property actually belonged to bondspeople, who by definition could not legally own anything. Even as Jefferson tried to deny a particular *peculium*, he legitimated the concept and also conceded the distinction between what was his and what was theirs: "I thank you for putting an end to the cultivation of tobacco as the peculium of the negroes," he wrote to Thomas Mann Randolph in 1798. "I have ever found it necessary to confine them to such articles as are not raised on the farm. There is no other way of drawing a line between what is theirs & mine." The fruits of Jefferson's laborers' work in his earth were his. Yet when he needed extensive digging done at Poplar Forest, he paid his bondspeople for their extra work. Once again, certain kinds of labor on Jefferson's property were his, but certain kinds were not, even when he claimed the laborers as his.[41]

In another kind of ad hoc concession, Jefferson could even base important decisions about his slaves on their preferences or behavior. Short of using violence or running away, the most effective exercise of personal power or influence by slaves was to persuade their owner to sell them to another owner of the slaves' choice. Omitting his many sales to cover debts, Jefferson claimed "delinquency" and "their own request" as his two criteria for sales.[42] The sales of Martin in 1792 and of Robert Hemings in 1794 confirm Jefferson's willingness to accede, albeit grudgingly and in special circumstances, to strong persuasion by slaves who wished to be sold.[43] The manner in which runaway Jamey Hubbard forced his sale in 1812 is only a more extreme example of the influence a slave could have on a master in spite of the owner's overwhelming legal power.[44]

On the other hand, Jefferson was capable of angrily asserting his rights when slaves claimed at least by their behavior that they had customary rights that clashed with his. No incident reveals this more clearly than his battle with some James River boatmen, many of whom were enslaved African Americans. In March 1809 all of Jefferson's goods were supposed to be transported from the White House to Monticello after he left the presidency. He directed that some trunks be carried up the James River rather than overland. Jefferson soon discovered that the trunk that contained his collection of Indian vocabularies as well as writing paper, a telescope, and a dynamometer (used to calculate the strength of farming animals) had been stolen.[45] Two weeks later, Ned, the possession of the estate of James B. Couch of Buckingham County, was to be tried for the theft and, Jefferson hoped, would "doubtless be hung for it. Some such example is much wanting to render property waterborne secure." Yet Ned was only whipped and burned in the hand.[46]

Jefferson expressed no opinion concerning this verdict in any of his extant writings, but he had already declared himself with sufficient animosity in favor of the execution of an unknown African American to make clear his attitude. Ned was found guilty only of theft. (The criminal law of slavery allowed for execution of a slave found guilty of burglary—breaking and entering with intent to steal—but executions for even this offense had become rare by 1809.) That Ned was not given a more severe punishment reveals the wide discrepancy between the manner in which Jefferson the enraged victim thought the criminal law could and should operate and the way Jefferson the lawmaker, former lawyer, and enlightened reformer thought it should. After this episode, Jefferson continued to emphasize the need to protect waterborne items against plunder.[47] Yet between the theft and the trial, he revealed his perception of the boatmen's point of view when he referred to "the system of plunder which our watermen carry on with respect to whatever of mine is put into their hands, and which they say is a matter of right." It was not at all unusual for the slaves among the boatmen to claim a customary right to white people's property.[48]

Jefferson may have been forced to face the implications of slaves' exercise of their own ethical judgment in such cases. But even in the trunk incident, which did not involve any of his slaves, he came into conflict with his own earlier thinking and expression about the nature of the slave society in which he lived. In the 1780s he had written:

The man, in whose favour no laws of property exist, probably feels himself less bound to respect those made in the favour of others. When arguing for ourselves, we lay it down as a fundamental, that laws, to be just, must give a reciprocation of right: that, without this, they are mere arbitrary rules of conduct, founded in force, and not in conscience: and it is a problem which I give the master to solve, whether the religious precepts against the violation of property were not framed for him as well as his slave? And whether the slave may not as justifiably take a little from one, who has taken all from him, as he may slay one who would slay him?[49]

There is no evidence that Jefferson made any special effort to secure a capital conviction of Ned, so his animosity toward an unknown thief before he knew Ned was accused may only reflect his desperation concerning the loss of a valuable instrument and of thirty years' worth of work on a collection of Indian vocabularies.[50] But his assumption that the slave courts could condemn the thief to death is instructive concerning his understanding of the weapons at the disposal of slave owners in their struggle with slaves accused of violating the criminal laws of the Commonwealth. After all, it was Jefferson who during the Revolution had opposed making theft a capital crime for whites.[51]

Also instructive are the public and private accusations of criminal behavior against Jefferson's own slaves. Few criminal prosecutions of Jefferson slaves appear in available slave court records. The earliest concerned the same alleged offense in the summer of 1781. Will and Jack, two Poplar Forest slaves in Bedford County, were charged with breaking into a storehouse and stealing some whiskey and miscellaneous objects. Jack was found guilty and sentenced to twenty-five lashes; Will, also judged guilty, was to suffer thirty-nine lashes. Jefferson, however, who had just ended his term as governor the previous month, apparently had nothing to say about these convictions.[52]

Jefferson did have something to say about other infractions of his rules or of the criminal laws. "Misbehavior" or violations of Jefferson's mostly spoken customary law of the plantation occurred fairly regularly, bringing into play his conception of himself as lawgiver and law enforcer. The most famous, but decidedly not the most harsh, application of Jefferson's "plantation justice" concerned a man whom Jefferson and his overseer accused of stealing nails from the Monticello nailery. Overseer Edmund Bacon remembered that when he told Jefferson about the theft, Jefferson

> was very much surprised and felt very badly about it. Jim had always been a favorite servant. He told me to be at my house next morning when he took his ride, and he would see Jim there. When he came, I sent for Jim, and I never saw any person, white or black, feel as badly as he did when he saw his master. He was mortified and distressed beyond measure. He had been brought up in the shop, and we all had confidence in him. Now his character was gone. The tears streamed down his face, and he begged pardon over and over again. I felt very badly myself. Mr. Jefferson turned to me, and said, "Ah, sir, we can't punish him. He has suffered enough already." He then talked to him, gave him a heap of good advice, and sent him to the shop. Grady had waited, expecting to be sent for to whip him, and he was astonished to see him come back and go to work after such a crime.[53]

As a result of this method of handling the slave's actions, James, or Jim, knew exactly what his "crime" was and could have had no doubt as to who made and directed the enforcement of the customary plantation laws of Monticello. Overseer Grady, a newcomer to Monticello, obviously did not know Jefferson's method of disciplining his "servants" and expected the usual corporal punishment. But Jefferson relied on his personal authority to shame James and added a large dose of judicial mercy, such as county judges and others could grant to enslaved suspects, to clarify his conception of himself as lawgiver and enforcer.[54] When merciful, he was relatively enlightened; when giving and enforcing the customary laws of the plantation on his own, however, he exercised the powers of an unlimited monarch.

Even though an anonymous correspondent reported to Jefferson that a Mr. Brown had awakened one morning at Monticello to see Jefferson "flogging in the most brutal manner a negroe woman," there is no other evidence that Jefferson acted in this way.[55] He ordered others to whip bondspeople, yet he consistently regarded flogging as an extreme measure. In 1801 he asked Thomas Mann Randolph to "speak to [overseer] Lilly as to the treatment of the nailers. It would destroy their value in my estimation to degrade them in their own eyes by the whip. This therefore must not be resorted to but in extremities. As they will be again under my government, I would chuse they should retain the stimulus of character."[56] So "the stimulus of character" was paradoxically supposed to motivate slaves to whom white Virginians customarily accorded no honor or dignity.

Jefferson would order a whipping, or even a far more severe punishment, when he thought it necessary. A whipping occurred in 1812, after runaway Jamey Hubbard had been captured. Jefferson had him "severely flogged." Jamey was a recidivist runaway whom Jefferson had been unable to control under "the stimulus of character."[57] In other cases, Jefferson resorted to sale. Three Poplar Forest slaves were accused of attacking their overseer with a knife in 1822. Indeed, the charges were stabbing, intent to kill, and consulting "on the subject of rebelling and making insurrection." However, two slaves were found not guilty of all charges, and the other, Billy, was convicted only of stabbing and attempted murder. The public court's not-guilty verdicts and, according to contemporary standards, relatively lenient punishment of whipping and burning in the hand did not satisfy Jefferson, whose quick and irrevocable private retribution was to transport all three men out of the state for sale in New Orleans.[58]

It is particularly interesting that these men had already been tried by courts of oyer and terminer. Jefferson had made a clear distinction in practice between his enforcement of plantation law and governmental enforcement of statutes. When Cary, a Monticello slave, allegedly assaulted Brown, another bondsman at Jefferson's home plantation, Jefferson wrote to Thomas Mann Randolph that if no prosecution were possible, he would still have to "make an example of him in terrorem to others" and sell him to Georgia. It was desirable that Cary be sold to a place "so distant as never more to be heard of among us, it would to the others be as if he were put out of the way by death."[59] So Cary's de facto transportation would be more than an example to other slaves: it would be sufficiently painful and wrenching that it would work "in terrorem." Distasteful, degrading, or impractical as Jefferson may have found whipping, he was in fact willing to resort to "selling to Georgia" to control his most defiant slaves. The laws of Virginia allowed for the public transportation of slaves found guilty of a capital offense but reprieved; by not interfering with owners who privately sold their defiant slaves, state government officials also allowed masters like Jefferson to perform the same role of transporter.[60] One was a public punishment, the other private, but Jefferson's use of de facto transportation had its own special sting at the same time that it made extremely clear that Jefferson the master and not the majesty of state law condemned an errant slave to transportation.[61]

Slave owners who considered themselves enlightened claimed to protect their slaves. It was part of the customary law of Jefferson's plantations for him to protect slaves against various dangers just as he would protect himself and his agents from certain slaves. "You have been quite misinformed as to my having any intention to lease my possessions in Bedford. Nothing could induce me to put my negroes out of my protection," Jefferson wrote to Henry Clark in 1820.[62] Consistent with his occasional statements about his duty to slaves, this absolute expression still needs to be tested. Jefferson did include provisos in various agreements that he would feed and clothe slaves he placed at the disposal of his daughters and their husbands. He also made it clear to various overseers that his slaves should not be worked "too hard," although he never specified in writing what "too hard" meant. While in Paris, he did outline some of the ways he meant to protect slaves he hired out in Virginia. One method was to resort to courts of law, another to exempt some favorite bondspeople from being hired out. Jefferson also followed the usual practice of including a clause in hiring agreements that required good care of slaves he hired out. Like other planters, Jefferson placed similar clauses in his agreements with overseers.[63]

Jefferson assumed, however, that the ultimate method of protecting his bondspeople, except those from whom he or other people needed protection, was to keep them in bondage, preferably in bondage to him. In 1814 he perceived two alternatives, both to him impossible: "The laws do not permit us to turn them loose, if that were for their good; and to commute them for other property is to commit them to those whose usage of them we cannot controul." Writing when Virginia law still required all emancipated slaves to leave the state within one year—exempting only those who successfully petitioned the legislature to stay— Jefferson saw manumission as an inhumane abandonment of "his people" to suffer the consequences of Virginia law. He therefore accepted the current manumission law as humane.[64] Nor would he sell his slaves in order to end his involvement in the peculiar institution, because sale would "commit them to those whose usage of them we cannot controul." This helps to explain why Jefferson accepted the 1820 offer of trusted relative John Wayles Eppes to exchange bank stock for some of his slaves.[65] If during the 1960s and 1970s "no one seemed to have more to answer for than the enlightened slaveholder of Monticello," this sort of justification for failing to free his human property left him open to many such questions.[66]

When Jefferson chose to free any of his human property—behavior utterly opposite to his strenuous attempts to recover them—he had to contend with statutes that both empowered and limited him in more complex ways than did any laws concerning runaways or alleged criminals. Since 1782 Virginia law had allowed individual manumission by deed or will. Jefferson rarely employed that power to emancipate; yet when he did, his legal strategy reflected some particularly important aspects of the statutory law of slavery. It is well known that Jefferson manumitted only blood relatives of his wife—members of the Hemings family—whom he had inherited upon her death. This history of Jefferson's acts of emancipation requires us to make sense of his opinion, expressed in 1789, that granting liberty to "persons whose habits have been formed in slavery is like abandoning children."[67]

Very few accounts of the passage of the 1782 law recognize its qualifications.[68] That act allowed manumission by will or by a witnessed instrument recorded in a county court, "*provided always* . . . That all slaves so set free, not being in the judgment of the court, of sound mind and body, or being above the age of forty-five years, or being males under the age of twenty-one, or females under the age of eighteen years, shall respectively be supported and maintained by the person so liberating them, or by his or her estate."[69] In other words, only "sound" male slaves between the ages of twenty-one and forty-five or female slaves from eighteen to forty-five years of age could be emancipated without remaining within the sphere of legal liability of their former owners. This law regarded all other former slaves as dependents, or (to use Jefferson's phrase) "children." The law's intention was to avoid "abandoning children" by preventing the manumission of people who might become a "charge" on the public, and who then would be dependent upon public funds or poor relief. (The requirement that emancipated people leave the state was not enacted until 1806 and was later modified.)[70]

Jefferson's attitude toward both bondspeople and the laws of Virginia influenced his decision to free several members of the Hemings family. The manner in which he freed them tells us how he dealt with the law of manumission. Those officially freed were Robert, in his thirties in 1794; James, also in his thirties in 1796; and five slaves freed by Jefferson's will, four—Burwell Hemings, John Hemings, Joe Fosset, and Madison Hemings—one year after Jefferson's death and one—Eston Hemings—at the age of twenty-one.[71] At forty-four years of age when the will stipulated one further year of slavery after Jefferson's death had passed, Burwell was close to, but not over, the limit of unqualified manumission, and he was a skilled painter and glazier. John Hemings, however, was fifty-one when his last year of slavery ended. His protection was that he was an accomplished carpenter who would undoubtedly be in demand, if only because of his woodwork at Monticello and Poplar Forest. At age forty-six, Joe Fosset was also potentially a "free child," but he too was a skilled blacksmith. Sally Hemings's children Madison and Eston, identified by some as Jefferson's own children, were protected either by age or by the terms of the will. Eston Hemings was still a "child" of eighteen in July 1826, so he was to be apprenticed to John Hemings until he was twenty-one (in May 1829), and then he would be free. Madison, born in January 1805, was already twenty-one when Jefferson wrote his will, so he would be free one year after Jefferson's death.[72] In the cases of John and Joe, the two men most vulnerable to the legal disadvantages of being "free children," Jefferson's will bequeathed each of them tools, a log house, and a curtilage of one acre.[73] So Joe Fosset, John Hemings, and even Burwell Hemings received special protection from Jefferson within the possibilities created by the laws of Virginia.

Five members of the Hemings family received their freedom in Jefferson's will. Sally Hemings, the most famous member, did not. Jefferson's racism and his debt problem surely influenced his decision to free so few people, yet why did he free some members of the favored Hemings family and not others? While Jefferson left no explicit explanation for his failure to free Sally Hemings, the legal circumstances he had to consider are clear. Born in 1773, Sally Hemings was at the advanced age of fifty-three, which would have placed her unambiguously in the category of "free child" if she had been manumitted. Gender and old age did not have to impede freedom, however. On January 10, 1827, less than six months after Jefferson's death, his executor recorded an act of manumission from the estate. Thomas Jefferson Randolph pronounced Critty, "sometimes called Critty Bowles, the wife of Zachariah Bowles a free man of colour," who lived in Albemarle County and was another member of the Hemings family, "to be entirely liberated from slavery." While Critty was fifty-seven when freed, she now became the legal responsibility of her husband, a free man. The fathers of Sally's children, however, might or might not have been able to ensure the independence of Sally. Whoever they were, the free white ones would probably not have admitted responsibility, and the enslaved black ones perhaps could not have taken it.[74] The legal and financial liabilities to which Jefferson's debt-ridden estate would inevitably have been subjected made it economically difficult and therefore legally risky to emancipate Sally Hemings. She was an aging woman who apparently lacked a trade or a husband; her brother John and nephews Burwell and Joe could not be legally bound to support her, and her young sons Madison and Eston could not fairly be expected to provide for her. Jefferson's estate would have been responsible for

Sally's welfare had no one else taken responsibility. These legal circumstances cannot explain Jefferson's decision, however. Emancipation was possible if Jefferson regarded other reasons in favor of freeing Sally as more compelling than those that militated against it, but he either did not or decided against Sally's freedom for some other reason.

The other trap of emancipation presented no problem to the members of the Hemings family whom Jefferson freed. Fueled by the reaction to the rising number of manumissions that followed upon passage of the 1782 law, legislators suspicious or fearful of the increase in the free black population decided in 1806 to limit that group's legal growth without taking measures against its natural increase. The 1806 "Act to amend the several laws concerning slaves" declared that African Americans who remained within the Commonwealth more than one year after being freed not only would forfeit their freedom but also might be "apprehended and sold by the overseers of the poor . . . for the benefit of the poor."[75] Thereafter, when slave owners like Jefferson freed only some members of a family, those owners and this law forced many former slaves to make a terrible choice between freedom on the one hand and home and family on the other. "The laws do not permit us to turn them loose," Jefferson falsely claimed in an 1814 letter to neighbor Edward Coles, who did set his bondspeople free in Illinois a few years later, but Jefferson made his last will and testament in 1826, ten years after the Old Dominion's legislators of 1816 had bowed to economic, social, and political realities and had allowed one "escape hatch" from the trap of emancipation.[76] Thereafter freedpeople could petition local courts to exempt them from exile on the grounds of their "extraordinary merit" and "good character."[77] Jefferson still relied on state authority when he included in his will a request that the legislature of Virginia grant permission for his former slaves to remain in Virginia.[78] As might be expected, Jefferson's status benefited his former slaves.

The legislature quickly granted his wish in 1827, with the usual proviso against allowing any of the men to remain in Virginia after conviction of a crime.[79]

JEFFERSON'S RELATIONSHIP TO THE SLAVE LAWS

Yet another way that Jefferson encountered the strictures of the slave code underlines the nature of his link to that body of laws. He encountered the slave laws when other people entrusted him with the disposition or protection of their slave property as a trustee, agent, legal adviser, or lawyer.[80] Bound by the laws of Virginia, by the ethics of his sometime profession, by his wish to uphold his reputation, and by the canons of his class, and living in a world of shared obligations, Jefferson, like every other slave owner, had no choice but to acknowledge the strength of the relationship between his power as master and the force of the law of slavery. While it is fair to expect more creative ways of ameliorating and ending bondage from Thomas Jefferson than from other slave owners of his time, his acceptance of the legal foundation of bondage stifled some of his creativity. Relatively vigorous in his public pronouncements on abolition in the 1770s and 1780s, he maintained relative silence thereafter. His most creative legal acts or thinking concerning his bondspeople, albeit not highly unusual, were the de facto manumissions of Beverley and Harriet, a son and a daughter of Sally Hemings, and his unusually clear articulation of his slaves' *peculium*.

Thomas Jefferson never was able to ignore the law of slavery, and as a slave owner he probably did not want to do so. While in public office, he was called upon to make legal decisions about slaves and slavery. During the same years he also occasionally made public antislavery pronouncements. His governmental actions, which carried much greater weight than did his pronouncements, rarely propounded antislavery ideas. Every time he expressed support for progress and enlightenment, he encountered his and others' racism and self-interest as well as the hard realities of economic and political life in the new nation.[81] Regularly sought for his opinion concerning slavery during his years of retirement, Jefferson insisted upon public silence. Under the heavy pressure of events such as the Missouri controversy, he privately pronounced on the nation's problem of slavery without being able to offer a solution.

This is not to say that Jefferson was a mere product of his times who failed to solve a problem that others were also unable to solve. In other respects Jefferson certainly helped to produce his times. Yet he refused to go at least as far as neighbor Edward Coles, who legally emancipated his slaves and then helped them get started on their road to independence outside the slave South. Jefferson also failed to emancipate more than a few slaves in his will— in contrast to such contemporaries as John Randolph of Roanoke and, indirectly, Thaddeus Kosciuszko.[82] In 1970 David B. Davis asked, "Was Thomas Jefferson an authentic enemy of slavery?"[83] Was Thomas Jefferson willing to act against his own interest in the matter of slaves? The latter question hits closer to home, because it touches on how Jefferson lived, on what the laws of his slave society allowed, and on his conception of himself as an enlightened ruler.

A simple analogy is in order. Like military leaders who, once they have accepted command and have encountered an enemy, have no choice but to lead some soldiers to their deaths and to cause the killing of enemy soldiers, slaveholders had to consent to certain realities once they took ownership of slave property. They were quite free to do some things, as Edward Coles and George Washington's different means of emancipating their slaves demonstrated, yet anything but free to do others.[84] Some owners learned how to motivate their bondspeople without using the whip, but there was nothing to stop them should they wish to use it, and many did so. All slaveholders knew that the unimpeachable power of government was behind them if their self-preservation hung in the balance: they needed to worry about insurrection, but they knew they could depend on a deadly governmental response to it. The power of government on which slave owners could rely on a day-to-day basis was the power to make and enforce the slave code. But that same power limited them to some degree with respect to aspects of self-hiring, manumission, and even control.[85]

Slave owners did enjoy a certain amount of independence from governmental oversight of their "management" of their slaves. In return for the protection provided by the laws and judiciary of the governments of any slave society, however, slaveholders had to pay the price of abiding by the regulations that laws and the judiciary applied to owners. Jefferson and other owners were unwilling to take the risk of rejecting governmental regulation of them and their human chattel because of the very nature of their legal relationship with bondspeople. They regarded slaves as their property. Had they rejected the governmental regulation of that "species of property," they would have jeopardized much of the law of property as well as the society and economy in which they lived.

Jefferson's legal transactions concerning his own human chattel reveal that he had the wolf by just one ear, a particularly precarious circumstance. It was as if slavery were the wolf, and the law of slavery could not always protect slave owners from trouble that could ultimately be blamed on that wolf. "In a word," declared an anonymous letter writer in 1800, "if we will keep a ferocious monster in our country, we must keep him in chains. . . . Slavery is a monster—the most horrible of all monsters."[86] The law of slavery only supported, and did not guarantee, the security of slave owners. That was to be expected: no law has ever been able to guarantee security. Although it did help to preserve the institution of slavery, the law of bondage was least successful when used to control African Americans who chose to resist bondage violently—short of mortal violence—or by running away. Jefferson implicitly recognized this paradoxical weakness of the harsh code when he either resorted to private rather than public action to discipline particularly recalcitrant slaves or supplemented public action with punitive measures of his own.

Even the civil law placed Jefferson in a difficult position. If he wished to emancipate all of the members of the Hemings family in his will, he knew that statutes potentially limited his wish as well as their security. He could have freed them by sending them to the North, but they could never thereafter have legally returned to Virginia. He might have emancipated more members of the Hemings family in his will, yet that might have had a legal— that is economic—impact on his heirs. He may even have found a legal way to free them all with relatively few consequences undesirable to them or him, but the law made that less likely. Besides artificially circumscribing the lives of African Americans, this limitation of Jefferson's manumission of his bondspeople— had he seen fit to do so—was a price he had to pay for the protection provided by government. Jefferson did not regard emancipation as fit, but he faced the same legal circumstances as did other slave owners.

It is this "bargain" between the ostensibly independent slave owner and the government that helps to explain the sharp conflict between Jefferson's pronouncements about slavery and his actual ownership of slaves. Jefferson could not have it both ways: as a slave owner, he either had to obey the laws of slavery while he kept African Americans in bondage or else he had to free all of his slaves and not abide by the slave code with respect to his human property. Anyone who acted like an enlightened monarch could not be a republican leader of human beings when they were in bondage. No matter how beneficent a master he was—and relative to many other owners, he was—he still owned personal chattel. That committed him to support of the law of slavery, to the preservation of the peculiar institution. Unique and extraordinary in some ways, and often the beneficiary of the laws, he was just as subject to the law of slavery as any other slave owner. Approximately 97 percent of his enslaved laborers remained in bondage as the property of at least twenty-one new owners after Jefferson's death.[87] These people were living proof that the law of slavery was written on their skins immeasurably more than on Jefferson's, that they lived under the government of men as well as of laws. Yet the legal liabilities that may have limited Jefferson's ability to free these slaves reveal the lesser extent to which the law of slavery was also written on Jefferson's skin.

3

SLAVES AND CAPITAL PUNISHMENT IN VIRGINIA

◆━

Images of enslaved men and women hanging by the neck create vivid impressions. In a famous print, English poet and engraver William Blake used a slave rebel hanging in chains to symbolize slavery. Public executions of large numbers of slaves after rebellions or plots paint a chilling picture of the human suffering that white authorities inflicted on black men and women to protect themselves and to defend the peculiar institution.[1] Like artists, novelists, and poets, historians of slavery have mostly concentrated on extraordinary or isolated examples of slaves dying on the gallows.[2] Few have systematically studied the use of capital punishment against African Americans in bondage, nor have such executions been analyzed within the context of the general history of capital punishment.[3] These interpretive gaps have stemmed for the most part from the relative lack of comprehensive data. Much more is known about inequality and injustice in the sentencing of black convicts to death during the twentieth century than about the frequently cruel and inhumane condemnation of "socially dead" slaves to physical death between the seventeenth and nineteenth centuries. Fortunately, the collection of data from Virginia—in which there were more slaves than in any other North American colony or U.S. state, at least until 1860—provides an exception to this rule. The existence of considerable information concerning the Old Dominion permits a comprehensive analysis of how the government of one major slave society applied capital statutes to slaves.

In Virginia, as in other slave societies of the New World, public hangings of slaves took a terrible toll, constituting a cruel but usual punishment. At the same time, however, there were temporary fluctuations as well as a general per capita decrease over time in the use of capital punishment against enslaved African Virginians. The system's toll, in other words, could have been worse than it was. Those hangings that did not take place need explanation, as well as those that did. In a polity such as the Old Dominion, committed to uphold lifetime, hereditary racial servitude, as well as to protect life and property, what was the basis for judicial decisions to execute or not to execute slaves found guilty of capital offenses? Analysis of this issue should help to explain the significance of capital punishment for the peculiar institution, for the criminal code and courts of Virginia, and for slaves themselves.

Both hangings and reprieves or pardons of condemned slaves arose from the steadfast intention of slave owners to use whatever power was necessary to protect slavery. In addition to safeguarding people and property, Virginia's rulers were determined to dominate slaves. They accordingly molded and administered the system of criminal laws and courts for bondspeople in order to rule those black men and women who refused to accept, or whose behavior contradicted, the law's definition of them as property, without wills of their own.[4] Yet the white leaders of the colony and later the state learned between the seventeenth and the nineteenth centuries that they could protect the slave regime from rebellious or dangerous slaves by resorting to capital punishment with a lesser degree of frequency and barbarity than had previously been the case. They learned how to control some rebellious or dangerous bondspeople without killing them, even as they continued to exercise the option of executing a large number of others.

The sine qua non of the Old Dominion's criminal justice system was that the general level of judicial punishments for slaves must be more severe than that for whites. Even though gaps exist in the evidence concerning capital punishment in eighteenth- and nineteenth-century Virginia, available statistics reflect this judicial discrimination (see tables 3.1–3.5). So many bondspeople died at the hands of the Old Dominion's judiciary that the numbers almost speak for themselves. While the number of slaves actually executed in eighteenth-century Virginia is hidden, the figures for 1785–1865 are in plain view.

In courts whose records survive, 567 bondspeople were condemned to death between 1706 and 1784.[5] Comprehensive, centralized records of executions are unavailable before the 1780s, so for only 152 of the 567 known cases is it possible to determine that the death sentence was carried out. Yet we need to consider the possible total of slaves hanged from 1706 to 1784 in order to begin to understand the known total of executions between 1785 and 1865. An educated guess suggests what the actual total may have been. Available county court records comprise roughly 60 percent of originally created records, so extrapolation hints that the total number of condemnations during those years may have been as high as 945. Allowing for differences among counties and for other variables, it is reasonable to suggest that between four hundred and eight hundred slaves may have been hanged in Virginia between 1706 and 1784. We know of only seventy executions of free people during the same period. The number of free people executed may have been considerably less than the actual number of slaves executed, yielding a suggestive but unfortunately inconclusive comparison.[6]

The complete and accurate data for the next eighty years, 1785–1865, show that 635 enslaved Virginians were hanged by the neck, with more than two-thirds of them having been convicted of violent crimes against black and white people, 13.1 percent of property crimes, 12.8 percent of insurrection or conspiracy to revolt, and 4.9 percent of unspecified felonies.[7] The simple ratio of slaves hanged to other people hanged in Virginia—that is, the two

Table 3.1

Slaves Sentenced to Hang, by Category of Crime, Virginia, 1706–1865

Crime charged	Sentenced to hang, 1706–84[a]	% of total	Hanged, 1785–1865	% of total	Extraordinary sentences, 1706–1809			
					Body or head displayed	% of total	Body quartered, displayed	% of total
Against property	312	55.0	83	13.1	3	12.0	0	—
Against persons	144	25.4	440	69.3	22	88.0	5[b]	71.4
Against system	7	1.2	0	—	0	—	0	—
Insurrection	14	2.5	81	12.8	0	—	2	28.6
Unspecified felony	89	15.7	31	4.9	0	—	0	—
Robbery and treason	1	trace	0	—	0	—	0	—
Total	567		635		25		7	

Sources: County court records; Condemned Slaves, Library of Virginia; Virginia Treasury Office, Cash Disbursements Journals; newspapers.

[a]Hanging sentences only; verification of actual hangings is available for 152 of the 567 cases.

[b]Includes two slave women burned to death, one in 1746 who was convicted of poisoning her master, and the other in 1737 who was convicted of murder.

Note: Percentages do not always total 100.0 because of rounding.

Table 3.2

Slaves Sentenced to Hang, by Offense, Virginia, 1706–1784

	Attempted murder	Murder	Attempted rape	Rape	Poisoning	Theft	Arson	Conspiracy/ Insurrection	Escape/ Runaway	Unspecified	Total
1706–9	0	1	0	0	0	6	0	0	0	2	9
1710–14	0	2	0	0	0	8	0	2	0	1	13
1715–19	0	0	0	0	0	3	0	0	0	0	3
1720–24	0	4	0	1	0	7	0	0	0	0	12
1725–29	0	2	0	0	0	6	0	0	0	0	8
1730–34	0	2	0	0	0	4	0	6	0	1	13
1735–39	0	2	0	2	0	10	0	0	0	1	15
1740–44	0	4	1	0	0	13	1	0	0	1	19
1745–49	0	5	0	0	1	18	0	0	0	1	25
1750–54	1	12	1	1	0	30	1	1	2	11	59
1755–59	0	5	0	3	3	8	1	0	0	1	19
1760–64	1	7	1	1	10	26	2	0	0	7	54
1765–69	2	12	0	6	4	31	1	0	0	17	74
1770–74	1	3	0	4	8	51	1	0	0	15	83
1775–79	1	10	0	6	4	30	3	5	4	20	83
1780–84	0	3	0	4	5	50	3	0	1	12	78
Total	6	72	3	28	35	301	12	14	7	89	567

Sources: County court records; legislative journals; miscellaneous manuscripts.

Notes: Figures are for hanging sentences only; verification of actual hangings is available for 152 of the 567 cases. "Poisoning" includes illegal "administration of medicine." "Theft" includes burglary.

Table 3.3
Slaves Hanged, by Offense, Virginia, 1785–1865

	Attempted murder	Murder	Infanticide	Assault	Attempted rape	Rape	Poisoning	Theft	Arson	Conspiracy/ Insurrection	Unspecified	Total
1785–89	0	6	0	0	1	1	2	9	3	0	6	28
1790–94	3	16	0	0	1	3	5	6	2	4	1	41
1795–99	2	28	1	3	1	6	3	16	3	6	4	73
1800–1804	2	16	0	0	0	4	6	1	0	36	1	66
1805–9	1	15	0	0	0	6	3	5	0	2	0	32
1810–14	1	9	1	1	1	3	0	6	1	0	2	23
1815–19	1	13	0	0	0	4	4	3	2	5	0	34
1820–24	1	29	0	0	1	7	0	3	2	0	1	44
1825–29	1	30	1	0	3	4	2	3	0	0	2	46
1830–34	1	18	0	0	2	4	3	3	0	23	0	52
1835–39	2	13	0	0	2	3	0	3	3	0	1	27
1840–44	2	9	0	0	10	5	0	1	0	2	3	32
1845–49	4	14	0	0	0	4	2	1	1	0	1	27
1850–54	6	17	0	0	3	2	1	0	2	0	1	32
1855–59	1	23	0	0	6	1	3	0	2	0	0	36
1860–64	5	18	0	0	1	1	1	1	3	2	8	40
1865	0	0	0	0	0	1	0	0	0	1	0	2
Total	33	274	3	4	32	59	35	59	24	81	31	635

Sources: Condemned Slaves, boxes 1–10, Library of Virginia; Virginia Treasury Office, Cash Disbursements Journals; Capital Punishment Research Project; county court records.

Notes: All hangings have been verified. "Poisoning" includes illegal "administration of medicine." "Theft" includes burglary.

Table 3.4
Types of Hanging Sentences, Virginia, 1706–1784

	Hang	Hang, display head	Hang, quarter, display
1706–9	9	0	0
1710–14	13	0	0
1715–19	3	0	0
1720–24	12	0	0
1725–29	8	0	0
1730–34	13	0	1
1735–39	15	1	0
1740–44	19	1	0
1745–49	25	3	0
1750–54	59	1	0
1755–59	19	0	1
1760–64	54	3	0
1765–69	74	0	1
1770–74	83[a]	2	0
1775–79	83	2	0
1780–84	78[b]	1	0

Sources: County court records, supplemented by legislative journals.

[a]Three are known to have been pardoned by the Council.

[b]Twenty-seven are known to have been pardoned by the Council.

Note: The figures in the first column include those in the second and third columns.

numbers compared without weighting each group in accordance with its percentage of the total population at risk of being hanged for crimes—was perhaps more than twelve to one during those eighty years.[8] Slaves were never more than two-fifths of the state's population, however; whites comprised between three-fifths and two-thirds between 1790 and 1860. Thus the meaningful social ratio—that is, the two numbers compared by weighting each group in accordance with its percentage of the total population— was significantly higher. On a per capita basis, the Old Domin- ion executed slaves at approximately the same rate as did South Carolina, the only other North American slave society for which we currently have a complete nineteenth-century time series. Virginia's record surpasses that of per capita executions of free

Table 3.5
Fates of Slaves Convicted of Felonies, Virginia, 1785–1865

Crime	Executed	Transported or hard labor	Escaped	Died in prison	Unknown outcome	Total
I. Against property						
Stealing	46	331	4	1	2	384
Robbery	13	19	0	0	0	32
Arson	24	121	0	0	0	145
Total	83	471	4	1	2	561
II. Against persons						
Murder (unspecified or first-degree)	274	96	0	1	3	374
Murder (second-degree or manslaughter)	0	32	0	0	0	32
Infanticide	3	15	0	0	0	18
Attempted murder	33	119	0	0	2	154
Poisoning or illegal medication	35	49	1	0	0	85
Rape	59	22	0	0	0	81
Attempted rape	32	32	0	0	0	64
Assault	4	21	1	0	0	26
Total	440	386	2	1	5	834
III. Against system						
Aid runaway	0	5	0	0	0	5
Forge pass	0	1	0	0	0	1
Print abolitionist literature	0	1	0	0	0	1
Total	0	7	0	0	0	7
IV. Insurrection	81	54	0	1	3	139
V. Unspecified	31	63	0	0	0	94
Grand total	635	981	6	3	10	1,635
(Percentage of convicted)	(38.8)	(60.0)	(0.4)	(0.2)	(0.6)	

Sources: Condemned Slaves, boxes 1–10, Library of Virginia; Virginia Treasury Office, Cash Disbursements Journals; Capital Punishment Research Project; county court records.

convicts in two free states, Massachusetts and Pennsylvania, although the time series on which this contrast relies are not so extensive as to be completely reliable.[9]

CAPITAL STATUTES IN COLONIAL VIRGINIA

All of these hard deaths occurred because of the well-coordinated and persistent effort of legislators and judges. Legislators began the process. Many laws of the colony and the Commonwealth mandated special penalties for African American convicts. The creation in 1692 of separate criminal courts for slaves accused of capital crimes reflected the growing belief of white legislators and judges that the government had to employ greater force to preserve slavery and protect slave owners than to protect citizens from white criminals. Special capital laws concerning black people convicted of conspiracy, insurrection, poisoning or dangerous "administration of medicine," assault with intent to kill any white person, and attempted rape appeared in Virginia's statute books year after year. Even bondage itself could "create" crimes: a slave could murder a master, mistress, or overseer, for example, committing a "status" crime that free people could not commit and the kind of offense— homicide of a social superior—that free people were less likely to commit. The absence of statutes could also reinforce discriminatory patterns between enslaved convicts and others. Until 1732 there was no law to affirm that slaves could plead for benefit of clergy—a one-time reprieve from execution extended to slaves convicted of certain crimes, mostly against property. It was not until 1792 that a slave could plead self-defense when "wantonly assaulted" by a white; only after 1848 would the law distinguish between first- and second-degree murder in convictions of slaves; and the state penitentiary never housed slave convicts other than those awaiting transportation. Finally, even though owners and other free people petitioned the state executive for pardons and reprieves

71

for slaves, no slave's conviction could be appealed to a higher court until 1848, and even after that time only one case appears in the records.[10]

Judges added another weapon to statutes. Reliance on both the common law and slave codes ensured that per capita hangings of slaves would be more frequent than per capita executions of other people for the same offenses. Even when common law definitions of crimes covered all accused people, as in the case of first-degree murder, enslaved Virginians suffered greater risk. Slaveholding judges were not about to apply the same criteria of premeditation and malice to both black and white defendants in homicide trials. The special situation of bondspeople, who were in most contexts legally extensions of the wills of their owners, led judges to construe almost all killings by slaves of people in authority over them as first-degree murder. The fact that many of these enslaved men and women had retaliated against owners or overseers who had beaten or whipped them led few judges to exercise mercy.[11] While most definitions of and sanctions against crimes allegedly committed by slaves were based on positive statutes and only indirectly on common law, a separate "common law of slavery" developed in Virginia as more and more judges of county courts of oyer and terminer (which tried slaves for capital offenses until 1785 and tried them for all felonies thereafter) applied the changing slave code to accused slaves.[12]

Old Dominion judges even made certain to reserve the extreme forms of capital punishment for condemned slaves. If both free and enslaved people were to be hanged for the same offense, it was essential to maintain the distinction between the two groups. Hanging by strangulation, so well known to Anglo-Americans, African Americans, and perhaps even to newly imported Africans, was the dominant mode of execution, but courts ordered sheriffs to display the executed slave's head or body in at least twenty-six cases, twenty-one before 1785 and five thereafter. Eleven of these sentences were definitely carried out. In five cases, all before 1785, judges decreed that the condemned must also be quartered after the hanging, with the sections of the corpse to be displayed in prominent places. The fact that no evidence of the use of the same techniques of hangings against other Virginians appears in available records for the eighteenth and nineteenth centuries makes it highly likely that these extraordinary forms of capital punishment were reserved for slaves (even though judges imposed such measures regularly in Great Britain all through the eighteenth and even into the nineteenth century).[13] The rationale of perpetuating slavery and dominating blacks also led white authorities to place slaves at a much higher risk than whites of suffering punitive death by other means than execution.[14]

WAS A STATISTICAL DECLINE EQUIVALENT TO AN INCREASE OF MERCY?

The public officials of the Old Dominion always found reason to hang some, and at times many, slaves. But historians wish to discern variety and change, and it is precisely the primary developments in the capital punishment of slaves—that is, the temporary and long-term decreases in its use—that raise the central question of motivation. In the face of the powerful forces that encouraged so many executions of slave convicts, how could anyone limit the use of capital punishment against the legally powerless? What possible chance was there for any waning in frequency? Slaveholders were as determined to dominate enslaved African Virginians in the months before Appomattox as they had been in 1692. Racism, proslavery ideology, economic considerations, public opinion, the impetus and harshness of capital statutes, and tradition all seemed to guarantee that slave convicts would suffer an even larger number of hangings than they did. Instead, there was a long-term decrease in per capita hangings of slaves in Virginia.

One can explain this only by resisting the temptation to reify the forces enumerated above. Those seemingly irresistible forces actually resulted from the decisions of thousands of people at thousands of different times and in highly diverse circumstances. In fact, some of the very same people who advocated the hanging of one slave for one offense were among those who opposed the execution of another slave. (Judges are the most obvious people to have done this.) This resulted not only from inconsistency but also from many of the same assumptions that guided those who supported capital punishment. Hegemony must be maintained over slaves, but this could be done in a variety of ways and in consideration of different circumstances.

First, improved penal conditions for free people could create the opportunity for decreases in capital punishment for the unfree. The general movement for reform of penal systems throughout the United States made possible a large reduction in the number of executions of free black and white convicts.[15] The Virginia state legislature abolished benefit of clergy, created the penitentiary, and confined capital offenses to first-degree murder for whites and many free blacks in 1796. Aiding or conspiring with slave rebellion, treason, and certain forms of arson were the only additions to Virginia's capital statutes for free whites from 1796 through 1865.[16] (The protection afforded free black defendants steadily decreased after 1800.[17]) These marked improvements in the state's penal system for free people also helped to save the lives of some slaves, to whom none of these changes applied. Using the de facto system of transportation that existed in the eighteenth century, then relying on the transportation laws of 1801 and later, judges and other white authorities kept more and more slaves out of the hands of the hangman. Between 1801 and 1865 more than twice as many slaves were transported (983) as were hanged (485) for capital crimes (see chapter 4).

The connection was an old one: criminal sanctions against slaves had to be more harsh than sanctions against free people. The more lenient sanctions against free people became, the less the leaders of the slave society of Virginia had to rely on capital punishment to preserve slavery. The distinction between free people and slaves survived inviolate. The revised code of 1849 made the connection quite explicit. Should a slave be convicted of a capital crime for which whites would suffer fewer than three years in the penitentiary, it would be possible for the governor to commute the sentence of death to sale and transportation.[18] As long as slaves could be executed for more offenses than could free people, then slavery was safe. This condition prevailed from the 1790s through the 1860s, and the per capita number of executions of slaves generally decreased from 1800 through 1864.

Amelioration in the criminal code for whites explains the opportunity, but not the motives, for judges to lower the number of per capita executions of enslaved African Americans. The obvious question to ask about these judges' behavior is whether it constituted judicial mercy. Mercy was a judicial prerogative that European Virginians ordinarily honored. Men who saw themselves as Christian, just, and professional were going to take the opportunity on occasion to try to appear merciful. We cannot normally know whether they were sincere in this wish; we can only observe their effort to appear merciful. The records of slave trials contain frequent requests from oyer and terminer court justices to the governor and Council to grant some form of clemency to slaves condemned to death.

Judges asking for mercy cited the youth or "ignorance" of some convicts. The justices of the Richmond County oyer and terminer court found a slave named Jack guilty of burglary and felonious theft. The law required them to sentence him to death. They noted in the trial record sent to the governor, however, that this was Jack's first offense and that "from the circumstances of the case," it was doubtful to them "whether he was sensible of the crime." They believed Jack to be a proper object of mercy. Condemned to death for the same offense in 1761, Fielding Lewis's slave Ned was also recommended for mercy. The judges stated that this was his first offense and cited his "good character." The Hanover County oyer and terminer judges attributed the slave Braxton's participation in a 1792 burglary to the influence of his accomplice. Braxton, they declared, was "only about the age of seventeen or eighteen years" and had been "corrupted" by the slave Isaac. (The governor and Council pardoned Braxton.) Although sentenced to hang by Richmond city judges, a slave named Albert was instead transported in 1828 because he was "16 or 17 years old."[19]

Provocation was grounds for a pardon, but only if the victim was another slave. The Stafford County oyer and terminer court condemned Will to death in 1777 for murder of another master's slave. But the governor and Council saw reason for clemency, "the Negro who was killed having given provocation of the highest Nature, & . . . the killing happened in the course of a mutual fighting." Benjamin Clements of Southampton County hoped for the pardon of his slave Pierce in 1774. Pierce's white accomplice had induced Pierce to steal a horse, Clements insisted.[20]

Some judges pointed out that the sentence of death was too harsh for the offense, almost always a crime against property. A Patrick County slave named Randolph was transported rather than executed in 1825 because the governor and Council noted the "great disproportion between the offence [of burglary and theft of sugar from a storehouse] and the punishment." In 1785 the Henrico County oyer and terminer justices ordered that murder charges be dropped against William Morris's slave Will because "at the time of committing" the crime, "he was a Lunatic & not in his proper Senses."[21]

It would seem reasonable to ascribe such judicial behavior to the desire of oyer and terminer judges to exercise the same kind of restraint as that which Douglas Hay argues that eighteenth-century English gentry displayed in not using the full force of capital statutes against the many convicts in their courts.[22] That is, slave court justices may have sacrificed punishment "when necessary to preserve the belief in justice." Many oyer and terminer justices wished to perceive themselves and to be perceived by other slaveholders, nonslaveholding whites, free blacks, and slaves as benevolent, even as patriarchs. What better way to display this benevolence than to grant "mercy" to bondspeople who were subject to the judges' seemingly absolute power? Such merciful acts could also result from owners' pleas for clemency on behalf of their slaves, further strengthening the social bond among slave owners.

Yet there is a problem with facile application of the Hay model of judicial benevolence to oyer and terminer judges in Virginia slave courts. First, it is difficult to know whether many slaves ever accepted the legitimacy—as opposed to the power—of the judicial process. In addition, the justices could not act as independently as could the English judiciary. They were under pressure to convince other whites that they could keep slaves under control. For every slave owner who might praise a judge for showing mercy to an enslaved defendant, another would condemn him for weakness in the face of challenges from the "inferior orders" of society. In addition, the local judicial authorities in the Old Dominion were jealous of their powers. The county court justices, who also acted as oyer and terminer judges, had steadily lost power as the result of the state's late eighteenth-century creation of new court systems to handle civil and criminal cases, leaving them with little control over criminal prosecutions of free defendants. The only plenary power they continued to exercise was to try and to condemn to death slaves accused of felonies, even if that power was somewhat circumscribed.[23]

This was the power of life and death. The state executive let many death sentences stand, and the slaves so executed often belonged to elite slave owners. All of this would seem to allow or even to encourage oyer and terminer justices to be heavy-handed.

77

However, not-guilty verdicts in capital cases before 1785 support the notion that judges often restrained their seemingly limitless power to execute slaves. Approximately 30 percent of slaves tried in courts whose records have survived were judged innocent of capital offenses between 1706 and 1784. Others benefited from the judges' decision to "down-value" the goods they were convicted of stealing so that their conviction would be for a clergyable offense—an offense for which a slave condemned to death could be granted benefit of clergy—or a misdemeanor.[24] Judges bent on distorting the judicial process and using the death penalty to eliminate troublesome and dangerous slaves certainly would not have allowed so many reduced sentences or verdicts of innocent. The decrease in per capita hangings of slaves from 1785 through the 1860s also indicates that judges and other white authorities regularly showed self-restraint or were restrained by higher authority.

The results of the trials of 395 slaves for crimes against persons (excluding insurrection) and crimes against property in four representative Virginia counties between 1790—that is, after the first major revisions in the state court system—and 1864 illustrate this. The counties considered are (Tidewater) Essex and Southampton, (Piedmont) Spotsylvania, and (Southside) Henry. Eighty-eight (62.4 percent) of the 141 accused of crimes against persons in these four locales were found guilty, leaving 53, or 37.6 percent, not guilty. Of those found guilty, 57 received death sentences, or 64.8 percent of those found guilty. Only 54.4 percent of those sentenced to death (31 of 57), however, actually went to the gallows. Slaves convicted of property crimes fared better: 137 (53.9 percent) of 254 accused slaves were convicted, and only 20 (14.6 percent) of these convicts were sentenced to hang. Just 2 of the condemned did hang.[25] This was only partly the work of the judges. In some cases they had recommended transportation; in others, the state executive pardoned the convict; in still others, the state governor and Council exercised clemency without the recommendation of the oyer and terminer judges.[26] The judges and their superiors placed limits on themselves, and they all were subject to legal limitations.

But this still does not explain why judges and other white authorities would protect some slaves from hanging. The question of the role played by the interests of enslaved defendants in oyer and terminer courts is an essential one. No statute of Virginia bound any oyer and terminer justice to respect the rights of accused slaves *as slaves*. If a purpose of oyer and terminer courts was to help protect slavery, does it then follow that slave-owning judges had to refuse concessions to bondsmen and bondswomen? Would this only "honor the dishonored"?[27] But a slave standing before a court was not just a slave: he or she was a defendant in a court of law. The justices were supposed to be just that—administrators of justice. If they concluded that evidence was weak or that the prosecution had not proved the commission of a capital offense, they would be violating the canons of the bench to convict even a slave of a capital offense. That some judges could still ignore such judicial ethics is obvious; that all judges were bound by oath to uphold these standards of justice is equally clear.

Justices were also bound by law and custom to honor the rights of slave owners to their human property. Every time any judge made any decision about a slave, he was simultaneously acknowledging the rights of owners concerning human chattel and upholding the authority of government over the questions of property and social control raised by bondage. Thus when judges or the state executive granted clemency to a slave, or took away the labor or life of that person (only while compensating the owner), they were upholding the authority of slaveholders and the legitimacy of slavery. As long as they did not grant "too many" acquittals, reprieves, or pardons, they were not threatening the domestic institution. Of course, some judges could, in spite of all these judicial and legal requirements, ignore the evidence and perpetuate injustice. But the acquittals, reductions of charges, and pleas for mercy show that compliance with the law and the search for justice also influenced the fate of slaves in capital trials.

This left room for the apparent exercise of clemency. Many judges and petitioners cited the dictates of humanity as their motive for requesting reprieves or pardons for condemned slaves. Suspicious as such expressions may be, there is no reason to reject them out of hand. What is necessary is to recognize, as did white leaders, the limits of such appeals. As long as pleas for humanity did not threaten the institution of slavery, authorities at the local and state levels could accept them. It was nearly certain, however, that if the trial of a slave for a particularly feared or hated offense stirred up community feelings, then petitions and letters would come to the state governor in favor of execution. Few pleas for mercy followed the trials of slaves for insurrection or conspiracy to revolt. There might be occasional miscalculations of public opinion in favor of a particular hanging, as when Governor Joseph Johnson approved the 1852 transportation of Jordan Hatcher, a slave convicted of murdering a white factory foreman in Richmond. But Johnson survived the political fallout from this controversy, and later governors reprieved more and more slaves without incurring serious political injury.[28]

When exercised, the prerogative of mercy had to limit hangings. Several other forces, however, would appear to guarantee more hangings but in fact sometimes reduced them. Among the most important of these was the behavior of slaves themselves. Many appear to have adjusted their actions to changing socioeconomic and political conditions, whether those actions constituted resistance to the conditions of slavery, conscious opposition to slavery itself, deflected aggression, or mere self-seeking.[29] Thus the most dangerous form of major slave resistance or aggressive activity handled by Virginia's slave courts appears to have been poisoning between the 1740s and the 1770s, killing and insurrection between the 1790s and 1831, and arson from 1831 until

1865.[30] Large-scale stealing, always the most prevalent object of slave courts' attention, fluctuated in frequency partly because of the booms and busts in the larger economy or in the fortunes of individual slaveholders.[31] In reaction to apparent and often real increases in certain kinds of slave behavior that endangered the slave society of Virginia, legislators created harsher sanctions or judges gave tougher sentences. This was particularly true during wartime.[32]

Yet the changing behavior of slaves also could influence the decisions of officials not to sentence slave convicts to death. Just as judges reacted harshly to perceived increases in certain kinds of dangerous behavior of slaves, they also restrained their use of hanging when they perceived a waning of those kinds of behavior. Between 1740 and 1784 more slaves stood before courts of oyer and terminer under suspicion of the capital crime of having poisoned or illegally given medicine to other Virginians than for any other capital offense except burglary. But after 1784 these offenses seemed less prevalent to prosecutors, less dangerous to judges, and, to legislators, less in need of stringent laws.[33] Insurrection and conspiracy held the attention of the Old Dominion's white authorities between 1790 and 1831. There were at least 242 capital trials of slaves for insurrection or conspiring to rebel during those years. While more than 60 of these occurred in response to Gabriel's Plot and another 80 took place in connection with Nat Turner's Revolt, such trials were a regular occurrence from the 1790s through the 1820s. During those decades and through 1831, no fewer than 76 slaves suffered death by hanging for alleged insurrectionary speech, plotting, or action; another 41 were transported. But then a remarkable change occurred after the Turner Revolt and through the 1860s. There were two more executions in 1840 and three during the Civil War; otherwise, ten alleged insurrectionaries were transported or sent to hard labor on the public works from 1832 to 1865. One can speculate about the reasons for this rapid decrease in such punishments, but one can be certain about how quickly judges and the state executive put the hanging of numerous slave rebels behind them.[34]

While a controlling assumption in judges' decisions to deliver fewer sentences of death for particular offenses was perforce that previous hangings had successfully deterred slaves from committing as many of those offenses, in some instances judges and legislators concluded quite the opposite. Sometimes white authorities decided that hangings could not prevent certain kinds of behavior. A case in point is stealing in all its felonious forms, the offense for which slaves stood trial most often. In a verified case of 1706, five slaves simultaneously met the hangman in Westmoreland County. Their statutory offense was not supposed to have been insurrection, murder, or any other crime against persons. Instead it was purportedly burglary and the theft of goods worth more than twenty shillings.[35] Such executions continued to occur regularly until enslaved defendants could plead benefit of clergy, which at least three hundred did successfully between 1734 and 1784. (The total number of successful pleas may have been as high as five hundred, assuming that the three hundred known pleas are approximately 60 percent of actual pleas in property cases.) Only seven such pleas were successful in known murder cases, and forty in known poisoning or illegal administration of medicine trials, during the same years. Benefit of clergy thus significantly reduced the number of potential hangings of slaves for offenses against property.

It would not be until the nineteenth century that even more men and women convicted of property crimes would escape the noose. Executions for these alleged offenses continued through the eighteenth century because some convicts had been granted benefit before and others were convicted of nonclergyable offenses. Through 1784 there were at least 271, perhaps as many as 450, sentences of slaves to death for nonviolent property crimes. The trend continued through the late 1780s and 1790s: 31 slaves went to the gallows for alleged burglary or robbery between 1785 and 1799. But in all the years from 1800 through 1864, only 28 did so. Most of those 28 suffered death after being convicted of robbery or using violence against persons while committing a burglary and/ or theft. One key to this sharp reduction in hangings of slaves for property crimes was the room for discretion allowed by the 1796 reduction to noncapital status of all crimes against property committed by free whites. Another key was the even greater discretion allowed by the institution of the 1801 transportation law.

That such discretionary powers became available to judges and the state executive by 1801 does not, however, explain why they so frequently used them to reject capital punishment of slaves for crimes against property. Indeed, the number of major stealing incidents for which white authorities believed slaves were responsible increased throughout Virginia as a whole during the eighteenth century, yet judges and legislators reduced the number of executions of bondspeople for these incidents. This "crossing" of trends suggests that white leaders concluded that capital punishment could not reduce crimes against property and that its use should be reserved only for such problems as recidivism or for theft aggravated by assault or threats. The alternative of transportation of such convicts could both remove the slave from the Commonwealth and save public money.

Racist and proslavery public opinion were also highly influential in both executions and reprieves. The few antebellum lynchings or attempted lynchings of individual slaves (some resulting from charges of rape but others occurring because of mounting anger against marauding maroons), the many lynchings that followed Nat Turner's Revolt, the public outcry among whites after groups of slaves killed any white authority, and many petitioners' insistence that it was necessary to "make an example" of particular slaves in order to counteract rising attacks by slaves on people or property—all reflect the power of public opinion or, in some cases, panic and hysteria, to encourage or even compel authorities to carry out executions.[36]

The powerful, yet hardly irresistible, force of public opinion is apparent in some episodes. When nine slaves faced execution for allegedly killing John Hamlin, their Lunenburg County owner, in 1827, the defense counsel petitioned the governor to transport four of them. "The general excitement which prevails in the county . . . and the serious apprehensions entertained, by many, of a repetition of the like tragedies, should these go unpunished," he reported, meant that "the people of the county . . . are, in general, strongly opposed to the transportation of any." Yet the judges had recommended just that for two of the convicts, and Governor William B. Giles followed their advice.[37]

As often as racism could support hangings of blacks, it could still sometimes lead legislators or judges to ignore or de-emphasize certain kinds of behavior. In 247 homicide cases resulting in hangings between 1785 and 1864, Virginia's records identify the people whom enslaved defendants had been accused of murdering. Only 50 of these executed slaves had allegedly murdered other slaves. Among the 97 convicted of murder and transported whose victims can be identified, 55 had been judged guilty of murdering other slaves (see table 3.6).[38] In other words, slightly more transported slaves had supposedly murdered other slaves than had purportedly murdered whites. On the other hand, slightly fewer slaves were hanged than were transported after being found guilty of murdering slaves. No slave was ever executed or even transported for attempted murder of a slave. The special statutes of 1823 and 1832 concerning assault with intent to kill covered only those cases in which whites were the victims. Oyer and terminer judges did not bother to apply the common law to slaves who had assaulted other slaves, with or without intent to kill. Slaveholders as a rule could not conceive of applying, or simply did not apply, the common law

Table 3.6

Victims of Slaves Hanged, Transported, or Sent to Hard Labor for Attempted Murder or Murder, Virginia, 1785–1864

| | Attempted Murder | | | | | | Murder | | | | | |
| | Hanged | | | Transported or Labor | | | Hanged | | | Transported or Labor | | |
	White Victim	Slave Victim	Unidentified Victim	White Victim	Slave Victim	Unidentified Victim	White Victim	Slave Victim	Unidentified Victim	White Victim	Slave Victim	Unidentified Victim
1785–89	0	0	0	0	0	0	3	1	2	0	0	0
1790–94	3	0	0	0	0	0	10	6	0	0	0	0
1795–99	2	0	0	0	0	0	19	6	3	0	0	0
1800–1804	2	0	0	2	0	1	12	3	1	3	2	0
1805–9	1	0	1	0	0	0	14	0	0	0	1	0
1810–14	1	0	0	1	0	0	6	3	0	2	0	2
1815–19	1	0	0	1	0	0	10	2	1	3	3	1
1820–24	1	0	0	3	0	0	21	6	2	2	6	0
1825–29	1	0	0	14	0	0	24	3	3	6	1	3
1830–34	1	0	0	11	0	0	11	2	3	5	4	2
1835–39	2	0	0	9	0	0	12	1	0	9	1	1
1840–44	2	0	0	7	0	1	5	3	1	0	5	2
1845–49	4	0	0	7	0	0	8	4	1	2	3	3
1850–54	6	0	0	19	0	0	10	3	3	3	9	1
1855–59	1	0	0	32	0	0	16	6	0	3	12	3
1860–64	5	0	0	10	0	1	16	1	1	4	8	4
Total	33	0	1	116	0	3	197	50	21	42	55	22

Sources: Condemned Slaves, boxes 1–10, Library of Virginia; county court records.

Note: Figures for slaves convicted of infanticide (three executed and fifteen transported) or of murdering a free black person (six executed and nine transported) do not appear in this table.

of rape to a slave when another slave was the alleged victim, although records of at least two cases do exist.[39] The racist, ethnocentric, and proslavery assumptions that could help produce these distorted results are too well known to require elaboration here. The conviction prevalent among whites that black lives and bodies mattered less than those of whites did not always control the judicial process, but the idea certainly had a significant impact on it.

Considerations of owners' investment in slave property often reinforced but also frequently blocked decisions to execute slaves. As early as 1705 the colony's government compensated slave owners for what legislators intended to be the full market value of any executed slave. The state continued that practice through 1865, which accounts for the extensive records of post-1784 executions.[40] (Most pre-1785 documentation has disappeared.) The purpose of compensation was threefold. It was supposed to encourage slave owners to cooperate with governmental efforts to control slaves' most dangerous behavior, thus discouraging "selling down the river" as a private sanction against the most recalcitrant slaves. It was also meant, as the word *compensation* indicates, to cushion the economic shock suffered by slaveholders whose capital assets were destroyed when slaves were executed. Finally, the compensation system spread among all taxpayers, large and small slaveholders and nonslaveholders alike, the cost of protecting lives, property, and the vulnerable slave system itself from dangerous slaves.[41]

Although some planters might doubt the compensation system's efficacy at times, it often reinforced the decision to execute. In 1772 the House of Burgesses required that four judges, being a majority, assent to guilt when death sentences were issued. Prominent planter Landon Carter was incensed. The result, he predicted, was that "a negro now cannot be hanged" because it would be impossible to get such a vote. He thought he knew why the law had passed: "I understand the Public frugality occasioned this law that they might not have too many Slaves to be paid for.

Frugality go on with your destruction; and prosper thou the country whom thou intendest to serve if thou canst. My word for it, this law will not stand long." Carter's prediction was wrong on both counts. Slaves continued to hang then and even after the Virginia legislature later required a unanimous vote for a slave to be condemned to death.[42]

Economic interest supported hangings in other ways. For example, some slaves did suffer hanging for killing other slaves. Blacks who endangered slaves were a major problem for both the owners and the owned. Attacks of bondspeople on one another endangered their community's solidarity as well as depriving the already deprived. So, when slaves could not exercise control over fellow African Americans, they would be affected by the outcome of judicial control of those people. While that surely created a difficult problem for those slaves otherwise hostile toward the slave courts, it was a simpler matter for owners. The interest of slaveholders in preventing these injurious or deadly attacks was strong. Serious injuries sustained by wounded laborers affected their value, while dead slaves represented lost capital as well as labor. Such assaults also threatened some slaveholders' objective of maintaining harmony in the quarters.

But economic factors were no more deterministic than others. Just as economic considerations could encourage capital punishment of slaves, so did they sometimes discourage it. Trials of slaves were expensive, but most white leaders believed they were worth the cost. Executions of slaves were even more expensive.[43] They entailed all the costs of jailing the condemned while the governor and Council considered appeals from owners, petitioners, or court officers. Actually executing the slave and compensating the slave owner in accordance with the value ascribed to the man or woman by slave court justices, who were usually the owner's friends, the owner's neighbors, fellow slave owners, or residents of the same county, added to the expense. The total cost of compensation for executed slaves in Virginia from 1791 through 1800 was nearly $36,000. For 1820–31 it was $44,020.[44] The "return" perceived by whites was that execution removed a dangerous slave from the slave society.

Transportation, however, accomplished somewhat the same purpose as execution, but at less cost. The system of transporting slave convicts out of Virginia and the United States did require disbursements for jailing in the county, transferring reprieved slaves to the penitentiary in Richmond, providing for their stay there, negotiating with prospective buyers, and, as with executed slaves, compensating owners. But sale of reprieved slaves to the highest bidders made up much of that expense at the same time that it promised to remove the convicts from Virginia forever.

Some less obvious but still powerful factors affected the use of capital punishment against slaves. The wish to "make the system work" was an important determinant. When in the 1730s all of Virginia's slave courts began to allow slaves to plead benefit of clergy when convicted of capital crimes, the colony's and later the state's legislators put some offenses beyond this protection. These were the nonclergyable offenses, such as conspiracy to murder or to make insurrection.[45] There were enough clergyable offenses, however, that many slaves avoided hanging even after being convicted of capital offenses. Yet benefit of clergy contained a threat that put slaves at risk. Should the slave who had received benefit of clergy later be convicted of another capital crime, there could be no appeal to benefit. Under these circumstances, at least fourteen slaves received death sentences before 1785, and more than eleven were hanged thereafter. These condemnations occurred not because of the offense of which these slaves were found guilty per se. Instead they reinforced benefit of clergy as a suspended sentence of death.[46]

Executions of slaves could also result from the unexpressed, general expectations of the white population concerning the outcome of capital trials of slaves or white callousness toward the fate of black victims. Hangings became standard operating procedure. The regular hangings of black bondspeople, an average of 78 per decade between 1785 and 1865—as many as 67 or 72 occurring during two five-year periods in which insurrectionary activity or planning was feared, extensive, or intensive—and the long-established system of laws, courts, and compensation gave capital punishment against enslaved Virginians the look of permanence, reinforcing many whites' belief in its legitimacy. Apathy, brutality, hysteria, racism, and oppression were surely involved in this cycle of official violence, but calm assurance as well as utter indifference also kept the cycle going.

Several examples underscore the indifferent or matter-of-fact approach some people took to the system. In 1763 Archibald Campbell succinctly characterized the forthcoming execution of a slave for breaking open a store in Norfolk: "I think you are well quit of such a rogue," he wrote to Henry Tucker, the man's owner. A state Auditor's Office employee showed how institutionalized the execution procedure had become by 1786 when he endorsed the record of a condemned slave's trial. "No doubt the negroe was hung," he noted, "but there must be produced a Cert[ification] of the execution." At seventy years of age in 1828, James Monroe remembered that "several" slaves had been executed for their part in Gabriel's Plot of 1800, which occurred while Monroe was governor. The actual number exceeded twenty-five. And in 1809 Miles King of Gloucester County wrote William Wirt—a lawyer subsequently famous for his biography of Patrick Henry and for his anti-Masonic presidential candidacy of 1832—in order to secure compensation of $1,533.33 for four of his slaves who had recently been hanged by the neck after being convicted of murdering their overseer. The heads of two were also displayed in public. Having said nothing at all about the overseer or the slaves, King asked Wirt not to let "this trifling matter" of the compensation interfere with other business. He quickly changed the subject to a horse race.[47]

On the other hand, positive human emotions could motivate opposition to certain executions. Personal attachment might act as a powerful incentive to strenuous efforts to save slaves from the gallows, although public officials frequently rejected such appeals. In 1843 the Richmond Hustings Court condemned Virginia, the property of Archibald Govan of Hanover County, for starting a fire in a residence. Govan quickly filed a fervent petition with the governor, arguing that the offense itself did not warrant execution and pointing out that Virginia was the daughter of one of his favorite house servants. Govan promised to sell Virginia out of the state should the governor pardon her. Lucy H. Govan shared that estimation of the offense, but she emphasized even more strongly than Archibald Govan the personal cost of execution both to other Govan slaves and to herself. "I am so much attached to Linney," Lucy wrote to a correspondent about Virginia's mother. "She nursed me in my infancy—and was the property of my brother, all these things make me feel it much more keenly." Governor James McDowell granted the pardon, and Archibald Govan prepared to sell Virginia in North Carolina so that she could be as close to her family as Govan's promise to the governor allowed.[48]

Some whites believed it inadequate to argue only that the sparing of black convicts' lives would often be as effective a deterrent as taking their lives. Such people showed something more than the reluctance of authorities to be as harsh as the law allowed them to be, which is so well known to students of criminal justice systems.[49] Instead, they believed forbearance to be humanitarian, not just politic. Hints abound, for example, about the possible connection between religious beliefs and reduced use of capital punishment of slaves. It was partly Governor William Gooch's knowledge that a slave condemned to death in 1731 was a Christian that led him to raise the question of her eligibility for benefit of clergy. Gooch's questioning led to 1732 legislation that guaranteed that privilege to any slave when statutes concerning specific crimes allowed it. The spread of evangelical Christianity among the planter class by the early 1800s also fostered the growth of sentiments in favor of amelioration of conditions experienced by slaves, not the least of which was death on the gallows.[50]

Another motive for active opposition to some, if not all, hangings of enslaved human beings was political. American revolutionaries, it is well known, were at first deeply ambivalent about slavery, but later they found new ways to protect it within their developing republic. Once southern leaders gave up or openly rejected any idea of gradual or immediate abolition, many did concentrate on what they hoped would be amelioration of the condition of slaves as a republican enterprise. Building on this self-styled reform, others later attempted to foster an image of themselves as benign, paternalistic guardians of servants who labored in a serene, because well-ruled, "domestic" environment.[51] It was in the republican spirit that Thomas Jefferson first advocated transportation for slave convicts, counseled Governor James Monroe to limit bloodshed in reaction to Gabriel's Plot, and endorsed Virginia's 1801 transportation law.[52] It was not just the well-educated leaders who held the self-contradictory desire to find a way to extend the blessing of liberty to slaves even as they remained enslaved. "I have always been Averst to taking away the Life of a Slave for the Crime of Steeling," John Caruthers wrote to Governor William H. Cabell from Lexington in 1806. If Ned had to be executed, Caruthers went on, then he hoped Cabell would prevent the hanging from happening on July Fourth, "Celebrated by the Sons of Ammarica for the Liberties which we now Injoy."[53]

In 1849 two eminent jurists made clear their opinion that the good reputation of the Commonwealth of Virginia necessitated the limitation of capital punishment against slaves. The 1849 revisors of the Virginia code expressed shock that the 1848 legislature's revision of the criminal code prescribed no punishment between whipping and execution for slave convicts. "Our code would be a bloody one, and a disgrace to the state," they insisted, if that provision "should be adopted with any expectation of its being enforced." The legislature promptly reinstated transportation. The possibility that these actions reflected particular sensitivity to abolitionist criticisms of slaveholders is obvious but somewhat difficult to prove. It is equally possible that they derived from the wish of legislators to think well of themselves.[54]

Revulsion against the spectacle created by public hangings was sufficiently strong in some circles to contribute to sentiment against capital punishment for slaves. Samuel McDowell Reid articulated a white leader's attitude in 1854 in response to the gathering of an eager crowd in Lexington: "This was to have been, and indeed was, a great day in Lexington, it was the day appointed for the hanging of Jim the negro who killed Poagues man at the Boatyard, and a vast crowd collected from Mountain top and valley, such as you never see on ordinary occasions, people who really came, looking like they would enjoy the exhibition—but the sport was marred by a letter from the Governor granting a respite for 30 days, and the probability is that he will be removed for sale and transportation." Reid's rejection of the crowd's point of view led him to make an incorrect prediction. Jim Gooch had been convicted of first-degree murder and was executed at the end of the thirty-day respite. But Reid had still objected to the undesirable social impact of the public hanging of a slave. The judges of Henry County may have had similar feelings, or fears, about the impact of public hangings on slaves when they ordered that the execution of three men convicted of poisoning their master take place "within the walls of the jail."[55]

Still another factor that could motivate a few whites to oppose capital punishment against slaves was their understanding that it was a condemnation of the already condemned. As Robert Tinsley wrote to the governor and Council in 1826, slaves, "unfortunate as they are, in being doomed to perpetual slavery, deprived of the inestimable privilege of a trial by jury of their equals, and according to the forms of the Common law, are yet the more unfortunate, as on account of their condition of slaves, the wisdom of the legislature has not been able to devise, a scale of punishment graduated according to the several degrees of their offenses." The prosecutor in the case about which Tinsley was writing declared that he could not agree with these sentiments, but he did go on to argue against execution because of other weaknesses in the trials. The slave in question was transported.[56]

The reaction of slaves to capital punishment is just as important a subject as is the response of other Virginians, but evidence is much less abundant concerning the former than the latter. It is consequently possible to analyze only some aspects of that reaction. However much they may have held the slave owners' judicial system in contempt, slaves had to take the risk of suffering capital punishment very seriously. Even after running away, suicide, successful concealment, reduced sentences, benefit of clergy, pardons, and transportation lowered the number of actual or potential hangings, many enslaved people still went to the gallows. They were in more danger before the Revolution and in less peril after 1800. But as with whipping, the threat of execution was as important at times as the reality. Presumably some slaves ignored both threat and reality, especially when acting in passion. But condemned insurrectionaries regularly made it clear that they regarded death at the hands of government as but another prop upholding slavery.[57] Other slaves found one way or another to justify the actions that white authorities believed justified hanging those slaves. If the slaves did not make explicit statements, they could make clear where their loyalties lay by giving primary attention to any slaves who witnessed their execution.[58] Still others sang psalms while waiting in jail for their hanging, accepted consolation from a black or white clergyman just before they climbed the gallows, or even gave scaffold speeches exhorting fellow slaves to avoid lives of wickedness, speeches that became formulaic as they attained the status of ritual and that therefore may or may not have been sincere.[59]

We may speculate that slaves were impressed with the power of slave resistance when it provoked government to use the ultimate power of enforcement. Because we know that many slaves actively affirmed their customary right to "take" goods from their owners or even other whites, we can infer the resentment of those men and women against the execution of fellow bondspeople for alleged crimes against property.[60] We know that some slaves defended those who killed "sole drivers"—sometimes "soul drivers"—or vicious owners and overseers.[61] On the other hand, we can infer from the consequences of killings of slaves by slaves that bondspeople may occasionally have welcomed the execution of a slave responsible for such a death.[62] It is a fair inference that slaves often reacted to executions in one or more of these ways. Unfortunately, however, there is little or no direct evidence in court records and manuscripts, or in former slaves' autobiographies and narratives of slaves in Virginia, of slaves' actually making these judgments about capital punishment.

Two aspects of the numerous hangings of slaves stand out for twentieth-century observers, however. They are the disparity between executions of black and white Virginians and between African Virginian and European Virginian evaluations of some slaves' behavior. Quite often black men or women hanging from a rope represented far more than most whites' belief in capital punishment. They also reflected the profound division that was inherent in any slave society. In the extreme case of a slave killing a master or overseer, self-preservation was in the balance for other masters and overseers. Quite often, however, it was self-preservation that had been in the balance for the slave who killed the white authority. The law and courts refused to recognize this problem. Instead they almost always considered only the master and overseer, for to do otherwise would threaten the system of control that made slavery possible. Indeed, it is this aspect of capital punishment of slaves that separates it from capital punishment for free people in Virginia, the rest of the United States, or elsewhere in the world. It served another purpose in a slave state such as Virginia.[63]

One of the primary purposes of the slave code and courts was to help preserve slavery. If the decisions of many different white authorities in Virginia to use or not to use capital punishment against slave convicts are measured against that purpose, then the Old Dominion's officials succeeded. Numerous circumstances and many other kinds of decisions helped to preserve slavery; capital punishment was only one guarantor of the peculiar institution. But the statistics of hangings—635 went to the Old Dominion's gallows between 1785 and 1865 alone—are still most extraordinary.[64]

At the same time, white Virginian authorities learned that capital punishment was so effective in conjunction with the manifold other powerful methods of control exercised by slave owners and government that they did not have to rely on it every time the law allowed them to do so. In conception, slavery was the absolute control of some human beings by others; in practice, however, it was sufficient control. That meant that as long as the peculiar institution survived in the Old Dominion, blacks endured domination by psychological, legal, or physical terror. But "mercy" as well as terror helped to maintain slavery. To this extent, Hay's interpretation of English judicial benevolence intended to maintain social control does apply to the system of capital punishment in Virginia.[65] Whites might be impressed with the level of determined opposition to slavery that many condemned slaves represented; they might even see the humanity of slaves in the very men and women whom they categorized as the most dangerous. But they ultimately could rest assured that hangings and reprieves from hangings were but two sides of the coin that they used to help pay for making their world safe for slavery.

4

THE TRANSPORTATION OF SLAVES
FROM VIRGINIA, 1800–1865

On November 20, 1838, the oyer and terminer justices of Jefferson County, Virginia (now West Virginia), heard the prosecution
of John, the twenty-year-old slave of Humphrey Keyes, on the
charge of having attempted to rape a white woman. After John
entered a plea of not guilty, the court reviewed testimony from
the alleged victim, the defendant's mother, and a white man who
appeared as a character witness in John's favor. Believing the accuser, the members of the bench convicted John and sentenced
him to be hanged by the neck. They also assessed the value of John
at seven hundred dollars so the state government could compensate
Humphrey Keyes for that amount.[1]

The government of Virginia did pay Keyes the compensation,
but John did not hang. Instead the governor and Council decided
in February 1839 to reprieve John for sale to the highest bidder,
on the condition that he be transported out of Virginia and out of
the United States, to a place from which he could never return to
his home state. A majority of the officials had concluded that the
evidence against John was insufficient to warrant the death penalty. Numerous citizens of Jefferson County angrily disagreed and
threatened to form a lynch mob. The government, however, withstood this challenge to civil and judicial authority by calling up
sixty volunteers. The auditor remitted seven hundred dollars to
Keyes on March 16, 1840, and the Virginia Penitentiary received
John on March 26, in anticipation of his sale to a slave trader. That
sale occurred on September 16, when Rudolph Littlejohn signed a

bond for twenty-seven thousand dollars, to which William H. Williams was the security, promising to carry John and the twenty-six other convict slaves he had purchased out of the United States.[2]

Littlejohn's role quickly ended. Instead, Williams delivered the twenty-seven convicts as well as forty-six other slaves to the brig *Uncas*, bound for Mobile or New Orleans. Governor John Rutherfoord of Virginia somehow learned of this transaction and sent a warning to the mayor of New Orleans, who in turn saw to it that Williams was intercepted when he brought the slaves into New Orleans via Mobile on November 1, 1840. Three of the convict slaves had already been sold or had met another fate, so Williams was convicted of importing twenty-four slaves in violation of a Louisiana law of 1817 that prohibited the importation of slaves convicted of certain felonies in other states. After losing an appeal to the Louisiana Supreme Court, Williams faced a loss of nearly fifty thousand dollars. The slaves in question were auctioned off to the highest bidder once again, but this sale was in New Orleans and without residential qualifications, thus ironically ensuring that the convicts whom Virginia intended to export out of the United States would in fact probably remain within the country. The fate of John is unknown. Williams, on the other hand, successfully petitioned the Louisiana legislature for indemnity.[3]

THE PROCEDURE OF TRANSPORTATION

John's convoluted journey through Virginia's and Louisiana's judicial systems via the domestic slave trade was atypical in one important respect. We have some idea of the place to which he was actually transported. Otherwise, it is possible to answer some important questions about the procedure to which John was subjected. Historians are making great progress in the study of the domestic slave trade, the criminal code and courts for slaves as instruments of social control and the protection of slavery, and the nature of slavery in different slave societies. They have also studied the transportation of convict servants from Great Britain to its colonies.[4] Yet they have paid little attention to the transportation of condemned slaves. A look at the penal transportation of slaves from Virginia, a practice on which the Old Dominion's white leaders relied sporadically before 1801 and regularly thereafter, provides another international perspective on slavery, connects the domestic slave trade, the law of slavery, and the nature of the institution, and complements our knowledge of the transportation of convict servants.

In force from its passage on January 15, 1801, Virginia's law "to empower the governor to transport slaves condemned, when it shall be deemed expedient," declared that the governor, "with the advice of council," might sell any slaves under sentence of death to persons who would be required to enter into bond, with security of five hundred dollars for each slave, that they would "carry out of the United States" the reprieved convicts. The same law limited the reprieve of transported slaves, subjecting them to capital punishment should they return to Virginia. County courts were thereafter to send to Richmond the testimony from trials that resulted in the sentence of death, to provide the basis for the decisions of the governor and Council. Owners of transported slaves were to receive compensation just as did owners of executed slaves. Basically the same transportation law remained in effect as long as the peculiar institution survived. Because of the state executive's active role in the transportation process, full records are available concerning the government's disposition of transported slaves.[5]

White authorities in Virginia used the penalty of transportation from 1801 to 1865 against slaves convicted of capital crimes and also, after 1849, of certain other felonies. The questions of why, how, how often, and how effectively they did so embrace considerations of slave resistance and insurrection, the gradual abolition of slavery in the Western Hemisphere, the protection of white

supremacy and slavery, the state government's search for an adequate means to protect people and property in a slave society, the
creation of the convict-lease system, the economics of the slave
trade, economic development in Virginia, government finance, interstate comity, civil war, politics, public opinion, proslavery "re-
forms," and constitutional and legal change. The simple answer
to the question of why is that the governmental practice of 1801
and later not only reflected earlier private practice but was also a
reuse or modification of measures employed temporarily by previous governments of Virginia. Indeed, it can be said that the law
of 1801 actually legalized a de facto procedure of the previous quarter century. The more complex answer to the same question of
why has to do with white Virginians' guarded application of the
evolving penal philosophy of the nation to the peculiar and changing conditions of a slave society.

The declarations of Thomas Jefferson on the subject are illumi-
nating. As a member of the state legislature, Jefferson included
transportation of convict slaves in his 1778 proposal for reform
of the Old Dominion's criminal code. As president, Jefferson
encouraged Governor James Monroe to ask the Commonwealth's
legislature to pass the 1801 law.[6] But the words of some common
citizens testify more fully to the general, shared understanding
of the reason why most white citizens would allow the transportation of some slaves in lieu of execution. According to approximately one hundred Brunswick County petitioners in March 1808,
the only just decision for Governor William H. Cabell was to reprieve for sale and transportation another slave named John, the
possession of William Lashly. On February 22, 1808, the Brunswick slave court had convicted John of burglary and the theft
of goods valued at four dollars and had sentenced him to hang
on April 1. There were several reasons not to execute John, the
Brunswick signatories declared: "Takeing into consideration the
bad effects of frequent Capital punishments—the fatal conse-

quence of punishing crimes of greater and lesser magnitude alike—the Cruelty of takeing the life of a fellow Creature when the possibility of his innocence may exist; and when his Crime is not such an one as to evince the plainest proof of a Soul utterly depraved:—circumstances of the Crime for which John . . . was condemned to death, we feel ourselves induced from motives of policy and feelings of humanity to intercede in his behalf."[7]

The petitioners' arguments as well as the suspicion that John had violated the law under the command of his owner, against whom he could not testify in court, persuaded Governor Cabell and his Council to commute John's sentence to transportation.[8] They and other executives would save the lives (even as they exposed the reprieved to new dangers) of nearly a thousand slaves, many of whom benefited from petitions similar to that submitted by the Brunswick citizens. The prevailing assumption was that in some instances it was not only expedient and economical but also humanitarian to be merciful to slave convicts.[9]

THE ORIGINS OF VIRGINIA'S TRANSPORTATION LAW

The pre-1801 history of Virginian slave owners' relation with defiant slaves supported the notion that punishments short of death could maintain control. George Washington accepted this idea when he took action against a slave whom he characterized as a "Rogue and a Runaway" who should be kept handcuffed until at sea, bound for a West Indian slave market.[10] Indeed, the practice of "selling to Georgia" was later so prevalent that petitioners on behalf of a slave who had killed a Mississippi trader in 1836 while in transit through Virginia declared that Maryland and Virginia slaves' "hatred to the south and southern purchasers of their Race has been increased to a degree of *desperation* so much so that the *best* of them has no *morral* hesitancy in killing what they call a sole driver."[11]

Not only private sales had helped whites to maintain control over slaves. In 1706 the Council of Virginia ordered that a slave owned by the colony be transported to another English colony "for offering violence to Mr. Cary." In 1723 the House of Burgesses passed a special law to transport to the West Indies eight slaves convicted of plotting an insurrection. The Council intervened in the precedent-setting case of Mary Aggie in 1731, granting the Christian slave a pardon on the condition that she be sold in another English colony, and referring to English authorities the question of whether slaves could plead benefit of clergy—a one-time reprieve from execution extended to slaves convicted of certain crimes, mostly against property. The authorities answered in the affirmative. A slave who was convicted in 1735 in York County of running away and receiving stolen goods was also found guilty of theft in Elizabeth City County in 1736. He was ordered by the latter county's court to be transported out of the county and never returned. The Caroline County justices issued the same order in 1744 concerning a slave suspected of poisoning, even though he was found not guilty of that offense. In 1756 the Charles City County oyer and terminer justices decided on the West Indies as the destination of a slave whom they had convicted of burglary and theft. The fledgling state government similarly relied on transportation of runaway or rebellious slaves to the West Indies in several instances in order to protect the Old Dominion during the American Revolution. Finally, during the same dangerous times, the Northampton County authorities responded similarly to the threat they perceived from a slave convicted of attempting to rape a white woman. They not only sentenced him to be castrated but also stipulated that he be taken out of the county and never returned.[12]

The maturing government of the Commonwealth soon institutionalized the means of forcing the private transportation of numerous slaves whom officials deemed dangerous but would not allow to be hanged. Benjamin Henry Latrobe learned of the practice while in Virginia. A slave whom Latrobe saw hanged in 1796 "had always entertained hope of a reprieve or at least that some Gentleman would buy him, as the phrase is, from under the Gallows, in order to carry him out of the State. This it seems is often done." Latrobe was probably quite right, as the entries for the 1780s and 1790s in the Virginia Council journals suggest. Pardon after pardon appears for slaves condemned to death for a variety of offenses—forty-one convicts between 1782 and 1786 alone. Had these slaves all been returned to their homes, the outcry by citizens would have been deafening, but statements against governmental leniency were not widespread at the time. The obvious inference is that *pardoned* usually meant "on the condition that the owner privately sell the pardoned slave out of the state."[13]

By the 1790s the growing suspicion among whites about execution of slaves for various crimes was that it did not always work as a deterrent. Latrobe commented on how the religious conversion of the slave executed for repeated stealing enabled him to reduce "the dread of his example, the only *real* benefit attending a public execution." Some nineteenth-century observers similarly noted that slaves about to be hanged could somewhat neutralize the terror their hangings were supposed to provoke by expressing evangelical precepts, by actively affirming solidarity with slaves in attendance, or even by attempting to justify the behavior for which they had been condemned.[14] White officials would still hang at least 635 enslaved men and women from 1785 to 1865, but the 983 whom they transported and the countless others bought "from under the Gallows" would testify to the strong opinion of whites in power that the penalty of transportation was a good substitute for execution in many cases.

TRANSPORTATION LEGALIZED

The strongest evidence that most white Virginians believed transportation to be an efficacious deterrent is that it became the de facto practice and then was legalized at the very time that slave resistance appeared to be growing. When Virginia's white authorities transported slaves from revolutionary Virginia and Jefferson proposed the legalization of transportation as a general and not a special penalty, they did so in full knowledge of the many slaves who had either taken arms against American forces or who had run away. More significant still was the timing of the 1801 law. Some slaves convicted of crimes had been acting solely for themselves; many others, however, had quite different motives. Imbued with their own revolutionary or defiant notions, aware of and perhaps adopting the natural rights theory of American revolutionaries, and encouraged by the example of the St. Domingue rebels, more and more Old Dominion slaves attacked the property or persons of their owners and other whites through the 1780s and 1790s.[15] If that were not enough to convince white leaders that slave resistance was substantial, the discovery in 1800 of Gabriel's Plot confirmed the worst fears. Indeed, the Virginia legislature passed the transportation law, apparently an ameliorative measure and a law that received Monroe's assent, only four and one-half months after Monroe had received the first reports of Gabriel's conspiracy. Moreover, scare after scare as well as some substantial plots surfaced in the next twenty years, yet there was no powerful effort to eliminate the penalty of transportation in favor of more hangings. Instead the use of transportation steadily increased from an average of 6.8 per year between 1801 and 1804 and 6.6 per year in 1805–9 to 12.0 per year in 1810–14 and 13.8 per year for 1815–19. Sentences reduced to transportation also increased in relation to hangings: the ratios were 1 to 0.8 in 1801–4, 1 to 1 in 1805–9, 2.6 to 1 in 1810–14, and 2 to 1 in 1815–19 (see tables 3.3 and 4.1).[16]

Opinions about mercy and deterrence obviously did not alone determine the heavy reliance on the penalty of transportation. The state could also benefit economically from the practice. When

Table 4.1
Slaves Transported or Sent to Hard Labor for Various Offenses, Virginia, 1801–1864

	Stealing	Robbery	Arson	Murder, white	Murder, slave	Other murder	Attempted murder	Poisoning	Rape or attempted rape	Insurrection	Misc.	Unspecified	Total
1801–4	5	0	0	3	2	0	2	0	1	12	1	1	27
1805–9	20	2	3	0	1	1	0	1	2	2	0	1	33
1810–14	32	1	5	2	0	3	3	1	1	5	1	6	60
1815–19	41	3	5	3	5	1	1	3	0	6	1	0	69
1820–24	28	2	4	2	8	1	3	2	3	0	2	2	57
1825–29	34	2	5	6	2	3	14	5	5	0	3	2	81
1830–34	35	1	9	5	5	2	11	2	3	21	2	7	103
1835–39	25	1	8	9	1	1	9	3	3	0	1	1	62
1840–44	30	0	4	0	5	2	8	1	6	5	0	8	69
1845–49	23	2	4	2	3	3	7	1	5	0	1	1	52
1850–54	20	2	17	3	13	2	17	14	5	0	6	5	104
1855–59	19 (3)	2 (0)	29 (4)	3 (1)	17 (3)	8 (2)	32 (5)	8 (2)	13 (0)	2 (1)	2 (0)	22 (0)	157 (21)
1860–64	19 (10)	0 (0)	26 (17)	4 (4)	8 (5)	4 (4)	11 (6)	8 (6)	7 (4)	3 (2)	5 (3)	5 (4)	100 (65)
Total	331 (13)	18 (0)	119 (21)	42 (5)	70 (8)	31 (6)	118 (11)	49 (8)	54 (4)	56 (3)	25 (3)	61 (4)	974 (86)

Sources: Virginia Auditor's Office, item 153, Condemned Slaves, boxes 1–10, Library of Virginia; Virginia Treasury Office, Cash Disbursements Journals, 1855–64; county court records.

Notes: The figures in parentheses indicate the number of slaves among those reprieved between April 1858 and 1864 who are known to have been sent to hard labor on the public works. The figures without parentheses indicate the slaves sent to the public works.

"Stealing" convictions were usually for burglary and theft combined. "Other murder" includes eight slaves convicted of murdering free blacks. "Attempted murder" involved white victims only. "Poisoning" convictions include those for illegal "administration of medicine." The "Miscellaneous" column includes one conviction for causing the printing of writings that denied the right of masters to property in their slaves (1839), one for forgery of a pass (1827), two for aiding a runaway (1864), and twenty for assault. "Unspecified" indicates those convicts whose offense was not recorded by the Auditor's Office. The figures for 1860–64 are probably too low because of the loss of some records for 1864 and early 1865.

the state executed slaves, the owner received the condemned person's market value as determined by the judges who pronounced the capital sentences. The funds for this compensation came from tax revenues. Even though this spread the cost of slave control among all taxpayers, capital punishment still was expensive.[17] When the state transported slaves, owners still received compensation, but the proceeds of the sales to the highest bidder partially reimbursed the state. Bids equaled valuations less frequently after 1801 than before, but the sales potentially could make up much of the expense.[18] The timing of this legalization was economically important. In 1801 there were still numerous markets for American-born slaves in the Western Hemisphere. The proviso of exporting the transportees outside the United States under pain of forfeiture of a bond erected a barrier to entry into U.S. markets, yet legislators must have known that the barrier would hardly have been insurmountable. They may have concluded that the proviso was at least a good-faith effort to uphold interstate comity and responsibilities.[19]

The willingness of the state executive to use transportation was apparent soon after passage of the law. Just eleven days after Monroe signed the legislation, the government sold nine slaves convicted of plotting with Gabriel to William Morris, John G. Brown, and others for $2,917.34. Moreover, the traders bought the convicted plotters for exactly what the oyer and terminer justices of Caroline and Henrico counties and the city of Richmond said they were worth.[20] When various courts convicted fourteen slaves of conspiring to rebel in the spring of 1802, the Commonwealth reduced the sentences of four of them and sold these slaves to well-known trader William Fulcher and one partner on September 20, 1802. At the same time the government sold Fulcher and his partner thirteen other slaves who had been convicted of capital crimes.[21] One could argue that some of the exported slaves had been convicted of insurrection only for political reasons and that

transportation was a way for the government to support its authority without bloodying its hands any further. This may have
been true in some cases, but such a rationale would not explain
the presence of Jack Bowler among the first group of transported
convicts. Bowler, a physically imposing and politically effective
man, had competed with Gabriel for leadership of the 1800 plot.[22]

Traders found markets for these convicts in diverse locations.
Morris and Brown requested that the 1801 group be delivered to
Staunton, Virginia, "from which place we think we can take them
on in safety." One can infer overland conveyance to the Ohio
River, thence to the Mississippi River and on to New Orleans,
which was still in Spanish hands and was already a larger en-
trepôt and slave-trading center than Richmond. The French ces-
sion and the eventual takeover of Louisiana by the United States
would close that market to legal trading of convict slaves, so
governmental officials in Virginia started helping traders find
other markets. At one point in 1801 they even suggested Haiti as
a destination for convicted rebels, a proposal quickly rejected by
legislators because of its implications for the safety of slaveholding
in the states. By mid-1802 attention focused on Surinam, Cuba,
and St. Croix. The Spanish West Indies wanted African slaves
only, while the British consul had made it clear that the last thing
British West Indian planters desired was to import insurrectionaries and other kinds of dangerous or rebellious slaves.[23]

In spite of preferences in the Spanish West Indies, it was to
Spanish territory that dealers transported some slaves between
1802 and 1819. William Fulcher reported to Governor Cabell in
1806 that he had taken more than a dozen men overland through
the Carolinas, across Georgia, and to the St. Marys River in East
Florida, where he delivered them to Jack Cooper, a speculator
trading with the Spaniards. A similar destination was probable
for two South Carolinians who purchased six convict slaves in
1810, among whom was still another convicted plotter. Two slaves

named Robin and Barnabas, who were found guilty of being accessories after the fact in the murder of their master in 1818, faced an
especially bleak and lonely future when they ended up on the Dry
Tortugas, the small, still-Spanish islands some sixty miles west of
Key West. Later, Dr. Samuel Mudd and three other men convicted
of complicity in the assassination of President Abraham Lincoln
would be imprisoned there.[24]

TRANSPORTATION TESTED

By 1820 the state had paid more than $150,000 in compensations
to owners of transported slaves. That amount had reached nearly
$476,000 by 1850 and continued to climb.[25] More and more citi-
zens began to ask a pertinent question, one that historians should
consider as well: How effective was transportation in helping to
protect people, property, and bondage? The sharp increase between
1801 and the 1820s in the number of slaves transported for crimes
against property—an increase matched only by the number of
slaves transported for insurrection—reflects the perception of oyer
and terminer justices that slaves particularly dangerous to property
alone could be removed safely by condemning them to death, with
the full expectation that the governor and Council would commute
the sentence to transportation. But the transportation system was
never foolproof. The regular reports of angry residents of Virginia
as well as embarrassed traders show the ability of some convicts to
evade the system. Some slaves managed either to reappear in the
Old Dominion or to escape from custody elsewhere.

There is no way to compute the exact number of such return-
ees and escapees because they were in private hands at the time
they freed themselves. But the story of Bob, "alias Bob Tucker,"
is instructive, showing how a resourceful convict could escape.
A skilled blacksmith who was at one time or another the slave of
William Gregory of Charles City County, Virginia, Nicholas Brani-

gin of Prince Edward County, Virginia, North Carolinian slave trader James Cunningham, South Carolinian Peabody Keyes, and Governor John Milledge of Georgia, Bob was tried by the Henrico County Court of Oyer and Terminer two days before Christmas 1803 for entering a home during the night, breaking open a trunk, and stealing from it some clothes—all while he was a runaway from South Carolina. On March 7, 1804, Tucker and several other men were purchased by Ellis Puryear and associates and taken to East Florida, where they were sold. One buyer immediately took Tucker back into the United States, an action that did not violate the letter of the transportation law but that certainly defeated one purpose—to keep transported people out of other slave states. The supposedly transported slave soon ran away from his new owner in Georgia and was back in Henrico County Court in May 1805, this time suspected of another burglary. He was instead convicted of returning to Virginia after having been transported, the penalty for which was execution. The Virginia Council was not eager to hang Bob, however. Instead they reprieved him six times. In March 1806 they arranged with Governor Milledge, who claimed to be Bob's current owner, that he should be sold to William Fulcher, who would then try to remove Bob from the United States. Veteran trader Fulcher was no more successful than Puryear had been. Bob Tucker escaped this time in Tennessee, perhaps forever.[26]

There were other escapes in later years.[27] One has to expect that any penal system will experience resistance, no matter whom it is trying to control. That is why some citizens demanded execution of slaves even under doubtful legal circumstances. They wanted to make certain they could get rid of dangerous slaves.[28] While some whites would claim that slaves feared transportation as much as they did hanging, others asserted that slaves knew transportation meant nothing more than sale to the Deep South.[29] While there is not much direct evidence concerning slaves' fear of transportation, it is readily apparent that slaves who left loved ones and friends behind and especially those who were committed to resistance would find either punishment abhorrent. Yet a slave transported was a slave who could continue to resist slavery, whether in a new environment or after escaping and returning to Virginia.

Slave traders apparently did not struggle mightily against this possible consequence of transportation. Instead they labored to sell transported slaves in the best market. This enterprise became a bigger and bigger challenge as the nature of the international and interstate market for slaves changed. The selling of Bob Tucker in Florida and his quick resale to a Georgian apparently reflected a regular practice. Reports began to flow into Richmond by 1817 that traders were freely shipping convicts, including several convicted of involvement in the Boxley Plot of 1816, straight to South Carolina and other states. After the state of Maryland passed its own transportation law in 1819, the supply of such convicts increased. Not only that, but Deep South officials began to complain about and take measures against the sale of convict slaves within their borders—Louisiana in 1817, Mississippi in 1822, and other states in reaction to the threat posed to slavery by slaves who supported Nat Turner's Revolt of 1831.[30] While the case of *Groves v. Slaughter*, decided by the U.S. Supreme Court in 1841, described but did not affirm such measures as exercises of police power, state laws were of little effect, if only because the abolition of slavery in many areas of the Western Hemisphere reduced the size of the slave market by the 1830s and 1840s.[31]

One of the most telling arguments against transportation turned out to be an economic one. Early in the life of the system, traders discovered that they could obtain good discounts on convict slaves. They became more and more particular about the "condition" of each slave as grounds for seeking reduced prices or as the basis for completely rejecting the purchase of some slaves so that they could not be transported at all. Rejection by traders would defeat the very purpose of transportation, because no matter how effective the Virginia Penitentiary was in preventing escapes by slaves reprieved for sale and transportation but unsold, it thereby ensured that they remained in the state, with white convicts, and in the penitentiary that had not been intended to hold slaves. Traders also discovered that they could argue the "objection as to *all*," as Lewis Collier put it in 1829, "on the score of *Character*."[32]

Thus traders added to Deep South officials' opposition to the regular sale of convict slaves in available markets at current prices. Virginia's legislators recognized this economic situation with a law of 1830 that explained "the duty of clerks of county courts, and the forms of certificates for owners of slaves to be removed to the State of Louisiana." Such certificates would affirm, among other things, that the slave or slaves had "not been guilty, nor been convicted of any crimes, within their knowledge." This measure would presumably prevent private punishment of the most defiant slaves by selling them through New Orleans. The legislators also attempted to impose price controls. Knowing that the difference between the level of compensation paid to owners of transported slaves and the price obtained from purchasers of such slaves from the state was increasing, lawmakers in 1840 attempted to reverse the trend by stipulating that oyer and terminer judges should set the value as if the slave were to be sold at public auction to buyers who knew the slave had been condemned and reprieved.[33]

TRANSPORTATION "REFORMED"

In 1841 Governor John Rutherfoord began his campaign to reform the transportation system. Citing the downward pressures on prices, the consequent losses accrued by traders, the *Creole* incident of 1841, and such evasions of the laws of both Virginia and states of the Deep South as that involving William H. Williams and Louisiana the year before, Rutherfoord asserted that "sale and transportation have not had the effect anticipated." Rutherfoord's proposal was that capital punishment for slaves be reduced. So many judges, he said, had been recommending "mercy"— that is, transportation—for convicted slaves because they rarely wanted to order execution. Perhaps because of his suggestion for improvement, Rutherfoord's reform measure failed. Instead an apparently extraordinary hardening of the slave code provoked the first real change. In March 1848 Virginia legislators revised the state's criminal code. Their formula for the punishment of slaves was simple and deadly: conviction of a slave for an offense that would result in the death penalty or imprisonment of at least three years of any free person would in turn require execution of a slave.[34]

The law inexplicably did not mention transportation. Governor John B. Floyd spoke in favor of reducing the costs of transportation in December 1848, after passage of the revised criminal code. He seems not to have known that transportation had been abolished, perhaps because he did not expect it. The judges of Gloucester County do appear to have noticed. In August 1848 they condemned a slave named William to death for petty larceny, and William hanged in September. No other slave received such an extreme penalty for that offense in 1849 and 1850, however. It is probable that the legislators had been dangerously careless in 1848. Two eminent jurists, John M. Patton and Conway Robinson, led a successful reaction to the perhaps inadvertent abolition of transportation. Patton and Robinson, revisors of the Code of Virginia, submitted a report in July 1849 on their suggested revisions of the entire code. They included a proposed measure that became part of the newest code: as before, the governor and Council would have the power to reduce any capital sentence of a slave except for a crime that would result in the execution of a white person—that is, first-degree murder, certain kinds of arson, con-spiring with slaves to murder someone or to "make insurrection," and treason, an offense impossible for slaves to commit.[35]

The immediate result of the reinstatement of transportation in 1849 was a marked increase in the number of slaves trans-ported as well as in the ratio of transported to executed slaves. By the late 1850s, however, the result was paradoxically the de-crease of the transportation of slaves out of the Old Dominion, but not a concomitant decrease of reprieves. The new state con-stitution of 1850, ratified in August 1851, influenced the use of transportation because it required all subsequent governors to publish their reasons for any reprieve or pardon of any convict, including slaves. Governor Joseph Johnson experienced a furious reaction when in 1852 he tried to justify transportation of Jordan Hatcher, a slave who had killed a Richmond factory foreman. Johnson's decision stood, but only at the price of lost political sup-port. The message was clear to later governors: Be careful about ordering reprieves. Yet the number of reprieves still continued to rise. Governor Henry A. Wise found a way out in 1857 and 1858. Citing the need for slave labor to reduce the high costs of such public improvements as railroads, Wise built on existing argu-ments in favor of the purchase or hiring of slaves for such work. Why not put free black and enslaved convicts out to hard labor on the "State works," such as the James River and Kanawha Canal Company? Wise forcefully reminded lawmakers that the trans-portation system was a sham. It also violated interstate comity, as the governor of Alabama had recently reminded him. The Ala-bama governor and other southern state authorities "very properly protest against being made a Botany Bay for the slave convicts of Virginia," Wise added. Wise concluded that everyone knew the bonds were fraudulent and a "mockery," which rendered the sys-tem "immoral."[36]

113

CONVICT LABOR

The Virginia General Assembly joined in Governor Wise's criticism of transportation. On April 7, 1858, Wise signed "An Act providing for the employment of negro convicts on the public works." This law did not prohibit transportation; it allowed another sentence on which state authorities would primarily rely until 1864. The public works included those partly as well as fully owned by the Commonwealth. There would be no governmental payment for the costs of conveying the convicts to and from work or for maintaining, supervising, or guarding them, except on works wholly owned by the state. Thus the state would get the most out of contracts with partly owned public works. Presumably slaves would have good reason to fear the kind of treatment they would receive from the companies only partly owned by the Commonwealth. The many extant contracts for the use of such convicts on the Covington and Ohio Railroad are ample testimony that state officials negotiated the most lucrative arrangements possible.[37]

Use of the reprieved slaves on the public works was, however, no more successful than transportation. While the need for requisitioned and hired slaves on the fortifications during the Civil War increased the demand for and use of convict labor, this ended up working against the employment of convict slaves. More and more citizens complained about the presence of such workers in their communities. They were a "perfect nuisance," exclaimed seventeen petitioners of Bath County. Others were not bothering with petitioning, argued Governor John Letcher in 1862. Instead they were threatening mob action. Some convict slaves began to escape behind enemy lines; others reportedly became "hard to restrain and keep in proper subjection, and . . . therefore much more likely to effect their escape." After trying to make small revisions to the system in 1861, the Virginia General Assembly finally tried to strengthen the option still available to the state executive of getting slaves out of Virginia.[38]

The law of February 1864 specified that the governor could sell such slaves upon receipt of the agreed price and a bond "in penalty of one thousand dollars, conditioned that the slave shall within three months be transported beyond the limits of the Confederate States, and shall never afterwards return into this state." Under the circumstances of war, this seemed ridiculous. Speakers against the bill had indeed insisted that its backers "wish to do what cannot be done—They wish to send the slaves out of the Confederate States." Was the law a veiled threat to send such slaves into Maryland, Kentucky, and other slave states in the Union, or simply a boost to the slave trade with Brazil or the few other remaining slave societies in the Western Hemisphere? Perhaps it was neither. Economic considerations had changed because of an increase in the number of female slave convicts during the Civil War, some of whom had given birth to children while incarcerated. Female slaves convicted of offenses other than arson or crimes for which a free black person would receive the sentence of death now might, but did not have to, be auctioned off unconditionally. This provision also applied to any children born to such women after conviction, but not to those living at the time of conviction.[39]

TRANSPORTED PEOPLE

Besides the legal and administrative nature of transportation, we know several important things about the impact of the system on slaves. No direct evidence of the attitude of slaves toward it has appeared, but there are clear data on the names and ages of 374 transportees that hint at their family histories. The listing of names is unusually revealing. As is well known, white perception of slave names was not regularly personal or complete. That is, slaves and their families could not always control the choice of first names, and white record keepers usually noted only first names. However, 23.8 percent (89 of 374) of the people on a list of slaves transported from 1816 through 1842 appear with their family names. These names are only rarely the same as the family names of the most recent owners. In contrast, court clerks or the state auditor noted the family names of only 7.0 percent (16 of 227) of slaves executed or transported for various kinds of theft between 1815 and 1844. For some reason the Virginia Penitentiary officials wished to keep track of many last names of slaves.[40]

Concerning ages, there is a similar contrast between court records and the penitentiary list of 1816–42. That list gives an age for each individual slave, while court and state auditors' records only rarely do so. There are too many ages of twenty, twenty-five, thirty, and thirty-five for the list to be trusted completely, but comparison of the age groupings of the transported slaves with other available data on the ages of enslaved Virginians reveals that between 1816 and 1842, most slave convicts were of roughly the same age as most slaves traded or taken out of Virginia to the expanding areas of the South (see table 4.2).[41]

The significance of these data is that the slaves of the age most desirable to traders—those in their late teens, their twenties, and their thirties—were the ones more likely to come into conflict with the criminal code of Virginia. The economic circumstances preclude the possibility of owners' using the system to get rid of sick or weakened bondspeople or of slaves toward whom they held a grudge of some kind. The demand for slaves was too high for an owner to pass up the price that could be obtained on the open market in favor of the uncertain prices available through state compensation. Moreover, there were too few women (only 35 of 374) to support an economic argument concerning owners' motives for seeking transportation. Judges obviously did not want to be manipulated in this way, especially because the legal exclusion

Table 4.2

Ages of Slaves Transported for Various Offenses, Virginia, 1816–1842

| | 10–19 | | 20–29 | | 30–39 | | 40–49 | | 50+ | | |
	N	%	N	%	N	%	N	%	N	%	Total
Male	58	17.1	159	46.9	73	21.5	33	9.7	16	4.7	339
Female	19	54.3	10	28.6	4	11.4	1	2.9	1	2.9	35
Total	77	20.6	169	45.2	77	20.6	34	9.1	17	4.5	374

Source: "A List of Slaves and Free persons of color received into the Penitentiary of Virginia for sale and transportation from the 25th June 1816 to the 1st February 1842," Virginia Auditor's Office, item 153, Condemned Slaves, box 10, Library of Virginia.

of judges from trials of slaves in whom they had any financial interest prevented them from directly manipulating the system to their own benefit. Instead these data suggest that young slaves were experiencing the kind of anger against slavery or showing the kind of determination that would often result in behavior that white authorities attempted to control judicially. The same age cohort appears most frequently in the criminal court records of many societies, yet slaves convicted of crimes were not necessarily "common criminals." Many were resisting aspects of slavery if not bondage itself.[42]

TRANSPORTATION AND THE PRESERVATION OF SLAVERY

The de facto or intentional resistance of slaves to the law of slavery means that the question of how effective the system of transportation was must be expanded to include the question of whether it helped to control slave resistance or other illegal slave behavior. The answer is that even though it did not prevent such behavior from continuing—some slaves, for example, would always be willing to challenge slavery or might prove dangerous to other slaves—it did help to prevent slave resistance from destroying slavery in Virginia. It did so in concert with slaves' own efforts to preserve their communities and values or to protect themselves, as well as with various kinds of public and private sanctions such as execution, whippings, or private sale out of the Old Dominion. Indeed, it is noteworthy that only a few Virginian slaves were executed, and relatively few were convicted, for insurrection after 1831.[43]

It is worth speculating whether whites had to pay a constitutional and political price for this use of the judiciary and the power of the state to protect people and the institution of lifetime bondage in Virginia. The Commonwealth exported convicted, rebellious slaves to other states. This not only violated interstate comity in some cases but also increased the chances of individual or collective slave rebellion and other kinds of dangerous slave behavior in the states of the Deep South. We can never determine the degree to which transportation had these effects. We can only perceive the possible connection between the practice and the higher concentration of the fear, and even the incidence, of insurrection in the Deep South after 1831. It is also interesting to speculate on the questions of whether this in turn made southern leaders more politically sensitive to the abolitionist issue, endangered the lives of slaves inaccurately and unjustly accused of conspiracy, or made Deep South leaders suspicious of the motives of border state leaders, thereby sowing seeds of disunity in the Confederate States.[44]

It is certain, however, that the use of transportation as a penalty for slaves convicted of violating the criminal statutes of Virginia directly affected the lives of 983 slaves and indirectly influenced the future of countless others. It saved them from hanging in the Old Dominion; it also forcibly placed them in new and unpredictable environments. Moreover, less than a decade before it would have been necessary to abolish transportation anyway because of the Thirteenth Amendment's prohibition of slavery, the Commonwealth of Virginia found an alternative punishment that it and many other states would use extensively after 1865. This was the convict-lease system. As two historians have put it, that system meant that "many blacks became familiar with the courts not as protective institutions but rather as places where labor contracts which reduced them to peonage were enforced." Not until after World War I did the convict-lease system disappear from Virginia. It is true that state use of black convicts on the public works arose partly as a means of controlling free blacks, but it also was clearly designed to curb and gain revenue from dangerous slaves, a task that the transportation system was previously supposed to carry out. In that sense, this study corroborates the judgment made by Thorsten Sellin and others that many punishments for free people originated as punishments for slaves.[45]

Above all, the sentence of transportation out of Virginia and the United States, with its penalty of execution for any transported slave who returned to the Old Dominion, merely continued the status of slaves as understood by Orlando Patterson. "The condition of slavery did not absolve or erase the prospect of death," Patterson writes. "Slavery was not a pardon; it was, peculiarly, a conditional commutation. The execution was suspended only as long as the slave acquiesced in his powerlessness."[46] Transportation was similarly a reprieve, with an important condition. Should transported slaves not accept permanent absence from their home, family, other loved ones, and friends, they faced the execution from which transportation had spared them. This necessitated an extremely painful choice between living or physical death. Thus were nearly one thousand Virginian slaves condemned to another variety of "social death" between 1801 and 1865.[47]

5

"THE FULL AND PERFECT ENFORCEMENT OF OUR RIGHTS": FUGITIVE SLAVES AND THE LAWS OF VIRGINIA

In November 1854 Charles Gilbert left Richmond, Virginia. The payment of ten dollars secured him passage on a boat to Old Point Comfort on the Chesapeake Bay. From there to a steamer that put him into Norfolk, and finally to a steamer that conveyed him to Philadelphia, he took a decidedly indirect route. After spending a week with a friend, he had to sleep for another eleven weeks in the crawl space beneath a hotel, under a washhouse, in thick woods, and in a swamp. There was a $550 reward for his capture, so he could trust almost no one. Officers searched for him more than once, and this explains why he stayed in such a variety of places. Gilbert had to suffer these perils because he had violated the laws of the Commonwealth of Virginia concerning runaway slaves and because, through running away, he had challenged the contemporary conviction of most white Virginians that northern abolitionists and southern slaves had to be stopped in their efforts to undermine the peculiar institution.[1]

Lott Mundy, a free African American resident of New York, was in the galley of the schooner *Danville*, for which he was the cook, when it was docked at the port of Richmond in late July 1856. Mundy was not alone. Hearing a noise, another crew member inspected the "chain box" in the galley, where he found an alleged fugitive slave. Upon reinspection, another suspect was found. Lott Mundy was soon convicted of aiding the escape of these two slaves and was sentenced to fifteen years in the Virginia Penitentiary.[2]

About two years later, William D. Bayliss of Delaware, the white skipper of the schooner *Keziah*, faced an extremely hostile and potentially violent crowd of white Petersburg residents after being seized by state officials on the charge of secreting and aiding five fugitive slaves on his boat. The Petersburg authorities protected him from the crowd and delivered him to court, where he was sentenced to forty years in the Virginia Penitentiary.[3]

After people like Charles Gilbert successfully eluded capture and found safety in the North, Virginian legislators tried to tighten the laws of their state to block future escape attempts. As if modeling their measures on the federal Fugitive Slave Act of 1850, they gave special powers of search and seizure to state inspectors so they could find fugitives on steamers bound for Philadelphia, New York, Boston, and other northern ports. State and local authorities successfully intercepted some fugitives. When Mundy and Bayliss arrived at the Virginia Penitentiary, they kept company with eleven other men and one woman who had also been convicted of violating the laws of Virginia concerning fugitive slaves. The inspection law and all of the other laws concerning fugitive slaves were supposed to protect slave property from itself—that is, to keep slaves from "stealing themselves"—as well as from free allies, whether Virginians or not.

The statutes were supposed to keep the chains of slavery around bondspeople and build a wall of security around human property. Historians have discussed the manner in which the federal government dealt with the question of the interstate rendition of fugitive slaves under the U.S. Constitution.[4] Almost completely missing from the history of fugitive slaves, however, is an understanding of slave states' laws concerning runaways and fugitives, the first line of defense on which slave owners relied. The laws—their origins, execution, and impact—reveal one reason why so many white southerners found the federal Fugitive Slave Act of 1793 to be so weak and campaigned for passage and rigorous enforcement of the revised, stringent law of 1850. The states could not possibly protect the "property" of their citizens without help from the federal government. State laws could not do the job by themselves.[5]

The history of Virginia's laws concerning runaway slaves encompasses nearly two centuries of diverse efforts to counter the efforts of bondspeople to challenge by escape their condition as legal chattel. The law declared them to be slaves; they asserted their claim to be free. These actions of bondspeople and the responses of owners and authorities were partly predictable. African Americans learned the dominant culture, explored the terrain, and watched for opportunities to escape. Owners remained vigilant and evolved some effective techniques of prevention and persuasive negative sanctions for running away, while legislators continually developed institutional measures for buttressing the efforts of owners to retrieve "slaves who stole themselves." Each group—fugitive slaves and their owners—countered the other's tactics even as the conflicting strategies of liberation and domination stayed more or less the same.[6]

The most fundamental modification of tactics occurred after the American Revolution. Isolated episodes occurred during the colonial period when slaves fled with the help of "outsiders." The Stono rebels of South Carolina, for example, in 1739 relied on the promise of the Spanish in Florida to grant them freedom if they escaped.[7] Also, many anonymous men and women fled to the diverse sanctuaries of towns and cities, backcountry North Carolina, or other secluded regions, secure in the knowledge that there would always be some urban shopkeepers and frontier settlers who needed labor and who were unlikely to ask too many questions. Other men answered Lord Dunmore's call to arms in 1775 because of the promise of freedom for doing so, and men, women, and children were emancipated by the British under Lord Clinton's proclamation of 1779.[8] But in spite of the importance of the ideology of liberty to the formation of the United States, those white Americans who could and would end bondage in the new republic were largely confined to the states north of the Mason-Dixon line. Most white slaveholders in South, however ambivalent they may have been about slavery, still would not give up their slaves.[9]

The North Star would rise later, yet some Virginian and other southern African Americans knew by the 1780s and 1790s how to reach possibly legal sanctuary north of Maryland and Delaware. As they fled north in increasing numbers, southern slave owners looked for new ways to stop them. Such historians as Larry Gara have effectively laid to rest any claims of widespread organization and success on the part of white abolitionists who aided fugitives and have argued instead that the slaves themselves and their free black allies were primarily responsible for the escapes that did occur—how many we will never know.[10] If we accept that African Americans were the central figures in the flight to the North, one aspect of the fugitive slave question becomes more clear. Slave owners' efforts to retrieve runaways in free states had long provoked some controversy, but after the 1820s the escalation of northerners' efforts to give sanctuary to fugitives helped to create the fierce national controversy over fugitive slaves. There was nothing particularly new about slaves running away, so most white southerners focused less on slaves' behavior than they did on the behavior of whites and free African Americans. They believed they already knew how to deal with fugitive slaves. The new problem was how to deal with Yankees and others who were willing to give runaways direct aid and comfort.

THE EARLY DEVELOPMENT OF VIRGINIA'S
FUGITIVE SLAVE LAWS

The slave owners of Virginia developed laws concerning runaway slaves with the obvious precedent of laws related to runaway servants. While Gerald Mullin correctly observes that colonial

Virginia "was notoriously lax about enforcing codes for runaways" and that "runaway codes were generally unsuccessful throughout the [eighteenth] century," there was certainly no lack of law-making concerning runaways. Laws addressing the problem of runaway servants appeared regularly for 150 years, from 1642 through 1792.[11] Court cases appeared as early as 1640 in which different punishments were imposed on white servants and African American runaways.[12] Statutes designed to control runaway slaves appeared for two centuries, from 1660 to 1864. Beginning with a statute passed in 1660 that fell more heavily on runaway servants than on slaves, yet recognized the danger of these servants' having as confederates "negroes who are incapable of making satisfaction by addition of time," the laws of the Old Dominion never explicitly defined a runaway and simultaneously developed numerous techniques of dealing with them. During the colonial period lawmakers frequently amended and supplemented the original statutes. After the slave population of Virginia increased and the colonies experienced rapid growth from the 1720s through the 1760s, the problem of controlling runaways changed in character.[13]

The basic features of the laws were clear enough. Rewards were set for "taking up" runaways, and justices of the peace, prison keepers, constables, and sheriffs were empowered to deal with and even to put to work runaways brought before them, as well as being held responsible for them. The main means of returning runaway slaves to their owners was to "whip them from constable to constable" across the necessary distance within Virginia.[14] By 1748 the colony's lawmakers had to provide special measures for slaves taken up in Virginia who belonged to Maryland or North Carolina owners, specify publication of an advertisement concerning the runaway in the *Virginia Gazette*, empower any sheriff, constable, "or other officer" to impress men and horses in order to convey and prevent the escape of a runaway, require the claimant of a runaway to "apply to the court of the county where he resides, and make proof of his having lost a slave, answering the description published . . . in the Gazette, and obtain certificate thereof," and allow county authorities to send an unclaimed slave to the public jail in Williamsburg. The Williamsburg jailer had to put on the runaway's neck a "strong iron collar, with the letters PG [Public Gaol] stamped thereon," preparatory to hiring out the person. Should the slave remain unclaimed, the government could sell her or him at public auction, with the proceeds going to the public treasury.[15]

What should be apparent about all of these laws is that they lack any special measures for addressing the problem of runaways who attempted to leave Virginia. While both temporary and permanent escape constituted running away, it is useful to make a distinction between temporary runaways and permanent fugitives. The colony's laws had recognized permanent fugitives as especially threatening in 1691. These were "outlying" slaves who could be outlawed—that is, killed with impunity by persons delegated to capture them.[16] But it would not be until the British enemy attracted escaping slaves to their lines during the American Revolution that the new Commonwealth of Virginia would develop legal weapons against slaves' escaping beyond the Old Dominion with the help and protection of outsiders. Virginia stipulated in 1775 that slaves who voluntarily escaped to the British would, if recaptured, be transported to the West Indies. Running away in a group was also made a conspiracy.[17] Many owners, including Thomas Jefferson and George Washington, were bedeviled by the impossibility of their ever reclaiming bondspeople who had survived their escape to the British and by the likelihood that the state and federal governments could not assist them in this.

THE NEW COMMONWEALTH OF VIRGINIA
AND FUGITIVE SLAVES

The war ended, but the next "enemy" came from a more difficult source: the new enemy was within the United States. The first hint of "trouble" appears in the preamble to a law passed by the Virginia Assembly at the end of 1795: "Great and alarming mischiefs have arisen in other states of this Union, and are likely to arise in this by voluntary associations of individuals, who under cover of effecting that justice towards persons unwarrantly held in slavery, which the sovereignty and duty of society alone ought to afford; have in many instances been the means of depriving masters of their property in slaves, and in others occasioned them heavy expenses in tedious and unfounded law suits." The legislature responded by setting the form of court petitions for freedom and by levying fines on anyone who aided an unsuccessful suit.[18]

Two more harbingers of what was to come were published in the statutes of the state in 1798. Angered by what they saw as outside interference in the relationship between master and slave, a handful of slave owners in northern Virginia won the state assembly's approval for the law that prohibited members of abolitionist societies from serving as jurors in suits for freedom. That prohibition was the third part of a law that first decreed the death penalty without benefit of clergy for free people who advised or conspired with a slave to "rebel, or make insurrection, or who shall advise or assist such slave in the murder of any person whatsoever," and that secondly stipulated a fine for free people found guilty of "harbouring or entertaining any slave without the consent of his or her master, mistress, or overseer." The rest of the same law covered the process of identifying for trial slaves charged with a felony but fugitive from justice and retaken, raised to a felony a free black person's transfer of her or his "register" of freedom to a runaway slave who thereby managed to book passage on vessels leaving Virginia, demanded that all masters and skippers of vessels obtain certificates from magistrates verifying the identity of any free black passenger and giving details about that person's intended journey, and laid down a penalty of five hundred dollars to be recovered by suit from any master or skipper of a vessel who did not obtain such a certificate.[19]

The level of suspicion by Virginia's white leaders of abolitionists, outsiders, and northerners in this law foretells much of the hostility toward abolitionists from the northern free states that would become so obvious in later decades. In January 1805 Virginia's white leaders strengthened their capability to keep slaves within slavery and within Virginia. They did so by tightening statutory protection against slave stealing. Normally the action of people seeking "free slave labor" for their own or a client's benefit, the "carrying away" of slaves had by 1805 taken on an abolitionist cast. What to some abolitionists was a heroic act of liberation was of course infamous theft as far as slave owners were concerned. The language of part of the statute is so precise and determined that it makes clear how concerned legislators had become:

And as doubts may arise as to what shall be considered a carrying away or removal, within the meaning of this act, *Be it further enacted,* That not only all those who shall willingly and designedly carry away slaves as aforesaid, but all masters of vessels who, having a slave or slaves on board their said vessels, shall sail beyond the limits of any county with such slave or slaves on board, shall be considered as carrying off or removing such slave or slaves, within the true intent and meaning of this act. And any person travelling by land who shall give countenance, protection, or assistance to such slave or slaves, for the purpose of preventing him, her or them, from being stopped or apprehended, shall also be considered as carrying off or removing such slave or slaves, within the true intent and meaning of this act.[20]

The message was clear by the time the four main clauses of this law were enacted: "Any master or skipper of a vessel," and by implication any crew member, was to observe the strictest propriety in any transaction with slaves. Granted permission by their owners to deal with bondspeople, even to transport them to another port, masters, skippers, and crews were safe from suspicion. Caught with unauthorized slaves on their boat, however, they would pay a heavy price in fines, a form of restitution, and two to four years in the state's new penitentiary in Richmond. This law turned out to be preparation for war, not war itself. The teeth of the law were apparently only bared, not frequently shut on the law's prey, however. Five years later, only two convicts in the penitentiary had been incarcerated for slave stealing, and none explicitly for carrying off a slave, the offense more feared by the legislators who wrote the law of 1805.[21]

THE COMMONWEALTH ADJUSTS TO THE EXPANDING NATION

Aside from passing two acts meant to adjust the code concerning runaways, Old Dominion lawmakers saw no need for major changes in laws concerning fugitive slaves until an old external enemy came back during the War of 1812 to haunt slave owners.[22] Looking for the same chance as any enemy of a slave power had for centuries, the British made their promises of freedom to Chesapeake slaves. Enough of them responded positively that the government of Virginia tried once again, as it had during the Revolution, to accomplish the nearly impossible task of preventing slaves' escapes. In early 1814 and early 1815 two new statutes focused particularly on the problem of enemy vessels. Building on the old understanding that it was necessary to keep unsupervised slaves off any vessel if they were to be protected from capture or prevented from "deserting to the enemy," the statutes directed various militia officers to take action to put smaller boats out of the reach of slaves and to watch ferries particularly closely.[23]

After the War of 1812, the Assembly produced in 1817 "An Act to amend the several laws concerning runaways," whose preamble revealed that the enemy was in the North once again. The law's preamble stated: "Whereas it is represented to the General Assembly of Virginia, that serious inconveniences have been experienced by many citizens of this Commonwealth, from the frequent elopement of slaves to states north of the Potowmac [sic] and elsewhere; and whereas, the compensation now authorized by law, for the apprehending and securing of runaways, has not been found sufficient for the recovery of slaves so eloping."[24] The objective of the law was to widen the geographic coverage of runaway laws. Higher compensations and mileage allowances were offered to people who apprehended runaways from Virginia in Maryland or Kentucky; still higher compensations and mileage allowances were made available to those who returned fugitive slaves from Delaware, New Jersey, New York, or Ohio. The many coastal vessels in the East created a fluid "border" between Virginia and Delaware, New Jersey, and New York, while Ohio was within easy reach of western Virginians. This widened scope of the runaway laws by no means meant that the old dangers of ferries would be ignored. Slaves would now have to have a permit to use a ferry or even to cross a bridge. Owners and keepers of bridges and ferries were held responsible for checking these permits. Finally, because of the widened scope of the law, it was now required that runaways committed to jail must be advertised not only in the newspapers published closest to the point of capture but in a Richmond newspaper as well.

Northern abolitionists began to realize by this time that Virginian slaves were not the only African Americans who might try to escape from bondage. Indeed, New Yorkers were aware of the mad scramble of some of the slave owners of their state to sell their human property to the South before the state's gradual emancipation law affected them. If New York slaves had to flee from New York to avoid being sold to Virginia, what might free African American northerners have to do to avoid the fate of enslavement or reenslavement?

The plight of James Harris made that clear. Harris, who was born free in Philadelphia in 1786, was kidnapped while still a teenager. Taken to New Orleans, he managed to escape by ship back to Philadelphia. He fought in the War of 1812, but needing work thereafter, he fell into the hands of a man who hired him to move wood from Blackbird Creek in Delaware. This ruse delivered Harris to kidnappers, who took him as far as North Carolina before he was able to escape. He wrote to the Pennsylvania Abolition Society first in March 1816 from Greensville County in Southside Virginia. Harris managed to flee and dodge through Virginia, but only by spending time in the jails of Sussex County, then of Petersburg, and finally of Mathews County on the Virginia shore of the Chesapeake. In his letters he pleaded for the society to send his freedom papers to him. Otherwise he feared he would be sold into slavery. The problem he faced was strictly legal: by the law of Virginia, if he failed to prove he was free and no one claimed him within a year, the jailer of the county or town in which he was confined had to sell him outright as a slave. Although officials of the Pennsylvania Abolition Society were able to identify him, they could not locate his papers, so there was little they could do for him. The records of that organization do not record his fate.[25]

This pattern of enlarging the scope of the Old Dominion's statutes concerning runaways continued through the 1820s. A law of February 17, 1823, for example, set fees for the recovery of fugitives not only in the states named in the law of 1817 but also in places as far away as Indiana, all of the New England states, and "either of the British Provinces." The fee structure was undoubtedly attractive to some people: for returning fugitives from Ohio, Pennsylvania, or Indiana, the agent returning the slave received twenty cents per mile and a reward of $50; the reward was $120 dollars for returns from the more distant locations.[26]

Rivers, bridges, ferries, and northerners were the focus of the most significant revisions or creations of statutes concerning runaways in the 1830s. Preexisting law had included some effort to check waterborne escapes, but efforts were made in the 1830s to cover all means of conveyance on or over the waters of the Old Dominion.[27] Tightening of these statutes would continue into the 1840s.[28] The 1837 "Act prohibiting the transportation of slaves on rail-roads without proper authority" merely applied some of the rules concerning water transportation to the new mode of rail transportation.[29] Far more important than these laws, however, was the Commonwealth's reaction to the growth in the 1830s of organized abolitionism in the North. The existence of the North as a sanctuary for fugitive slaves and the willingness of some northerners to help those fugitives were well known before the 1830s. It was the increasing numbers and assertiveness of those northern abolitionists that caused greater worry for slave owners in Virginia after 1830.

VIRGINIA REACTS TO THE "ABOLITIONIST THREAT"

White Virginians tried to mount a counterattack against northern abolitionist "interference" with the southern "domestic institution." Part of their strategy was to suppress opinions dangerous to bondage, such as those expressed by David Walker in his 1829 pamphlet.[30] Proslavery apologists successfully defeated the efforts of some white Virginians to begin the gradual abolition of slavery in the Old Dominion. Unusual though it was to hear antislavery sentiments expressed in the chambers of the Virginia Assembly, some were indeed uttered there in the debates of 1829 and 1832. But the majority dominated, leaving opponents of the peculiar institution with few options. The increasing restiveness of bondspeople and the mounting fears of white people had become quite apparent in the Vesey Plot of 1822 in South Carolina, the Virginia insurrection scare of 1829, and Nat Turner's Revolt of 1831. Less dramatic but still indicative were the increasing assaults of slaves on white owners, overseers, and other whites in Virginia, the greater outpouring of sentiment concerning freedom in the new newspapers and pamphlets issued by growing antislavery associations in the North, and the undercurrent of concern about the safety of the peculiar institution that accompanied the nullification crisis of 1832–33.[31]

The intensity of action and fear associated with Nat Turner's Revolt obscured for a time the greatest threat faced by slave owners. Turner's Revolt was overt; the response was obvious and overwhelming. Careful as Nat Turner was to limit the number of his confederates so as to avoid detection and achieve surprise, and aggressive as he was in his use of terror to put his foes at a disadvantage, white leaders were still able to crush Turner's attack with the aid of state and local militia. Had these forces been unsuccessful, they would have received the assistance of federal troops that were dispatched from Norfolk. Indeed, the very few prosecutions of Virginian slaves for insurrection between Nat Turner's Revolt and the beginning of the Civil War lead one to believe that slaves understood that, under the circumstances, there were other, sometimes more effective ways to fight bondage.[32] Henry Box Brown certainly saw the situation in those terms, as he recounted the brutal response of whites in Richmond to the news of Turner's Revolt.[33] So Brown and others like him eventually relied on escape, a method of opposing slavery that carried great risk for slaves of being sold into an even worse condition yet still caused significant damage to the owner.

Amid all the measures to prevent northern abolitionists from fomenting slave rebellion in the South were even more vigorous efforts to stop slaves of the Old Dominion from escaping to the increasingly attractive North. Northampton County, Virginia, which was at the center of the fugitive slave problem because of its location on the Chesapeake Bay, within fairly easy reach of New Jersey and New York by water, also was well situated to be a "lookout" for the rest of Virginia. As if fated to be on watch, proslavery, states' rightist Eastern Shore native Abel Parker Upshur, defender of slavery at the 1829 Virginia Constitutional Convention, member of the Virginia General Court since 1826, and later member of President John Tyler's cabinet, fired off a heated letter to Governor John B. Floyd in late 1832 in reaction to the escape of seventeen or eighteen slaves from Northampton to New York City in a stolen whaleboat. This sort of thing had happened before, Upshur reported, but the situation was growing worse:

You will readily suppose that these circumstances proving the utter insecurity of this property among us, have rendered it of very little value. It is therefore of the utmost importance to all slave owners here, that the slaves should know that there is a power in the laws, to render abortive, all future attempts of that kind. Indeed, the protection uniformly afforded by individuals and private societies in the North, to fugitive slaves from the South, is too notorious to be denied, and presents, as it seems to me, a fit occasion for the interference of the public authorities of the aggrieved states. It is perfectly certain that unless this abuse can in some mode or other, be speedily corrected, the Eastern Shore of Virginia, affording as it does and must continue to do, by its very position, every facility for the escape of slaves, will soon be wholly without that species of property. The impoverishment and ruin of the people, will be the necessary consequence. It is obvious that the exertions of the original owners, can effect very little in reclaiming their slaves, from communities, organised against their rights. Hence, almost every attempt of that kind, has not only failed of success, but has subjected the party to public insult, and personal danger.[34]

The hyperbole in this appeal to the chief executive aside, the recommended course of action is clear: The Commonwealth must legislate further protection of human property belonging to its citizens because of the concerted, collective nature of the aid that fugitive slaves are receiving from abolitionists.

The first legislative response to the situation described by Upshur and experienced by many other slave owners came in early 1834, when laws concerning enticement or aid of fugitive slaves were tightened. One year later the Assembly gave the Virginia Slave Insurance Company a twenty-year charter to insure owners against absconding slaves.[35] But there was no sense of general alarm at this time. The Society for the Prevention of the Absconding and Abduction of Slaves, which met in Richmond from 1833 to 1849, spent most of its time trying to secure its funds from the estate of its late treasurer. In Richmond as well, a meeting of citizens in August 1835 "to consider and report what measures are proper to be adopted, in regard to the attempts making in some of the northern States, to interfere with the slave property of the South," adopted as part of its seventh resolution that Virginians "give no support, to any line of Steam boats, where the Captains thereof, shall *knowingly* give facilities to the transportation of persons or papers of an incendiary character." Yet nowhere else did this group refer to any potential of steamboat captains or anyone else to aid fugitive slaves. Richmonders would feel more threatened by fugitive slaves and steamboat captains later.[36]

An interstate war of words would bring home to white Virginians the degree of opposition to slavery they might encounter in the North. Private societies presented a threat to be sure, but when Governor William H. Seward of New York, the largest state in the Union, could successfully refuse to extradite three free African Americans accused of stealing a slave—that is, helping a slave escape—by a court of Virginia, a large sister state, it became obvious that the government of the Old Dominion faced a severe challenge should this sort of thing happen frequently.[37] But Virginia's legislators could produce only so many revised and new laws. Rewards were increased for the apprehension of fugitives close to the boundaries of Ohio, Pennsylvania, and Maryland, and special penalties were set for persons helping free black fugitives from justice.[38] It was also made clear that unregistered free blacks were to stay out of the state. In others words, the kind of people involved in the 1840 incident were now to be watched even more closely.[39] Nothing else was done for some time after these laws were passed.

An 1845 report from the Virginia Penitentiary and a roster of inmates in that institution in 1850 show that authorities were on guard and courts had concluded that some people were actively working to help slaves escape. Fourteen people were in the penitentiary in 1845 for "carrying off slaves feloniously," "aiding slave to abscond," "enticing slave to abscond," "stealing slaves," and "enticing a slave and stealing a horse." The 1850 census indicated that twelve people were incarcerated in the penitentiary for stealing a slave, which was apparently an umbrella designation for all of the offenses named in the 1845 report. The identity of the 1850 inmates suggests that slave owners had something to fear from a group other than northern abolitionists or free African Americans (see table 5.1). That group was white craftsmen. There were four black inmates and one "mulatto"; only one person, an African American, was a native of a northern state. But the group of twelve comprised four wheelwrights, four shoemakers, two carpenters, a blacksmith, and a seamstress. This striking phenomenon bears further analysis, but it does show that public pronouncements concerning external "interference" with southern slaves completely missed or covered up one source of opposition to slavery.[40]

THE CRISIS OF THE 1850S

Whether or not Virginia officials realized that the potential for concerted opposition to slavery existed within a southern socioeconomic group, they were very much aware of the crisis to which the interstate controversy over fugitive slaves had come by 1850. More incidents like the 1832 and 1840 escapes from Northampton County had occurred.[41] There had also been a series of events in other states and in the national government that caused proslavery southerners great concern. The Supreme Court had pronounced upon some aspects of the issue in *Prigg v. Pennsylvania* and *Jones v. Van Zandt.*[42] Whatever the debated points of the two decisions were, they both unmistakably upheld the constitutionality of the 1793 Fugitive Slave Act. At the same time, however, *Prigg* left an opening into which northern legislators jumped to write the Personal Liberty Laws, hoping to protect free blacks from kidnapping and also to weaken the capacity of southerners to recover fugitives. The result was that white Virginians, like many other white southerners, concluded that the federal government was virtually unable to protect slave property in the free states.

Virginians made their own contribution to this crisis. An Assembly committee wrote resolutions concerning fugitive slaves that were adopted by the legislature in February 1849. The resolutions naturally defended the constitutionality of the original Fugitive Slave Act and attacked northern abolitionists and legislators for violating the Constitution. But more germane to Virginia's situation were the accusations that abolitionists' "emissaries have

136

Table 5.1

Persons Incarcerated in the Virginia Penitentiary for
Offenses Involving Fugitive Slaves, 1850

Name	Date incarcerated	Age/Sex	Occupation	State of birth	Race
J. Wm. Wingfield	1849	29/M	Carpenter	VA	White
S. Brooks	1848	46/M	Blacksmith	MD	White
H. Morrisett	1849	27/M	Wheelwright	VA	White
Abby Ann Dixon	1849	?/F	Seamstress	VA	Black
Cato Ricketts	1847	33/M	Wheelwright	NJ	Black
S. A. Smith	1849	44/M	Shoemaker	MA	White
P. [R?] Smith	1842	41/M	Shoemaker	VA	Black
John A. Blevins	1848	55/M	Shoemaker	TN	White
A. Ewing	1848	53/M	Carpenter	TN	White
H. Charous	1844	27/M	Wheelwright	VA	"Mulatto"
B. Jackson	1844	33/M	Wheelwright	VA	Black
Thms Blackson	1850	52/M	Shoemaker	VA	?

Source: U.S. Manuscript Census, 1850, City of Richmond, 340.

Note: While the 1850 census listed Blevins as white, the 1870 census identified him as "mulatto"; U.S. Manuscript Census, 1870, Virginia, Henrico County, Jefferson Ward and City of Richmond, 431. In 1870 Blevins was living with several other African Americans, one of whom was a blacksmith, another a shoemaker.

penetrated into the very hearts of the slaveholding states, and aided the escape of slaves whom they had seduced from the service of their owners." The small number of non-Virginians held in the Virginia Penitentiary the next year for committing such acts suggests that these remarks represented either exaggeration or frustration—exaggeration of the dimensions of the problem or frustration with the inability of Virginia authorities to capture all of those responsible. The reference in the legislature's resolutions to the special vulnerability of the state's frontier counties—that is, those on its borders with free states—gives credence to the resolutions' expression of frustration. It was Virginia's frontiers that were the special problem of the state that contained more enslaved people than any other.[43] But the resolutions never mentioned the marine "borders" of the Old Dominion, which would prove to be far more porous than any frontiers on land.

In spite of the resolutions' vigorous charges against abolitionists and the earnest calls for federal action, pessimism informed the last section of the document: "Against such a current of popular feeling and prejudice as now prevails on this subject in the non-slaveholding states, it will therefore be difficult to legislate, so as to accomplish the full and perfect enforcement of our rights, at all times and under all circumstances."[44] Yet it was Virginia senator James Murray Mason who, on January 3, 1850, introduced the bill in Congress to revise the Fugitive Slave Act of 1793.[45] The state legislature's 1849 resolutions had been delivered to him, and he certainly would have been in contact with fellow Virginians who were outraged over what they regarded as unconstitutional actions concerning the "domestic institution." Indeed, Mason declared in the Senate that he introduced the bill "to discharge a duty which he owed to his constituents and in obedience to instructions from the General Assembly of Virginia." Nevertheless, with pessimism like that of the Assembly, he declared that "the disease was too deep-seated to be reached by ordinary legislation."[46]

Once the Fugitive Slave Act of 1850 went into effect, some of Virginia's slave owners may have thought their problems with runaway bondspeople would decrease. Certainly the legislature paid little or no attention to the matter when the Commonwealth's regulations were adjusted in early 1851 to conform to the new federal law.[47] In 1853 and 1854 the Richmond Common Council took action against slave escapes from the growing city, while other localities undoubtedly did the same. But the main focus of attention was the attempted and successful rescues of escaped slaves in the North in spite of the new powers available to federal judges and officials to remand fugitive slaves to the South. That Frederick Wilkins, alias Shadrack, the first man rescued after 1850, was from Norfolk, Virginia, and that Anthony Burns, a slave from Alexandria, Virginia, was successfully remanded from Boston only after the most extraordinary measures were taken certainly were reasons for proslavery Virginians to worry. Such cases, however, were in the realm of interstate and federal-state relations, not within the exclusive jurisdiction of the Old Dominion.[48] It was the alleged intervention of abolitionists to aid Virginian slaves who were trying to escape from the state that eventually provoked the greatest activity of the state's legislators.

Two days after the December 3, 1855, opening speech of Governor Joseph Johnson to the Virginia House of Delegates, in which he decried northern abolitionist opposition to southern slave owners' attempts to return their fugitive slaves from north of the Mason-Dixon line, a House delegate made an unsuccessful proposal on behalf of preventing the abduction of slaves from within the state. The radical nature of this proposal doomed its chances of acceptance, yet revealed the level of concern among some legislators concerning the abduction problem. The delegate moved that "the committee for courts of justice enquire into the expediency of so amending section 19 of chapter 176 of the Code of Virginia, as to admit the testimony of negroes against white persons charged with abducting or attempting to abduct slaves from the Commonwealth, when said persons so charged shall be citizens of such states as admit negro testimony in cases in which white persons may be parties." The Courts Committee soon referred the matter to a joint committee of both houses that was investigating the abduction of slaves, and the proposal died. So sacred was the long-term prohibition of African American testimony in any case concerning white people that only the most desperate mood would have led any delegate to make such a proposal.[49]

Within three months the House heard resolutions from a Democratic Party meeting in Gloucester, a Tidewater county with coastline on the York River and Chesapeake Bay, "relative to the recapture of fugitive slaves, and complaining of the tardiness of the Legislature in providing measures for the recapture of slaves and of retaliation for their abduction." Recapture and retaliation both raised national and constitutional problems that most legislators wished to avoid. But "abduction" was within the purview of the lawmakers. Francis Mallory, from Norfolk, another particularly vulnerable area of the state, chaired the committee investigating fugitive slaves. Mallory assured the House that there would soon be bills "providing for the protection of every part of the state exposed to the operations of the emissaries from the North." Twelve days later Mallory presented a bill to prohibit Virginians from hiring slaves in the District of Columbia and a bill to increase rewards for arrest of runaway slaves. The first was passed on March 5, and it created a special measure to deal with Congress's termination of the slave trade in the federal district and to prevent Virginian slaves from being hired or hiring themselves out there, presumably thus exposing them to the hated abolitionist "emissaries."[50]

Far more important parts of the Commonwealth's counterattack against the Yankee "emissaries," however, were the "Act providing additional protection for the slave property of citizens of this commonwealth," the "Act to amend the . . . Code of Virginia, so as more effectually to prevent the escape of slaves," and the "Act to amend the . . . Code so as to increase the rewards for the arrest of runaway slaves," all passed on March 17, 1856. This trio of statutes set up an inspection system for all boats leaving Virginia ports and laid down stiff penalties for noncompliance with the system. It increased the penalties for helping slaves escape, including the requirement of a public whipping and a penitentiary term for free people and sale out of the state for a slave. It also significantly raised the reward for arresting runaway slaves, adding a bonus of 25 percent of the value of the slave if the apprehension occurred in a nonslaveholding state. Special inspection commissioners were to be appointed, and existing river pilots were also to be licensed as inspectors.[51]

Within two weeks Governor Henry A. Wise appointed the first commissioner. Flaws in the system soon appeared, and Wise attempted to correct them.[52] In January 1857 one inspector exultantly informed Wise that "our Inspectors have been enabled to overawe the 'Yankee' spirit of rebellion that at first threatened defiance to the law."[53] While it is impossible to determine how well the system worked—that is, there can never be accurate data on how many slaves slipped by the inspectors—it is possible to investigate typical instances of detection and apprehension of fugitives or their helpers.[54] Not only did the inspectors and pilots discover intentional as well as unintended violations of the 1856 laws, but citizens who were well aware of potential rewards did upon occasion help the authorities discover fugitives or their allies. The state auditor's records of rewards disbursed from 1856 to 1859 suggest, however, what seemed obvious to many citizens of the Commonwealth. In ten of the fifteen disbursements, which involved twenty slaves and five aiders or abettors, the reward was for capturing a fugitive outside Virginia; only five of the rewards were for helping to capture fugitives or their helpers within the state. The trio of 1856 laws was clearly more successful as a means to alleviate the major interstate and national problem of the rendition of fugitive slaves from outside the South than it was as a means of detecting and apprehending people operating from within the state. In other words, the laws gave Virginians more help in the jurisdictions essentially beyond that state's control than they could in the area within its control.[55]

Nor could white Virginians have taken heart from the obvious fact that all five of the aiders and abettors apprehended because of information or assistance given by the rewardees had been caught within Virginia. There was a widespread conviction that too many fugitives and abettors were avoiding detection in spite of the state's best efforts. Some of the records of the trials of the alleged abettors show why there was reason to suspect that the number of apprehended people indicated a larger number of "emissaries" at work.

The trial of Lott Mundy, for example, revealed part of the problem that many Virginians perceived. An 1841 law had expressly prohibited free blacks from entering the Old Dominion, the sole exception being people like Mundy, a hand on a vessel that navigated waters beyond the state. Mundy's felonious attempt "to defraud and deprive" the master of Martin and Thomas, the slaves discovered aboard the schooner docked at Richmond, was the very dangerous act against which the white leaders of the South had been inveighing for some years. This act was to them a pure and simple theft of property, no more to be tolerated by slave owners than by the owners of any other kind of property anywhere else in the Union. But there apparently had been no conspiracy. Both slaves testified that Mundy had agreed to help them once they approached him on the boat, but neither had ever seen Mundy before. It is easy to conclude that Mundy's alleged behavior, his race, his status, and his residency in New York contributed to the sentence of ten years in the Virginia Penitentiary for aiding Thomas and another five years for helping Martin. Virginians who knew about the trial, though, had to be aware of another implication of the event. Believing Mundy guilty, they still knew he was no "emissary" of the abolitionists, because there had been no prearrangement and the slaves had approached him. Such aid could be offered without planning, which made it all the more easy and possible for slaves to escape. How many more such arrangements had proved and would prove successful even though this one failed? The authorities in Norfolk knew that Charles Gilbert had escaped in spite of their strenuous pursuit. How many others had?[56]

A Norfolk trial of a white man from Delaware in 1858 had the potential to raise more fears. Convicted of abducting slaves, William Lambdin of Smyrna, Delaware, was the object of several petitions and letters to Governor Henry A. Wise from Lambdin's wife, from business associates, and from prominent Delaware citizens. These citizens of a slave state knew better than to argue

against Virginia's fugitive slave laws; they also knew too little
to contest the prosecution's presentation of evidence against
Lambdin. Instead they took the seemingly wise course of affirming Lambdin's personal character. But those testimonials could
only accentuate the problem. The more prominent and respected
Lambdin was made to look, the more inexplicable and despicable
his alleged behavior would appear to proslavery white Virginians. They might expect someone like Mundy, whom they held to
be without honor, to commit such acts, but abducting slaves was
the last thing they might suspect a man like Lambdin would carry
on. Once they were convinced it had happened, however, rage
might be the only response.[57]

That rage did erupt in 1858. During the same week at the
end of May and beginning of June, white citizens in Norfolk
and Petersburg expressed their disgust toward four white men
whom they accused of involvement in a slave-stealing ring. People
in the two places acted independently at first, but then each city
learned of the other's actions. Their common actions seemed quite
warranted to them in light of the conspiracy they believed they
had uncovered. In Norfolk, a citizens' meeting convened to discuss
news that Captain Thomas J. Allen of New Jersey had been captured in his schooner with a fugitive slave on board. Satisfied that
the courts would deal with Allen, the meeting turned its attention to Willard Mott, a New Yorker, to William Danenburg, a Yankee skipper, and to Samuel Bayliss and his brother William, two
Delaware steamboat captains. The citizens at the meeting were
convinced that these four men had been acting together for some
time. Someone had made a statement to the *Norfolk American*
nearly a year earlier, identifying the four men as part of a conspiracy. The only effort to ascribe a motive to the men was a description of an argument they allegedly had over shares of money
they might obtain from fugitive slaves willing to pay for passage. Whatever the motive, the proslavery meeting decided to take

action against Mott and Danenburg, who were in Norfolk. A delegation of twenty men visited them and told them the meeting's resolutions: they should leave Norfolk forever or "be tarred and feathered, ridden on a rail and shipped North" to their "abolition friends."[58]

When captured downriver from Petersburg, Captain William Bayliss, skipper of the *Keziah*, was in even more personal danger than Mott and Danenburg. According to a newspaper report, word of the apprehension arrived at Petersburg before Bayliss, his first mate, and five suspected fugitives did, giving a crowd the chance to assemble. The people were so aroused by the time Bayliss and his first mate were brought onto a wharf that "a wild shout of indignation went up from the populace and a desperate effort made to take possession of them, and but for the most vigorous measures and the assistance rendered by several of the calmer citizens they must have been taken, when they would have been lynched upon the spot, as in the excitement of the moment that seemed to be the purpose."[59] A court of examination was supposed to meet the next day but could not "in consequence of the great excitement in the public mind." When Bayliss's trial was finally held, he was sentenced to a total of forty years in the Virginia Penitentiary, eight years for each slave he had been accused of aiding and abetting.[60]

Evidence from such sources as William Still's *Underground Railroad* confirms the Virginia authorities' suspicions. Bayliss had been involved for some time in the rescue of slaves. Indeed, he pleaded guilty to the charge of abduction. Although found not guilty, Bayliss's first mate may also have been involved. And certainly other people, both black and white, were engaged in the same kinds of operations as Bayliss. The *Richmond Daily Dispatch* declared that "it is probably [*sic*] that the prompt justice administered in this case will have a salutary effect on the underground agents." Some evidence indicates that escapes decreased after the *Keziah* affair, but other evidence implies that they were never stopped (see table 5.2).[61]

Table 5.2

Persons Incarcerated in the Virginia Penitentiary for
Offenses Involving Fugitive Slaves, 1860

Name	Date incarcerated	Age/Sex	Occupation	Place of birth	Race
John A. Blevins	1848	65/M	Shoemaker	TN	White
Washngton Asbury	1854	47/M	Blacksmith	VA	White
James Smith	1856	40/M	Blacksmith	VA	Black
Lot Monday	1856	37/M	Cook	NJ	Black
Wm. Reynolds	1856	27/M	Laborer	VA	"Mulatto"
George Johnson	1857	50/M	Wheelwright	VA	White
John McKinney	1857	41/M	Blacksmith	VA	White
Thos. J. Dunn	1857	49/M	Carpenter	MA	White
A. Cottingham	1858	52/M	Sailor	MD	White
Wm. B. Bayliss	1858	49/M	Sailor	DE	White
Paul Dallas	1858	59/M	Shoemaker	France	White
W. H. Thompson	1858	21/M	Blacksmith	NJ	Black
Jackson Ottinger	1858	33/M	Blacksmith	VA	White
Armstead McGuire	1859	49/M	Stonemason	VA	White
Ab. Nelson	1859	36/M	Blacksmith	VA	White

Source: U.S. Manuscript Census, 1860, 3d ward, Richmond, 472–76.

Perhaps no native white Virginian expressed his despair over the fugitive slave situation more bluntly than Edmund Ruffin, who published an 1859 article in the *Southern Planter,* later issued as a pamphlet entitled *Two Great Evils of Virginia, and Their One Common Remedy.* Besides what he called "the nuisance of the class of Free Negroes, as now existing and increasing in Virginia," Ruffin identified the second of the "great evils" as "the attempts, and partial success, of Northern Abolitionists, in seducing our slaves to abscond, and assailing and endangering the institution of negro slavery." Ruffin proposed the complete banishment of free African Americans from the Old Dominion and the enslavement of any who remained. He believed that this policy would have a dramatic effect on the North. Many free blacks would flee to Ohio, Pennsylvania, Massachusetts, and other states that had welcomed fugitive slaves as part of antislavery policy. Some Virginia slaves would continue to run to the North. The result, Ruffin gleefully predicted, would certainly be that the same northern states that welcomed fugitive slaves before would be forced to legislate and guard against such migration for fear that "lazy," "improvident," "criminal," and "worthless" blacks would cause severe social problems. The "slave-stealing" states would become the slave-excluding states. With northern asylum for fugitive slaves eliminated, there would be no more fugitive slaves from Virginia, and the other slaveholding states would follow Virginia's lead.[62]

VIRGINIA'S FUGITIVE SLAVE PROBLEM DURING THE CIVIL WAR

As if to confirm the worst fears of slave owners such as Ruffin, the fugitive slave problem grew considerably worse during the Civil War, even though the Confederate States of America was using battle-trained troops to defend its soil. One problem was that federal troops were eventually able to protect fugitive slaves as contraband, and after January 1, 1863, African Americans escaping from Confederate territory were beneficiaries of the Emancipation Proclamation. Senator Henry Clay had foretold the other problem in 1850 when he supported the Fugitive Slave Act along with the other compromise measures as a much better alternative than secession. Among other troubles, he said, secession would "mean that where one slave now deserted his master, thousands would thereafter flee."[63]

Clay was correct. Confederate authorities knew they had to adjust fugitive slave policies to the new conditions. The Confederate Constitution included strong clauses concerning fugitive slaves; the Convention of 1861 also issued an ordinance that allowed county courts to establish a police force to carry before justices of the peace any person suspected of "tampering" with slaves—that is, aiding escape or insurrection.[64] The Virginia legislature resorted to fugitive slave measures for wartime just as in the American

Revolution and the War of 1812.[65] When the Union adopted the policy of confiscation of enemy slaves and later made the momentous decision to emancipate slaves within Confederate-held territory as a war measure, the Commonwealth of Virginia responded with special protection for slave owners affected by such measures.[66]

When African Americans took advantage of the war, the confiscation measures, and the Emancipation Proclamation, they created a fugitive slave situation never before encountered by Virginian slave owners. So many slaves were leaving because of the war that numerous owners were even more unwilling than usual to give up slaves for the war effort. Farms and plantations with a small number of laborers could not produce enough food for the war effort, and slaves sent to work on fortifications and other public works were finding new ways to run away.[67] The state tried to gather data on such runaway slaves. The Auditor's Office recorded that between April 1861 and early 1863 at least five thousand Virginian bondspeople had fled to the enemy.[68] Even more were undoubtedly listed in records now missing. So the state government had to adjust to the fugitive slave situation once again, first exempting owners from supplying slaves when those owners had lost at least one-third of their slaves to the enemy, then setting the threshold of exemption at one-fourth.[69]

The courts continued to hear more prosecutions of people who had allegedly stolen slaves, advised them to abscond, or tried to help them get to Union lines. What was particularly new was the number of slaves convicted of these crimes. Bondspeople had helped fellow slaves run away for nearly two centuries. That was not new. The state had threatened to prosecute some slaves for helping runaways during the Revolution. That was not unfamiliar either. What had changed was that the federal military allies of the fugitive slaves fully intended to undermine slavery, which meant that all fugitives would receive official, armed encouragement from the Union. The British had stopped short of measures destructive of the institution of slavery during the Revolution; the Union consciously fought to eliminate bondage in the Confederate states from January 1863 until Appomattox. Slaves knew this and answered the call.[70]

AN INCOMPLETE AND IMPERFECT "ENFORCEMENT OF OUR RIGHTS"

Virginia's slave owners would not enjoy "the full and perfect enforcement of our rights" they hoped for. It was in the nature of the intense sectional, political, and moral conflict of the 1840s and 1850s that the proslavery and antislavery combatants would use every measure available to achieve their ends. It is also in the nature of the relationship between law and society that "full and perfect enforcement" was impossible. Yet Virginia had a special problem with respect to fugitive slaves.

The problem was that no matter how the government of the Commonwealth tried, it never caught up with the determination, ingenuity, and intensity of fugitives and their allies. The charged political situation of the 1830s, 1840s, and 1850s only accentuated Virginia's dilemma. When the problem appeared to be the weakness of the 1793 federal Fugitive Slave Act, proslavery politicians could pressure Congress for a stronger law. But when the stronger act of 1850 was passed—albeit not as strong as many southerners wished it to be—and it failed to satisfy many white Virginians, the state's legislators tried in 1856 to tighten up the laws over which they had full control. Even though the *Keziah* affair and other cases slowed down fugitive activities, they were enough to convince many that all options to stop fugitives had been unsuccessfully tried. Stanley Campbell has argued that the federal government was statistically successful: the overwhelming majority of allegedly fugitive slaves brought under federal jurisdiction after

1850 were remanded to the South. But the costs became excessive, and it had become quite difficult to get slaves into the hands of federal authorities. So white southerners mostly gave up expecting the federal government to help them. What, then, could they do when their own Virginia government could help them only so much?[71]

This is anything but an argument that the failure of Virginia to provide "full and perfect enforcement" of the rights white Virginians claimed to their human property was the cause of the Civil War. Most of Virginia's citizens did wait until after Fort Sumter to vote for secession. But this "domestic" problem added fuel to the slowly burning fire that secessionists would fan to full flame. Proslavery Virginians were pessimistic about the chances that the federal government would catch their fugitive slaves, but many of them were left no reason for any hope at all when their own state government proved equally powerless in spite of strenuous efforts over a long period.

CONCLUSION

The minute books of the county court of Henry County, Virginia, describe only ten felony prosecutions of slaves belonging to any member of the white Hairston family between 1783 and 1865. In the thirty-five years between 1865 and 1900, however, 230 men and women with the surname of Hairston—almost all of them African Americans—were prosecuted for all kinds of criminal offenses, including stealing, stabbing, unlawful shooting, murder, willful trespass, housebreaking, receiving stolen goods, disturbing religious worship, sodomy and bestiality, arson, unlawful gaming, "keeping private entertainment," horse racing on a public road, carrying a concealed weapon, cruelty to animals, perjury, lewd and lascivious cohabitation, obtaining goods under false pretenses, rape, carrying a pistol to a place of worship, shooting at a passenger train, forgery, fornication, lewdness, selling liquor to a minor on Sunday without a license, seduction, robbery, adultery, aiding the escape of prisoners, and even voting twice in the 1872 election. During the ten-year period 1875–84, 19 men with the Hairston name were locked into the Virginia Penitentiary in Richmond. Thirteen of them had been convicted in Henry County; the others had been found guilty in the courts of adjacent Patrick and Pittsylvania counties.[1]

Under bondage, these African American Hairstons had been connected with a powerful family. Members of the white Hairston family were solidly entrenched in the social and political elite of Southside Virginia. One in particular, Samuel Hairston, was almost legendary. A Floridian who had heard the Hairston legend claimed that Samuel was the "richest man in Virginia" and owned as many as sixteen hundred or seventeen hundred slaves, whose rate of natural increase was nearly one hundred each year. The Hairston homes were part of the legend: in 1851 a local minister exclaimed that Paradise itself was as beautiful as Samuel Hairston's house. However rich the Hairstons may have been, much of their wealth was held in human property. That meant not only that the Hairston wealth decreased dramatically because of the Union victory in the Civil War and the Thirteenth Amendment to the Constitution but also that many of those former slaves who had chosen the surname of Hairston for themselves were now going to test the waters of freedom.[2]

The pattern of Hairston prosecutions might lead those ignorant of the larger picture to fall into the dangerous trap of casting highly derogatory aspersions on African American members of the Hairston family. There were obviously many black Hairstons who prized freedom and aspired to be good citizens, as a small sampling of biographical sources reveals.[3] "The Freedmen of both sexes, generally are very industrious, and quite saving, showing a decided desire to own small tracts of land themselves," Freedman's Bureau agent William L. Fernald reported in 1867 to General Oliver Brown from Martinsville, the seat of Henry County.[4] Furthermore, some of those Hairstons prosecuted were acquitted and never appeared in a criminal court again. So the issue that their presence in court raises is not an alleged deterioration of family life, social responsibility, and individual values after emancipation. Instead it is the manner in which the diverse experiences of emancipation of many African Americans, especially of those who had belonged to one family, paradoxically constituted still another development in the law of slavery.

Elimination of much of the law of slavery was but the last development in that law, yet it was at first a deceptive change. The free Hairstons were no longer subject to the slave code, but they were still in danger from the white supremacist foundation of the code. Most of the statutes from the old slave code disappeared, but some old wine was poured into new bottles, and many of the old attitudes of the makers of the slave code persisted. After Radical Reconstruction, African Americans could legally testify in civil and criminal cases concerning whites, but could they in fact? And if they did, would their testimony have weight if it conflicted with that of respected white people? The only part of the Civil Rights Act of 1875 to survive the *Civil Rights Cases* of 1883 was the guarantee of black membership on juries.[5] White southerners found ways to get around that provision. No one could be bought and sold anymore, but debt peonage became a widespread problem. Any student of the postbellum South could cite numerous other examples of old wine in new bottles. One in particular is quite telling: the disenfranchisement of most African American voters in Virginia placed them in somewhat the same quandary as that in which free people of color found themselves before 1865. They could own a stake in society, but any claim to vote on the basis of that stake was generally rejected.

The most important social and political aspect of these new laws and customs—or "understandings"—was the assumption of white supremacy. Any thorough analysis of the African American Hairstons' experience with the law would therefore have to deal with the civil as well as the criminal law and with actual behavior as well as with the official records. It makes no sense for historians not to "look behind the laws." A majority of U.S. Supreme Court justices in *Plessy v. Ferguson* explained the laws only as they appeared on the books.[6] Those justices insisted that there was no inherent discrimination or implication of inequality in laws that required *both* black and white passengers to sit in railroad cars separate from each other. The assumptions that made this sort of logic palatable to most whites were so strong that, as Charles Black has stated, the biggest intellectual breakthrough in the process of deciding to challenge *Plessy* was the realization that "separate but equal" is a self-contradiction.[7] Yet the imperative of white supremacy forced the denial of what appears now to be a self-evident contradiction.

So the African American Hairstons were held to the law, and many laws dealt with them, sometimes protecting them, sometimes restraining them—as in those prosecutions that were accurate and just—and sometimes subordinating them. The African American Hairstons were no longer slaves. That was clear. The assumption of a single, uniform status—a slave is a slave before the law—had disappeared. Slavery survived, however, even though there could be small or far-reaching legal changes to adapt to new conditions or to respond to changing behavior, and the law of class and caste could show the same longevity. The assumption of unified white control over the black population had much of the power of the slave codes to render diverse African Americans as a mere abstract mass before the law. Hard law makes bad cases, one might say of the final change in the law of slavery—that is, its elimination. The hardness of slave law lived on in the hardness of the law of white supremacy. It would therefore be very difficult for lawmakers to perceive and to deal with distinctions among African Americans. They would become the butt of accusations of "inherent criminality" even though the great majority of them never violated the law. Any African American whose ideals, dreams, or behavior were perceived as a threat to white supremacy would be suspect before the law. The law would therefore change only with the old proviso: Any change was possible as long as it upheld white supremacy.

The different manifestations of the Old Dominion's laws concerning insurrection reflect this yoking of insistence on white supremacy with changes in the law. The Code of 1860 clearly condemned slave insurrections and white conspiracy with slave plotters. In 1866 the code for all free people declared: "If any person shall conspire with another to incite the colored population of the state to make insurrection, by acts of violence and war, against the white population, or to incite the white population of the state to make insurrection, by acts of violence and war, against the colored population, he shall, whether such insurrection be made or not, be punished by confinement in the penitentiary for not less than five nor more than ten years." From 1950 to 1975 the legislators modified the law to declare that "if any person conspire with another to incite the population of one race to acts of violence and war against the population of another race, he shall, whether such acts of violence and war be made or not, be guilty of a Class 4 felony."[8]

Evenhanded though the language of these laws seems to be, it is difficult to imagine a situation in which whites could have been prosecuted successfully before the 1970s. Since the law was changed to appear more abstract—from the use of "colored" and "white" to "one race" and "another race"—it has become even more difficult to apply. Is the latter revision more just? Does it make sense now that many anthropologists regard "race" as an outmoded classification of human beings? To what other "races" besides blacks and whites could it reasonably be expected to apply? Now that white supremacy is no longer enshrined in law, what sense can such a law make?

Other post-1865 laws of Virginia—and of the United States—reflect the relationship between assumptions of white supremacy and changes in the law. The many objections to the Black Codes passed during Presidential Reconstruction had a major theme: the codes were little better than modified slave codes applied to freedmen. After Congressional Reconstruction forced further revision of Virginia's code of laws, white supremacy could still figure in judicial actions. Many prosecutions of African Americans occurred after 1870. Indeed, the latest prosecutions of Hairston family members that I mentioned were from 1900, just two years before most African Virginian voters were disfranchised by the Constitution of 1902. Under the social and political circumstances of those years, such prosecutions were open to white supremacist distortion.

Since 1902 African Americans in the Old Dominion have gradually gained more influence over the law. The Voting Rights Act of 1965 forced a major change in state politics in Virginia. The same white man who had served as governor while a Democrat returned to that post several years later as a Republican. Soon there was a black majority in the Richmond City Council. Later L. Douglas Wilder became the first elected African American governor of Virginia (and of any state). Yet, even though "black-on-black crimes" are now a matter of deep concern among African Americans, who can confidently say that we have moved completely out from under the shadow of the law of slavery? Its development was so entrenched in the two hundred years between the 1660s and the 1860s that it has been difficult to move as far as is necessary beyond its influence between the 1860s and the 1990s. The many changes that were made in the law of slavery support either hope or despair concerning laws today. The law of slavery was constantly changed, but it usually upheld the peculiar institution. Laws that today encourage white supremacy, intentionally or not, certainly can be changed, but that will not happen if the assumptions of white supremacy continue in their present "half-life."

One moral of the story is that legal change and development are not necessarily positive. Africans who became African Virginians may sometimes have seen legal retrogression as they moved from their allegedly "primitive" and "savage" societies to "civilized" Virginia. While Thomas Jefferson certainly perceived himself as a benevolent lawgiver who applied statutory and customary laws of slavery for his slaves' benefit as well as for his own, the most obvious aspect of his slaves' relationship to laws is the perpetuation of their enslavement. The capital laws of the Old Dominion certainly changed from the seventeenth through the nineteenth centuries—both positively and negatively—but only under the rigid proviso of the protection of slavery and white supremacy. Fugitive slaves learned during the same period that legislators were determined to match every change in their tactics of resistance to slavery.

Taking hold of even one ear of a wolf is a precarious challenge, but keeping that hold is more precarious still. Slaveholders thought the wolf was the enslaved African American population. If one instead regards the wolf as slavery itself, its teeth bite in another way. Maintain the hold and slavery is maintained. Lose the hold and slavery can still endanger you, either immediately or as long as the wolf shall live—if the wolf roams free, hidden in the woods and not hunted down.

APPENDIX
SELECTED WORKS BY OBSERVERS
AND ETHNOGRAPHERS CONCERNING WEST
AFRICAN PRECOLONIAL LEGAL SYSTEMS

Page numbers refer to discussions of African laws and courts. Frank Cass has published reprints of several of the seventeenth-, eighteenth-, and nineteenth-century accounts of Africa, but none are edited and few contain a new introduction.

Adanson, Michael. *A Voyage to Senegal, the Isle of Goree, and the River Gambia.* Translated from the French. London: Printed for J. Nourse and W. Johnston, 1759.

Ajisafe, A. K. *The Laws and Customs of the Yoruba People.* London: G. Routledge, 1924. 28–31, 37–44.

Alexandre, Pierre, and Jacques Binet. *Le groupe dit Pahouin.* Translated by Isabella Athey. New Haven, Conn.: Human Relations Area Files, 1959. 94.

Atkins, John. *A Voyage to Guinea, Brasil, and the West Indies.* London: C. Ward and R. Chandler, 1735; London: Cass, 1970. 52–53, 68, 87, 149, 176.

Barbot, John. *A Description of the Coasts of North and South Guinea.* In *A Collection of Voyages and Travels,* compiled by Awnsham Churchill. 6 vols. London: J. Walthoe, 1732. 1:47, 56, 57, 119, 126–27, 236, 245, 299–303, 331–32, 337–38, 348, 352, 372–73, 415. (Also available in *Barbot on Guinea: The Writings of Jean Barbot on West Africa, 1678–1712,* edited by P. E. H. Hair, Adam Jones, and Robin Law. 2 vols. London: Hakluyt Society, 1992.)

Bascom, William R. "The Sociological Role of the Yoruba Cult-Group." *American Anthropologist* 46, no. 1, pt. 2 (1944): 67.

Benezet, Anthony. *A Short Account of That Part of Africa Inhabited by the Negroes.* Philadelphia: W. Dunlap, 1762. 19–21, 26, 40–41.

Bosman, William. *A New and Accurate Description of the Coast of Guinea.* London: J. Knapton, 1705; London: Cass, 1967. 148–49, 166–70, 177, 357–59.

Connolly, R. M. "Social Life in Fanti-Land." *Journal of the Anthropological Institute of Great Britain and Ireland* 26 (1897): 130.

Decapmaker, J. "Sanctions coutumières contre l'adultère chez les Bakongo de la région de Kasi." *Congo* (July 1939): 134–48.

Elias, T. Olawale. *The Nature of African Customary Law.* Manchester, Eng.: Manchester University Press, 1956. 216–17.

Equiano, Olaudah. *The Interesting Narrative of Olaudah Equiano; or, Gustavus Vassa, the African.* 2 vols. London: G. Vassa by T. Wilkins, 1789. In *Africa Remembered: Narratives by West Africans from the Era of the Slave Trade,* edited by Philip D. Curtin. Madison: University of Wisconsin Press, 1967. 71, 75.

Falconbridge, Alexander. *An Account of the Slave Trade on the Coast of Africa.* London: J. Phillips, 1788; New York: AMS Press, 1973. 15.

Forde, Cyril Daryll. *The Yoruba-Speaking Peoples of South-western Nigeria.* Ethnographic Survey of Africa, Western Africa, pt. 4. London: International African Institute, 1951. 24.

Fortes, Meyer. *The Dynamics of Clanship Among the Tellensi.* London: Oxford University Press, 1945. 236.

Great Britain, Board of Trade. *Report of the Lords of the Committee of Council . . . Submitting . . . the Evidence and Information . . . Concerning the Present State of the Trade to Africa . . .* London, 1789.

Great Britain, Parliament, House of Commons. *Minutes of the Evidence . . . Sessional Papers, Accounts and Papers.* Vol. 29, no. 698, 1790; vol. 30, no. 699, 1790; vol. 34, no. 745, 1790–91.

Green, John, and Thomas Astley, comps. *A New General Collection of Voyages and Travels.* 4 vols. London: Printed for T. Astley, 1745–47; New York: Barnes and Noble, 1968. 1:59, 245, 578, 582, 2:255, 259, 540, 629–30, 644, 686–92, 3:16, 38–40, 102–3.

Hambly, Wilfred D. *The Ovimbundu of Angola.* Field Museum of Natural History, Anthropological Series, vol. 21, no. 2. Chicago: Field Museum of Natural History, 1934. 201–3, 265.

Hawkins, Joseph. *A History of a Voyage to the Coast of Africa and Travels into the Interior of That Country*. Philadelphia: S. C. Ustick, 1797; London: Cass, 1970.

Ifemesia, C. C. "States of the Central Sudan." In *A Thousand Years of West African History*, edited by J. F. Ade Ajayi and Ian Espie. New York: Humanities Press, 1972. 72–112.

Jobson, Richard. "A Description and Historicall Declaration of the Kingdome of Guinea . . ." Translated from the Dutch. In *Hakluytus Pothumus; or, Purchas His Pilgrims*, compiled by Samuel Purchas. 20 vols. Glasgow: J. MacLehose and Sons, 1905–7. 6:266, 269, 312–18.

Kopytoff, Igor, and Suzanne Miers. "African 'Slavery' as an Institution of Marginality." In *Slavery in Africa: Historical and Anthropological Perspectives*, edited by Suzanne Miers and Igor Kopytoff. Madison: University of Wisconsin Press, 1977. 10–20.

Lemaire, Jacques Joseph. *Les voyages du Sieur Le Maire aux Iles Canaries, Cap-Verd, Sénégal, et Gambie*. Paris: J. Collombat, 1695. 124, 181–82.

MacCormack, Carol P. "Wono: Institutionalized Dependency in Sherbro Descent Groups (Sierra Leone)." In *Slavery in Africa: Historical and Anthropological Perspectives*, edited by Suzanne Miers and Igor Kopytoff. Madison: University of Wisconsin Press, 1977. 195–96.

MacLean, Col. John, ed. *A Compendium of Kafir Laws and Customs, Including Genealogical Tables of Kafir Chiefs and Various Tribal Census Returns*. Mount Coke: Printed for the Government of British Kaffraria, 1858; London: Cass, 1968. 35–45, 59–67, 113, 115.

Matthews, John. *A Voyage to the River Sierra-Leone*. London: Printed for B. White and Son, 1788; London: Cass, 1966. 79–81.

McCulloch, Merran. *Peoples of Sierra Leone Protectorate*. Ethnographic Survey of Africa, Western Africa, pt. 2. London: International African Institute, 1950. 24–25.

Meek, Charles Kingsley. "Ibo Law." In *Essays Presented to C. G. Seligman*, edited by E. E. Evans Pritchard et al. London: K. Paul, Trench, Trübner, 1934. 218–22.

———. *Tribal Studies in Northern Nigeria*. 2 vols. London: K. Paul, Trench, Trübner, 1931. 2:78.

Merolla da Sorrento, Father Jerom. *A Voyage to the Congo.* In *A Collection of Voyages and Travels,* compiled by Awnsham Churchill and John Churchill. 4 vols. London: Printed for A. and J. Churchill, 1704. 1:675–76.

The Modern Part of an Universal History, from the Earliest Account of Time. 44 vols. London: Printed for S. Richardson, 1759–66. 14:17–18, 66–67, 99.

Monteil, Charles. *The Bambara of Segou and Kaarta.* Translated by Kathryn A. Looney. New Haven, Conn.: Human Relations Area Files, 1960. 208.

Moore, Francis. *Travels into the Inland Parts of Africa.* London: E. Cave, 1738. 42–43, 88–89, 110, 133, 192.

Nadel, Siegfrid F. "The Kede: A Riverain State in Northern Nigeria." In *African Political Systems,* edited by Meyer Fortes and E. E. Evans-Pritchard. London: Oxford University Press, 1940. 181–82.

———. "The King's Hangmen: A Judicial Organization in Central Nigeria." *Man* 35 (July 1935): 129–32.

Newton, John. *Thoughts upon the African Slave Trade.* London: Printed for J. Buckland, in Pater-Noster Row, and J. Johnson, in St. Paul's Church-yard, 1788. In *The Journal of a Slave Trader (John Newton), 1750–1754,* by John Newton, edited by Bernard Martin and Mark Spurrell. London: Epworth Press, 1962. 105–8.

Notes on the Tribes, Provinces, Emirates and States of the Northern Provinces of Nigeria, Compiled from Official Reports by O. Temple, edited by Olive Susan Miranda MacLeod Temple and C. L. Temple. 2d ed. London: Cass, 1965. 194–95, 321–22.

Ogilby, John. *Africa, Being an Accurate Description of the Regions of Aegypt, Barbary, Lybia, and Billedulgerid, the Land of Negroes, Guinea, Aethiopia, and the Abyssines . . .* London: Thomas Johnson, 1670. 347, 352, 452, 475.

Paques, Viviana. *The Bambara.* Translated by Thomas Turner. New Haven, Conn.: Human Relations Area Files, 1959. 77, 92–96.

Proyart, Lievain Bonaventure. *Abbé Proyart's History of Loango, Kakongo, and Other Kingdoms in Africa.* Paris: C. P. Berton, 1776. In *A General Collection of the Best and Most Interesting Voyages and Travels in all Parts of the World*, compiled by John Pinkerton. 17 vols. London: Longman, Hurst, Rees, and Orme, 1808–14. 16:581–83.

Rattray, R. S. *Ashanti.* Oxford: Clarendon Press, 1923. 130–31, 227.

———. *Religion and Art in Ashanti.* Oxford: Clarendon Press, 1927. 87–92, 109, 211.

Rodney, Walter. "African Slavery and Other Forms of Social Oppression on the Upper Guinea Coast in the Context of the Atlantic Slave Trade." *Journal of African History* 7, no. 3 (1966): 438.

Schact, Joseph. *An Introduction to Islamic Law.* Oxford: Clarendon Press, 1964. 175–98.

Simmons, D. "Ethnographic Sketch of the Efrik People." In *Efrik Traders of Old Calabar,* edited by Cyril Daryll Forde. London: Dawsons of Pall Mall, 1968. 7.

Skinner, Elliott Percival. "An Analysis of the Political Organization of the Mossi People." *Transactions of the New York Academy of Science,* 2d ser., 19 (June 1957): 746–47.

Smith, William. *A New Voyage to Guinea.* London: Nourse, 1744; London: Cass, 1967. 198, 203–5, 216, 221, 246–48, 257–59.

Snelgrave, William. *A New Account of Some Parts of Guinea and the Slave Trade.* London: J., J. and P. Knapton, 1734; London: Cass, 1971. 138, 158, 161, 181–85.

Tauxier, Louis. *The Black Population of the Sudan, Mossi and Gourounsi Country, Documents and Analyses.* Translated by Ariane Brunel. New Haven, Conn.: Human Relations Area Files, 1960. 118.

"A True Relation of the Inhuman and Unparalleled Actions and Barbarous Murders of *Negroes* or *Moors,* Committed on Three *Englishmen* in Old *Calabar in Guinea . . .*" In *A Collection of Voyages and Travels,* compiled by Thomas Osborne. 2 vols. London: Printed for T. Osborne, 1747. 2:517.

Villault, Nicolas, Sieur de Belefond. *Relation des costes d'Afrique: Appeles Guinée.* Paris: Denys Thierry, 1669. Translated as *A Relation of the Coasts of Africk Called Guinea.* 2d ed. London: Printed for John Starkey, 1670. 135–36, 249–54.

Walker, S. W. "Gabi Figures and Edegi, First King of the Nupe." *Man* 34 (Nov. 1934): 170, 172.

Ward-Price, H. L. *Land Tenure in the Yoruba Provinces.* Lagos, Nigeria: Government Printer, 1939. 26, 42.

Winterbottom, Thomas. *An Account of the Native Africans in the Neighborhood of Sierra Leone.* 2 vols. London: C. Whittingham, 1803. 2d ed., with an introduction by John D. Hargreaves and E. Maurice Backett. London: Cass, 1969. 1:125, 127–29, 234–35.

NOTES

ABBREVIATIONS

AHR	*American Historical Review*
CCOB	County Court Order Book
CS	Condemned Slaves, Library of Virginia
CWH	*Civil War History*
HA	*History in Africa*
JAH	*Journal of American History*
JNH	*Journal of Negro History*
JSH	*Journal of Southern History*
PASP	Pennsylvania Abolition Society Papers, Historical Society of Pennsylvania
PTJ	*The Papers of Thomas Jefferson*, ed. Julian Boyd et al.
PTJ-CC	Papers of Thomas Jefferson, Coolidge Collection, Massachusetts Historical Society
PTJ-JC	Jefferson Collection, Henry E. Huntington Library
PTJ-LC	Papers of Thomas Jefferson, Library of Congress
PTJ-MD	Papers of Thomas Jefferson, Manuscript Department, University of Virginia
VEPLR	Virginia Executive Papers, Letters Received, Library of Virginia
VHS	Virginia Historical Society
VMHB	*Virginia Magazine of History and Biography*
WMQ	*William and Mary Quarterly*

INTRODUCTION

1. Richard S. Dunn, *Sugar and Slaves: The Rise of the Planter Class in the English West Indies, 1624–1713* (Chapel Hill: University of North

Carolina Press, 1972), 239–46; A. Leon Higginbotham Jr., *In the Matter of Color: Race and the American Legal Process: The Colonial Period* (New York: Oxford University Press, 1978); Alan Watson, *Slave Law in the Americas* (Athens: University of Georgia Press, 1989); William Wiecek, "The Statutory Law of Slavery and Race in the Thirteen Mainland Colonies of British America," *WMQ*, 3d ser., 34 (April 1977): 258–80; Peter H. Wood, *Black Majority: Negroes in Colonial South Carolina from 1670 to the Stono Rebellion* (New York: Knopf, 1974). See also Terri L. Snyder, "Legal History of the Colonial South: Assessment and Suggestions," *WMQ*, 3d ser., 50 (Jan. 1993): 18–27; and David Thomas Konig, "A Summary View of the Law of British America," *WMQ*, 3d ser., 50 (Jan. 1993): 42–50.

2. Edmund S. Morgan, *American Slavery, American Freedom: The Ordeal of Colonial Virginia* (New York: Norton, 1975); Orlando Patterson, "The Unholy Trinity: Freedom, Slavery, and the American Constitution," *Social Research* 54 (Autumn 1987): 543–77; idem, *Freedom*, vol. 1, *Freedom in the Making of Western Culture* (New York: Basic Books, 1991), 9–44.

3. David Levering Lewis, "Radical History: Toward Inclusiveness," *JAH* 76 (Sept. 1989): 473.

4. James Curtis Ballagh, *A History of Slavery in Virginia*, Johns Hopkins University Studies in Historical and Political Science, extra vol., 24 (Baltimore: Johns Hopkins Press, 1902), 27–115. I have discussed this study and Ballagh's assumptions in "James C. Ballagh and the Law of Slavery," a paper presented at a meeting of the Southern Historical Association, Norfolk, Virginia, 1988. Perhaps more influential than Ballagh's book is Charles S. Sydnor, "The Southerner and the Laws," *JSH* 6 (Feb. 1940): 3–23. Other relevant studies are Wilbert E. Moore, "Slave Law and the Social Structure," *JNH* 26 (April 1941): 171–202; Bertram Wyatt-Brown, *Southern Honor: Ethics and Behavior in the Old South* (New York: Oxford University Press, 1982), 362–401; James W. Ely Jr. and David J. Bodenhamer, "Regionalism and the Legal History of the South," in *Ambivalent Legacy: A Legal History of the South*, edited by David J. Bodenhamer and James W. Ely Jr. (Jackson: University Press of Mississippi, 1984), 3–29; J. Thomas Wren, "'A Two-Fold Character': The Slave as Person and Property in Virginia Court Cases, 1800–1860," *South-*

ern Studies 24 (Winter 1985): 417–31; Jonathan A. Bush, "Free to En-slave: The Foundations of Colonial American Slave Law," *Yale Journal of Law and the Humanities* 5 (Summer 1993): 417–70; Bradley J. Nicholson, "Legal Borrowing and the Origins of Slave Law in the British Colonies," *American Journal of Legal History* 38 (Jan. 1994): 38–54; and Andrew Fede, *People Without Rights: An Interpretation of the Fundamentals of the Law of Slavery in the U.S. South* (New York: Garland, 1992).

5. Ballagh, *History of Slavery in Virginia*, 27.

6. Stanley Diamond, "The Rule of Law versus the Order of Custom," in *In Search of the Primitive: A Critique of Civilization* (New Brunswick, N.J.: Transaction Books, 1974), 255–80; T. Olawale Elias, *The Nature of African Customary Law* (Manchester, Eng.: Manchester University Press, 1956), 37–55; Mark V. Tushnet, "Major Themes in the History of the Criminal Law in the United States: Some Implications of Method-ology," paper presented at the Conference on the History of Crime and Criminal Justice, University of Maryland, Sept. 4–7, 1980; idem, "Approaches to the Study of the Law of Slavery," *CWH* 25 (Dec. 1979): 329–38. See also John T. Noonan Jr., *Persons and Masks of the Law: Car-dozo, Holmes, Jefferson, and Wythe as Makers of the Masks* (New York: Farrar, Straus, and Giroux, 1976), 29–64; Sydnor, "Southerner and the Laws"; Wyatt-Brown, *Southern Honor*, 315–16, 364–65; and the articles in the "Law and Society in Early America" issue of the *WMQ*, 3d ser., 50 (Jan. 1993).

7. In "Louisiana Underlaw," Peter R. Teachout develops a conception of law quite useful to the historian of the law of slavery. "Underlaw" is the discretionary administration of law by local officials in order to maintain white supremacy. Under slavery, this "underlaw" was adminis-tered by slave owners and overseers. See Teachout, "Louisiana Under-law," in *Southern Justice*, edited by Leon Friedman (Westport, Conn.: Greenwood Press, 1965), 57–79.

8. See the exchange of 1977 and 1978 concerning the ways that statutes and behavior related to slaves: Wiecek, "Statutory Law of Slav-ery and Race," 258–80; A. G. Roeber, letter to the editor, *WMQ*, 3d ser., 35 (July 1978): 600; Jeffrey J. Crow, letter to the editor, *WMQ*, 3d ser., 34 (Oct. 1977): 696–97; and Wiecek's reply to Crow's letter, *WMQ*, 3d ser., 34 (Oct. 1977): 697.

9. Thomas D. Morris, "'As If the Injury Was Effected by the Natural Elements of Air, or Fire': Slave Wrongs and the Liability of Masters," *Law and Society Review* 16, no. 4 (1981–82): 569–99; idem, "'Society Is Not Marked by Punctuality in the Payment of Debts': The Chattel Mortgages of Slaves," in *Ambivalent Legacy,* ed. Bodenhamer and Ely, 147–70; idem, *Southern Slavery and the Law, 1619–1860* (Chapel Hill: University of North Carolina Press, 1996); Fede, *People Without Rights;* Michael Stephen Hindus, *Prison and Plantation: Crime, Justice, and Authority in Massachusetts and South Carolina, 1767–1878* (Chapel Hill: University of North Carolina Press, 1980); A. E. Keir Nash, "Fairness and Formalism in the Trials of Blacks in the State Supreme Courts of the Old South," *Virginia Law Review* 56 (Feb. 1970): 64–100; idem, "A More Equitable Past? Southern Supreme Courts and the Protection of the Antebellum Negro," *North Carolina Law Review* 48, no. 2 (1969–70): 197–242; idem, "Negro Rights, Unionism, and Greatness on the South Carolina Court of Appeals: The Extraordinary Chief Justice John Belton O'Neil," *South Carolina Law Review* 21, no. 2 (1968–69): 141–90; idem, "Reason of Slavery: Understanding the Judicial Role in the Peculiar Institution," *Vanderbilt Law Review* 32 (Jan. 1979): 7–218; Mark V. Tushnet, *The American Law of Slavery, 1810–1860: Considerations of Humanity and Interest* (Princeton, N.J.: Princeton University Press, 1981); Higginbotham, *In the Matter of Color;* A. Leon Higginbotham Jr. and Barbara K. Kopytoff, "Property First, Humanity Second: The Recognition of the Slave's Human Nature in Virginia Civil Law," *Ohio State Law Journal* 50, no. 3 (1989): 511–40; Robert B. Shaw, *A Legal History of Slavery in the United States* (Potsdam, N.Y.: Northern Press, 1991).

10. The following discussion is based on my *Twice Condemned: Slaves and the Criminal Laws of Virginia, 1705–1865* (Baton Rouge: Louisiana State University Press, 1988).

11. Suzanne Lebsock, *The Free Women of Petersburg: Status and Culture in a Southern Town, 1784–1860* (New York: Norton, 1984), 136–41.

12. Martin Chanock, *Law, Custom and Social Order: The Colonial Experience in Malawi and Zambia* (Cambridge: Cambridge University Press, 1985), 3–47, 219–24.

13. See Michael L. Nicholls, "'In the Light of Human Beings': Richard Eppes and His Island Plantation Code of Laws," *VMHB* 89

(Jan. 1981): 67–78; Janet Sharp Hermann, *The Pursuit of a Dream* (New York: Oxford University Press, 1981), 12–13, 30; and Thomas D. Morris, "Slaves and the Rules of Evidence in Criminal Trials," *Chicago-Kent Law Review* 68, no. 3 (1993): 1229–30.

14. John W. Blassingame, *The Slave Community: Plantation Life in the Antebellum South*, rev. ed. (New York: Oxford University Press, 1979), 323–31; Stanley M. Elkins, *Slavery: A Problem in American Institutional and Intellectual Life*, 2d ed. (Chicago: University of Chicago Press, 1968), 103–39; Eugene D. Genovese, *Roll, Jordan, Roll The World the Slaves Made* (New York: Pantheon, 1974), 25–49. In contrast, see Norrece T. Jones Jr., *Born a Child of Freedom, Yet a Slave: Mechanisms of Control and Strategies of Resistance in Antebellum South Carolina* (Middletown, Conn.: Wesleyan University Press, 1990).

15. Genovese, *Roll, Jordan, Roll*, 40.

16. Bernard Bailyn, *The Origins of American Politics* (New York: Knopf, 1968), 96.

17. Suzanne Schnittman, "Hired Slavery in Virginia's Tobacco Industry," unpublished typescript, kindly supplied to me by the author. See also Schnittman, "Slavery in Virginia's Urban Tobacco Industry, 1840–1860" (Ph.D. diss., University of Rochester, 1986); and Rodney Dale Green, "Urban Industry, Black Resistance, and Racial Restriction in the Antebellum South: A General Model and a Case Study in Urban Virginia" (Ph.D. diss., American University, 1980), 571–76.

CHAPTER 1: "LAWLESSNESS"

Earlier versions of this chapter were presented to the American Society for Legal History in 1980 and to the forty-first conference of the Institute of Early American History and Culture, at Millersville State College, in 1981.

1. Venture Smith, "A Narrative of the Life and Adventures of *Venture*, a Native of Africa," in *Early Negro Writing, 1760–1837*, edited by Dorothy Porter (Boston: Beacon Press, 1971), 557.

2. Some slaves in the Old Dominion came from other parts of Africa. I have only abided by the commonly accepted scholarly view that most of the Africans imported into Virginia came from West Africa.

3. Robert Farris Thompson, *Flash of the Spirit: African and Afro-American Art and Philosophy* (New York: Random House, 1983), 164. See also Sidney W. Mintz and Richard Price, *An Anthropological Approach to the Afro-American Past: A Caribbean Perspective* (Philadelphia: Institute for the Study of Human Issues, 1976). Winthrop D. Jordan expressed the need for this chapter quite well. After commenting that, happily, there are "signs of movement away from the sociology of the slave institution toward an anthropology of the slaves and their masters," Jordan said that scholars must focus on African origins to study slaves in North America in the same way that they must learn about Sweden to discuss the Swedish experience in the New World. See Jordan, "Planter and Slave Identity Formation: Some Problems in the Comparative Approach," in *Comparative Perspectives on Slavery in New World Plantation Societies,* edited by Vera Rubin and Arthur Tuden, Annals of the New York Academy of Sciences, vol. 292 (New York: New York Academy of Sciences, 1977), 36, 39. In "The Meaning of Africa for the American Slave," *Journal of Ethnic Studies* 4 (Winter 1977): 1–15, esp. 5–6, David Roediger argues that "the example of life as it was lived in Africa furnished the imported slaves a set of standards by which they could critically assess American values." This argument parallels my argument in this chapter. See also Thomas D. Morris, "Slaves and the Rules of Evidence," 1229.

4. See, e.g., George M. Fredrickson, *White Supremacy: A Comparative Study in American and South African History* (New York: Oxford University Press, 1981), 73–74; Mechal Sobel, *Trabelin' On: The Slave Journey to an Afro-Baptist Faith* (Westport, Conn.: Greenwood Press, 1979), 114–15.

5. Fredrickson, *White Supremacy,* 7–13, 35–36; Francis Jennings, *The Invasion of America: Indians, Colonialism, and the Cant of Conquest* (Chapel Hill: University of North Carolina Press, 1975), 6–12.

6. "What can we do with these savages?" asked a southern judge in 1908. See Thomas Manson Norwood, *Address on the Negro, by Judge Thomas Manson Norwood, on His Retiring from the Bench* (Savannah, Ga.: Presses Braid and Hutton, 1908), 21. See also Philip D. Curtin, *The Image of Africa: British Ideas and Action, 1780–1850* (Madison: Univer-

sity of Wisconsin Press, 1964), 9–15; Winthrop D. Jordan, *White over Black: American Attitudes Toward the Negro, 1550–1812* (Chapel Hill: University of North Carolina Press, 1968), 24–28, 305–10; George M. Fredrickson, *The Black Image in the White Mind: The Debate on Afro-American Character and Destiny, 1817–1914* (New York: Harper and Row, 1971), 52–55, 253–54; Kenneth Paul O'Brien, "The Savage and the Child in Historical Perspective: Images of Blacks in Southern White Thought, 1830–1915" (Ph.D. diss., Northwestern University, 1974), 32–35; Kenneth M. Stampp, *The Peculiar Institution: Slavery in the Ante-Bellum South* (New York: Vintage Books, 1956), 12–14; W. Robert Higgins, "The Ambivalence of Freedom: Whites, Blacks, and the Coming of the American Revolution in the South," in *The Revolutionary War in the South: Power, Conflict, and Leadership: Essays in Honor of John Richard Alden,* edited by W. Robert Higgins (Durham, N.C.: Duke University Press, 1979), 51–53; and works cited in the Appendix.

7. As slaves, Africans and African Americans were, of course, inevitably excluded from or subject to certain laws, just as Roman or Greek slaves were.

8. Julius Goebel Jr., *History of the Supreme Court in the United States,* vol. 1, *Antecedents and Beginnings to 1801* (New York: Macmillan, 1971), 3–8; Lawrence Henry Gipson, "Crime and Its Punishment in Provincial Pennsylvania," *Pennsylvania History* 2 (Jan. 1935): 3–5; A. G. Roeber, "'He read it to me from a book of English law': Germans, Bench, and Bar in the Colonial South," in *Ambivalent Legacy,* ed. Bodenhamer and Ely, 202–28.

9. See, e.g., Higginbotham, *In the Matter of Color;* and Fede, *People Without Rights.* For a thorough review of the pre-1979 literature on the treatment of slaves in American courts of law, see A. E. Keir Nash, "Reason of Slavery," 7–218.

10. I have tried to confine myself to the use of seventeenth- and eighteenth-century primary sources concerning Africa. However, I have used a handful of nineteenth- and twentieth-century sources that comment on the practices and institutions of earlier centuries. I have also tried to avoid secondary sources that confine their analysis to the colonial and postcolonial periods.

11. The works of observers I have used are listed in the Appendix. The list also includes some ethnographic observations from the nineteenth and twentieth centuries to demonstrate continuity of certain practices. Citations to specific works will appear in the notes as appropriate. Otherwise it should be understood that the conclusions of chapter 1 rest on the basis of evidence from all, or nearly all, of the sources listed in the Appendix.

A bibliography of such sources appears in Edward G. Cox, *Reference Guide to the Literature of Travel*, 3 vols. (Seattle: University of Washington, 1935), 1:354–401; Robin Hallett, *Penetration of Africa: European Exploration in North and West Africa*, 2 vols. (New York: Praeger, 1965), 1:399–407; George Peter Murdock et al., comps. *Outline of Culture Materials*, 4th rev. ed. (New Haven, Conn.: Human Relations Area Files, 1967); George Peter Murdock, *Outline of World Cultures*, 5th ed. (New Haven, Conn.: Human Relations Area Files, 1975); John N. Paden and Edward W. Soja, eds., *The African Experience*, 4 vols. (Evanston, Ill.: Northwestern University Press, 1970); and Robert I. Rotberg, ed., *Africa and Its Explorers: Motives, Methods, and Impact* (Cambridge, Mass.: Harvard University Press, 1970), 323–32. Besides the works of Hallett and Rotberg, other useful discussions of the African context are J. F. Ade Ajayi and Ian Espie, eds., *A Thousand Years of West African History* (New York: Humanities Press, 1972); and Curtin, *Image of Africa.* I have relied on twentieth-century editions of the seventeenth- and eighteenth-century works when possible, but I have used a few edited editions, as opposed to facsimile reprints with or without introductions. On the possibilities and perils of using seventeenth- and eighteenth-century European texts about Africa, see P. E. H. Hair, "Barbot, Dapper, Davity: A Critique of Sources on Sierra Leone and Cape Mount," *HA* 1 (1974): 25–54; idem, "Materials on Africa (Other Than the Mediterranean and Red Sea Lands) and on the Atlantic Islands in the Publications of Samuel Purchas, 1613–1626," *HA* 13 (1986): 117–59; Albert van Dantzig, "Willem Bosman's *New and Accurate Description of the Coast of Guinea:* How Accurate Is It?" *HA* 1 (1974): 101–8; idem, "English Bosman and Dutch Bosman: A Comparison of Texts," *HA* 2 (1975): 185–216, 3 (1976): 91–126, 4 (1977): 247–73, 5 (1978): 225–56, 6 (1979): 265–85, 7 (1980): 281–91, 9 (1982):

285–302, 11 (1984): 307–29; H. M. Feinberg, "An Eighteenth-Century Case of Plagiarism: William Smith's *A New Voyage to Guinea*," *HA* 6 (1979): 45–50; Adam Jones, "William Smith the Plagiarist: A Rejoinder," *HA* 7 (1980): 327–28; Robin Law, "Jean Barbot as a Source for the Slave Coast of West Africa," *HA* 9 (1982): 155–73; idem, "The Original Manuscript Version of William Snelgrave's *New Account of Some Parts of Guinea*," *HA* 17 (1990): 367–72; and J. D. Fage, "Hawkins' Hoax? A Sequel to 'Drake's Fake,'" *HA* 18 (1991): 83–91.

12. There are several valuable discussions of the problems of studying African institutions from a Western perspective. See Paul Bohannon, "Ethnography and Comparison in Legal Anthropology," in *Law in Culture and Society*, edited by Laura Nader (Chicago: Aldine, 1969), 401–18; Max Gluckman, "Concepts in the Comparative Study of Tribal Law," in *Law in Culture and Society*, ed. Nader, 349–73; idem, *Order and Rebellion in Tribal Africa: Collected Essays with an Autobiographical Introduction* (New York: Free Press, 1963), 178–206; R. S. Rattray, *Ashanti Law and Constitution* (Oxford: Clarendon Press, 1929), vii–viii, 285; J. van Velsen, "Procedural Informality, Reconciliation, and False Comparisons," in *Ideas and Procedures in African Customary Law*, edited by Max Gluckman (London: Oxford University Press, 1969), 137–52; and Roland Young, "Legal Systems Development," in *African Experience*, ed. Paden and Soja, 1:473–97. See also Elkins, *Slavery*, 90, 93; John K. Thornton, "African Dimensions of the Stono Rebellion," *AHR* 96 (Oct. 1991): 1101–13; and Mintz and Price, *Anthropological Approach*, 4–6. On treating West Africa as an area in which common perceptions, but not institutions, can be traced, see Albert J. Raboteau, *Slave Religion: The "Invisible Institution" in the Antebellum South* (New York: Oxford University Press, 1978), 7–8, 325–27n8.

13. Janet J. Ewald provides a short overview of some of the debates concerning African history in her review essay "Slavery in Africa and the Slave Trades from Africa," *AHR* 97 (April 1992): 465–85. See also the general introduction and introductions to each selection in J. E. Inikori, ed., *Forced Migration: The Impact of the Export Slave Trade in African Societies* (London: Hutchinson and Co., 1982). On competing interpretations of African legal history, see Chanock, *Law, Custom and*

Social Order, 3–10, 25–47, 219–39; and Martin Chanock, "A Peculiar Sharpness: An Essay on Property in the History of Customary Law in Colonial Africa," *Journal of African History* 32, no. 1 (1991): 65–88.

14. Joseph Schact, *An Introduction to Islamic Law* (Oxford: Clarendon Press, 1964), 175–87; Raboteau, *Slave Religion,* 5–16.

15. P. F. Gonidec, *Les droits africaines, évolution et sources,* 2d ed. (Paris: Librairie Générale de Droit et de Jurisprudence, 1976), 5–9; Richard W. Hull, *Munyakare: African Civilization Before the Batuuree* (New York: J. Wiley, 1972), 101–16; R. Verdier, "Ethnologie et droits africaines," Société des Africanistes, Paris, *Journal* 33 (Feb. 1963): 105–28; Mintz and Price, *Anthropological Approach,* 5–6.

16. Besides the selections in Inikori's *Forced Migration,* see David Eltis, "Precolonial Western Africa and the Atlantic Economy," in *Slavery and the Rise of the Atlantic System,* edited by Barbara L. Solow (Cambridge: Cambridge University Press, 1991), 97–119; Joseph C. Miller, *Way of Death: Merchant Capitalism and the Angolan Slave Trade, 1730–1830* (Madison: University of Wisconsin Press, 1988); Paul E. Lovejoy, *Transformations in Slavery: A History of Slavery in Africa* (Cambridge: Cambridge University Press, 1983); idem, "The Impact of the Slave Trade on Africa: A Review of the Literature," *Journal of African History* 30 (1989): 365–94; Patrick Manning, *Slavery and African Life: Occidental, Oriental and African Slave Trades* (Cambridge: Cambridge University Press, 1990); and Ewald, "Slavery in Africa," 465–85.

17. Eugene Cotran, "The Position of Customary Law in African Countries," in *East African Law and Social Change,* edited by G. F. A. Sawyer (Nairobi: East African Publishing House, 1967), 14–25; George Dalton, "Theoretical Issues in Economic Anthropology," in *Economic Development and Social Change,* edited by George Dalton (Garden City, N.Y.: Natural History Press, 1971), 214–17; Gonidec, *Les droits africaines,* 14–20; A. St. J. Hannigan, "The Imposition of Western Law Forms upon Primitive Societies," *Comparative Studies in Society and History* 4 (Nov. 1961): 1–9; Anthony Benezet, *A Short Account of That Part of Africa Inhabited by the Negroes* (Philadelphia: W. Dunlap, 1762), 26; Hull, *Munyakare,* 101–16; G. I. Jones, "Ecology and Social Structure Among the North Eastern Ibo," *Africa* 31 (1961): 133. See also the works cited in notes 13 and 14 above.

18. For the details and prevalence of the African use of slavery as a judicial sanction, see Basil Davidson, "Slaves or Captives? Some Notes on Fantasy and Fact," in *Key Issues in the Afro-American Experience*, edited by Nathan I. Huggins et al., 2 vols. (New York: Harcourt Brace Jovanovich, 1971), 1:64–66, 68; Marion Busser De Barenne Kilson, "West African Society and the Atlantic Slave Trade, 1441–1865," in *Key Issues*, ed. Huggins et al., 1:50; P. E. H. Hair, ed., *Liverpool, the African Slave Trade, and Abolition* (Liverpool: Historic Society of Lancashire and Cheshire, 1976), 27–29; Albert van Dantzig, "Effects of the Atlantic Slave Trade on Some West African Societies," *Revue Française d'Histoire d'Outre-Mer* 62, nos. 226–27 (1975) 258, 264; Orlando Patterson, *Slavery and Social Death: A Comparative Study* (Cambridge, Mass.: Harvard University Press, 1982), 114, 119, 126–29, 397n54; Joseph C. Miller, *Way of Death*, 116–17, 123, 131, 164, 197–98; Lovejoy, *Transformations in Slavery*, 43, 84, 87, 123, 125–26; Claude Meillassoux, "The Role of Slavery in the Economic and Social History of Sahelo-Sudanic Africa," in *Forced Migration*, ed. Inikori, 98; J. D. Fage, "Slavery and the Slave Trade in the Context of West African History," in *Forced Migration*, ed. Inikori, 164; Kwame Yeboa Daaku, *Trade and Politics on the Gold Coast, 1600–1720: A Study of the African Reaction to European Trade* (London: Clarendon, 1970), 28–29; Walter Rodney, *A History of the Upper Guinea Coast, 1545–1800* (Oxford: Clarendon Press, 1970), 106–9, 114–16; Roberta Ann Dunbar, "Slavery and the Evolution of Nineteenth-Century Damagaram," in *Slavery in Africa: Historical and Anthropological Perspectives*, edited by Suzanne Miers and Igor Kopytoff (Madison: University of Wisconsin Press, 1977), 162; Robert Harms, "Slave Systems in Africa," *HA* 5 (1978): 327–35; Svend E. Holsoe, "Slavery and Economic Response Among the Vai (Liberia and Sierra Leone)," *HA* 5 (1978): 290, 294; Joseph C. Miller, "Imangala Lineage Slavery (Angola)," *HA* 5 (1978): 216, 219, 226–27; James H. Vaughan, "Mafakur: A Limbic Institution of the Margi (Nigeria)," *HA* 5 (1978): 89, 91, 98; David Northrup, *Trade Without Rulers: Pre-Colonial Economic Development in South-eastern Nigeria* (Oxford: Clarendon Press, 1978), 69–73; Lovejoy, *Transformations in Slavery*, 43, 84, 87, 123, 126.

For accounts of observers, see John Barbot, *A Description of the Coasts of North and South Guinea*, in *A Collection of Voyages and Travels*, com-

piled by Awnsham Churchill, 6 vols. (London: J. Walthoe, 1732), 1:47,
299, 348 (also available in *Barbot on Guinea: The Writings of Jean Barbot on West Africa, 1678–1712,* edited by P. E. H. Hair, Adam Jones, and
Robin Law, 2 vols. [London: Hakluyt Society, 1992]); William Bosman, *A
New and Accurate Description of the Coast of Guinea* (London: J. Knapton, 1705; London: Cass, 1967), 168–69; William Snelgrave, *A New Account of Some Parts of Guinea and the Slave Trade* (London: J., J. and
P. Knapton, 1734; London: Cass, 1971), 158, 161; Francis Moore, *Travels
into the Inland Parts of Africa* (London: E. Cave, 1738), 42–43; John
Atkins, *A Voyage to Guinea, Brasil, and the West* (London: C. Ward and
R. Chandler, 1735; London: Cass, 1970), 176–77; Benezet, *Short Account,*
26; Lievain Bonaventure Proyart, *Abbé Proyart's History of Loango,
Kakongo, and Other Kingdoms in Africa* (Paris: C. P. Berton, 1776), in *A
General Collection of the Best and Most Interesting Voyages and Travels
in All Parts of the World,* compiled by John Pinkerton, 17 vols. (London:
Longman, Hurst, Rees, and Orme, 1808–14), 16:581–83; Anthony Bene-
zet, *Some Historical Account of Guinea,* 2d ed. (London: J. Phillips, 1778;
London: Cass, 1968), 83–87; Alexander Falconbridge, *An Account of the
Slave Trade on the Coast of Africa* (London: J. Phillips, 1788; New York:
AMS Press, 1973), 15; John Matthews, *A Voyage to the River Sierra-
Leone* (London: Printed for B. White and Son, 1788; London: Cass, 1966),
80–81; and Olaudah Equiano, *The Interesting Narrative of Olaudah Equiano; or, Gustavus Vassa, the African,* 2 vols. (London: G. Vassa by T. Wil-
kins, 1789), in *Africa Remembered: Narratives by West Africans from the
Era of the Slave Trade,* edited by Philip D. Curtin (Madison: University
of Wisconsin Press, 1967), 71, 75.

    See also Great Britain, Board of Trade, *Report of the Lords of the
Committee of Council . . . Submitting . . . the Evidence and Information . . .
Concerning the Present State of the Trade to Africa . . .* (London, 1789),
pt. 1, witnesses Elrid, Newton, Falconbridge, Miles, Barnes, Spaarman,
Dalrymple, Gandy, Yonge, Penny, Matthews, Deane, Norris, Weuves,
Dalzell, Edwards, Anderson, Arnold, and Baggs. See Great Britain, Parliament, House of Commons, *Minutes of the Evidence . . . Sessional Papers, Accounts and Papers,* vol. 29, no. 698, 1790, 6–7, 17–18, 49–50, 585,
612; vol. 30, no. 699, 1790, 81–82, 139, 141–43, 154; vol. 34, no. 745,
1790–91, 16, 40.

See Joseph Hawkins, *A History of a Voyage to the Coast of Africa and Travels into the Interior of That Country* (Philadelphia: S. C. Ustick, 1797; London: Cass, 1970), 97, 110–12; Falconbridge, *Account*, 82–83; Thomas Winterbottom, *An Account of the Native Africans in the Neighborhood of Sierra Leone*, 2 vols. (London: C. Whittingham, 1803; 2d ed., with an introduction by John D. Hargreaves and E. Maurice Backett, London: Cass, 1969), 1:128; Charles Monteil, *The Bambara of Segou and Kaarta*, translated by Kathryn A. Looney (New Haven, Conn.: Human Relations Area Files, 1960), 208; Charles Kingsley Meek, "Ibo Law," in *Essays Presented to C. G. Seligman*, edited by E. E. Evans Pritchard et al. (London: K. Paul, Trench, Trübner, 1934), 221; J. Decapmaker, "Sanctions coutumières contre l'adultère chez les Bakongo de la région de Kasi," *Congo* (July 1939): 134–38; Merran McCulloch, *Peoples of Sierra Leone Protectorate*, Ethnographic Survey of Africa, Western Africa, pt. 2 (London: International African Institute, 1950), 24–25; Cyril Daryll Forde, *The Yoruba-Speaking Peoples of South-western Nigeria*, Ethnographic Survey of Africa, Western Africa, pt. 4 (London: International African Institute, 1951), 24; Viviana Paques, *The Bambara*, translated by Thomas Turner (New Haven, Conn.: Human Relations Area Files, 1959), 77, 94–96; and Carol P. Mac-Cormack, "Wono: Institutionalized Dependency in Sherbro Descent Groups (Sierra Leone)," in *Slavery in Africa*, ed. Miers and Kopytoff, 195–96.

19. On the details and prevalence of the African use of slavery as a judicial sanction, see note 18 above; and Claude Meillassoux, ed., *L'esclavage en Afrique précoloniale* (Paris: F. Maspero, 1975).

20. Miers and Kopytoff, eds., *Slavery in Africa*; Suzanne Miers and Richard Roberts, ed., *The End of Slavery in Africa* (Madison: University of Wisconsin Press, 1988); Paul E. Lovejoy, ed., *The Ideology of Slavery in Africa* (Beverly Hills, Calif.: Sage, 1981); Meillassoux, ed., *L'esclavage en Afrique précoloniale*; Claude Meillassoux, *Anthropologie de l'esclavage: Le ventre de fer et d'argent* (Paris: PUF, 1986), translated as *The Anthropology of Slavery: The Womb of Iron and Gold* (Chicago: University of Chicago Press, 1991); Inikori, ed., *Forced Migration*; Manning, *Slavery and African Life*; Lovejoy, *Transformations in Slavery*; Harms, "Slave Systems in Africa," 327–35; Jonathon Glassman, "The Bondsman's New Clothes: The Contradictory Consciousness of Slave Resistance on the

Swahili Coast," *Journal of African History* 32, no. 2 (1991): 277–312. With Lovejoy's writings, these works provide a strong argument against a benign image of slavery in Africa.

For a regional comparison, see Frederick Cooper, *Plantation Slavery on the East Coast of Africa* (New Haven, Conn.: Yale University Press, 1977). For a comparative look at European enslavement of Africans in Africa, see John Edwin Mason, "Hendrik Albertus and His Ex-Slave Mey: A Drama in Three Acts," *Journal of African History* 31, no. 3 (1990): 423–45; and Fredrickson, *White Supremacy*, 54–93.

21. Miers and Kopytoff, eds., *Slavery in Africa.* See especially Barbot, *Description* 1:337; Bosman, *New and Accurate Description*, 358; William Smith, *A New Voyage to Guinea* (London: Nourse, 1744; London: Cass, 1967), 204. For a vivid description of the horrors of the execution of a European regicide, see Michel Foucault, *Discipline and Punish: The Birth of the Prison* (New York: Pantheon, 1977), 3–6.

22. Barbot, *Description* 1:303–4; William R. Bascom, "The Sociological Role of the Yoruba Cult-Group," *American Anthropologist* 46, no. 1, pt. 2 (1944): 67; Pierre Alexandre and Jacques Binet, *Le groupe dit Pahouin*, translated by Isabella Athey (New Haven, Conn.: Human Relations Area Files, 1959), 94; Elias, *Nature of African Customary Law.* On "Negro Election Day," see Joseph Reidy, "Negro Election Day and Black Community Life in New England," *Marxist Perspectives* 1 (Fall 1978): 102–17.

23. On professional advocates, see Matthews, *Voyage*, 79; and C. C. Ifemesia, "States of the Central Sudan," in *Thousand Years of West African History*, ed. Ajayi and Espie, 72–112. On execution for interrupted testimony, see Barbot, *Description* 1:299; Col. John MacLean, ed., *A Compendium of Kafir Laws and Customs, Including Genealogical Tables of Kafir Chiefs and Various Tribal Census Returns* (Mount Coke: Printed for the Government of British Kaffraria, 1858; London: Cass, 1968), 61.

24. Richard Jobson, "A Description and Historicall Declaration of the Kingdome of Guinea . . . ," translated from the Dutch, in *Hakluytus Pothumus; or, Purchas His Pilgrims*, compiled by Samuel Purchas, 20 vols. (Glasgow: J. MacLehose and Sons, 1905–7), 6:313–14; Nicholas Villault, Sieur de Belefond, *Relation des costes d'Afrique: Appeles Guinée*

(Paris: Denys Thierry, 1669), translated as *A Relation of the Coasts of Africk Called Guinea*, 2d ed. (London: Printed for John Starkey, 1670), 252–54; Barbot, *Description* 1:301–2, 337–38.

25. A. G. L. Shaw, *Convicts and the Colonies: A Study of Penal Transportation from Great Britain and Ireland to Australia and Other Parts of the British Empire* (London: Faber, 1966), 22–37; J. Thorsten Sellin, *Slavery and the Penal System* (New York: Elsevier, 1976); Patterson, *Slavery and Social Death*, 44–45. Indeed, some of the first white European settlers in West Africa appear to have been fugitives or banished criminals. See John Green and Thomas Astley, comps., *A New General Collection of Voyages and Travels*, 4 vols. (London: Printed for T. Astley, 1745–47; New York: Barnes and Noble, 1968), 2:245.

26. Francis Moore, *Travels*, 88–89; Walter Rodney, "African Slavery and Other Forms of Social Oppression on the Upper Guinea Coast in the Context of the Atlantic Slave Trade," *Journal of African History* 7, no. 3 (1966): 438. For the terms of this interaction, which differed from the terms of interaction in British America, see Philip D. Morgan, "British Encounters with Africans and African-Americans, circa 1600–1780," in *Strangers Within the Realm: Cultural Margins of the British Empire*, edited by Bernard Bailyn and Philip D. Morgan (Chapel Hill: University of North Carolina Press, 1991), 157–219, esp. 182–84.

27. Jobson, "Description" 6:317–18; "A True Relation of the Inhuman and Unparalleled Actions and Barbarous Murders of *Negroes* or *Moors*, Committed on Three *Englishmen* in Old *Calabar in Guinea* . . . ," in *A Collection of Voyages and Travels*, compiled by Thomas Osborne, 2 vols. (London: Printed for T. Osborne, 1747), 2:517; John Ogilby, *Africa, Being an Accurate Description of the Regions of Aegypt, Barbary, Lybia, and Billedulgerid, the Land of Negroes, Guinea, Aethiopia, and the Abyssines . . .* (London: Thomas Johnson, 1670), 452; Barbot, *Description* 1:119, 236, 301–3, 331–32; Matthews, *Voyage*, 80; Great Britain, Board of Trade, *Report*, witness Dalzell.

28. John Newton, *Thoughts upon the African Slave Trade* (London: Printed for J. Buckland, in Pater-Noster Row, and J. Johnson, in St. Paul's Church-yard, 1788), in *The Journal of a Slave Trader (John Newton), 1750–1754*, by John Newton, edited by Bernard Martin and Mark

Spurrell (London: Epworth Press, 1962), 107; Great Britain, Parliament, House of Commons, *Minutes*, vol. 30, no. 699, 1790, witness Newton.

29. Gerald W. Mullin, *Flight and Rebellion: Slave Resistance in Eighteenth-Century Virginia* (New York: Oxford University Press, 1972), 34–80; Wood, *Black Majority*, 95–166.

30. Mintz and Price, *Anthropological Approach*, 10–11; Mullin, *Flight and Rebellion*, 46–47; A. G. Roeber, "Authority, Law, and Custom: The Rituals of Court Day in Tidewater Virginia, 1720 to 1750," *WMQ*, 3d ser., 37 (1980): 29–52; Rhys Isaac, *The Transformation of Virginia, 1740–1790* (Chapel Hill: University of North Carolina Press, 1982), 88–94; Philip J. Schwarz, "Gabriel's Challenge: Slaves and Crime in Late Eighteenth-Century Virginia," *VMHB* 90 (July 1982): 283–309.

31. Mullin, *Flight and Rebellion*, 3–33.

32. Benezet commented on the disparity between African prohibition of adultery and the white American refusal to extend "those Christian laws, which prohibit fornication and adultery" to African American slaves (*Some Historical Account*, 31). See also Elkins, *Slavery*, 53–55.

33. Michael G. Kammen develops the notion of the refraction of British values and assumptions in the New World context. See Kammen, *People of Paradox: An Inquiry Concerning the Origins of American Civilization* (New York: Knopf, 1972), 6; see also Mintz and Price, *Anthropological Approach*, 27–31.

34. Mintz and Price, *Anthropological Approach*, 3; Frederick Barth, introduction to *Ethnic Groups and Boundaries: The Social Organization of Culture Difference*, edited by Frederick Barth (London: Allen and Unwin, 1969); Evon Z. Vogt and Ethel M. Albert, eds., *People of Rimrock: A Study of Values in Five Cultures* (Cambridge, Mass.: Harvard University Press, 1967).

35. H. Hoetink, *Slavery and Race Relations in the Americas: Comparative Notes on Their Nature and Nexus* (New York: Harper and Row, 1973). In an extended critique of Hoetink's study, Sidney W. Mintz has explored the role of class, status, and power in the formation of group boundaries. See Mintz, "Groups, Group Boundaries, and the Perception of 'Race,'" *Comparative Studies in Society and History* 13 (Oct. 1971): 437–50. The diverse modes of interaction between Europeans and Na-

tive Americans in French Canadian and British American colonies illustrate the importance of perceptions. See Gary B. Nash, *Red, White, and Black: The Peoples of Early America*, 3d ed. (Englewood Cliffs, N.J.: Prentice-Hall, 1992), 104–11.

36. See, e.g., Genovese, *Roll, Jordan, Roll*. Elizabeth Fox-Genovese and Eugene D. Genovese, however, argue that overreliance on anthropological models in the study of slavery can deflect historians from the essentially political character of slaves' interactions with slave owners. See Fox-Genovese and Genovese, *Fruits of Merchant Capital Slavery and Bourgeois Property in the Rise and Expansion of Capitalism* (New York: Oxford University Press, 1983), 179–212.

37. In my book *Twice Condemned*, I develop this interpretation with respect to the criminal law of slavery.

38. Elias, *Nature of African Customary Law*, 55; A. N. Allott, A. L. Epstein, and Max Gluckman, introduction to *Ideas and Procedures in African Customary Law*, ed. Gluckman, 1–81; Julian Pitt-Rivers, *The People of the Sierra* (Chicago: University of Chicago Press, 1971), 160, 178, 183, 201, 209; Walter Ullmann, *Law and Politics in the Middle Ages: An Introduction to the Sources of Medieval Political Ideas* (Ithaca, N.Y.: Cornell University Press, 1975), 62; George Lee Haskins, *Law and Authority in Early Massachusetts: A Study in Tradition and Design* (New York: Macmillan, 1960), 212; Gary B. Nash, "From Freedom to Bondage in Seventeenth-Century Virginia," review of *"Myne Owne Ground,"* by T. H. Breen and Stephen Innes, *Reviews in American History* 10 (March 1982): 35.

39. This paragraph is based on my discussions of slaves and crime in *Twice Condemned*. See also Thomas D. Morris, "Slaves and the Rules of Evidence," 1229–30.

CHAPTER 2: THOMAS JEFFERSON AND THE LAW OF SLAVERY

1. Louis P. Masur, "Reimagining Jefferson," *Reviews in American History* 17 (Sept. 1989): 391.

2. For conflicting viewpoints concerning Jefferson's choice, see Paul Finkelman, "Jefferson and Slavery: 'Treason Against the Hopes of the

World,'" in *Jeffersonian Legacies,* edited by Peter S. Onuf (Charlottesville: University Press of Virginia, 1993), 181–221; and Patterson, "Unholy Trinity," 543–77.

3. Jefferson to John Holmes, April 22, 1820, polygraph copy, PTJ-LC, 51. The Ford edition erroneously transcribes *ear* as "ears," which makes some difference in Jefferson's meaning. See Paul L. Ford, ed., *The Writings of Thomas Jefferson,* 10 vols. (New York: G. P. Putnam's Sons, 1892–99), 10:159. I am grateful to John Catanzariti, editor of the Thomas Jefferson Papers, and Elizabeth Blazejewski, editorial assistant, for checking a restricted microfilm copy of the original letter. The staff of the Jefferson Papers had discovered Ford's, and apparently everyone else's, error concerning *ear* shortly before I did. See also Dumas Malone, *The Sage of Monticello* (Boston: Little, Brown, 1981), 320–27; and John Chester Miller, *The Wolf by the Ears: Thomas Jefferson and Slavery* (New York: Free Press, 1977), 203–79.

4. Louis Philippe, Comte de Ségur, *Mémoires; ou, Souvenirs et anecdotes,* 2 vols., 5th ed. (Paris: Didier, 1843), 2:127. "Je travaille sur la peau humaine," she wrote.

5. Dumas Malone, *Jefferson and His Time,* 6 vols. (Boston: Little, Brown, 1948–81); Merrill D. Peterson, *Thomas Jefferson and the New Nation: A Biography* (New York: Oxford University Press, 1970); Bernard Bailyn, "Jefferson and the Ambiguities of Freedom," *Proceedings of the American Philosophical Society* 137 (Dec. 1993): 506–7; Guy A. Cardwell, "Jefferson Renounced: Natural Rights in the Old South," *Yale Review* 58 (Spring 1969): 388–407; William Cohen, "Thomas Jefferson and the Problem of Slavery," *JAH* 56 (Dec. 1969): 503–26; Robert Dawidoff, "The Fox in the Henhouse: Jefferson and Slavery," *Reviews in American History* 6 (Dec. 1978): 503–11; John P. Diggins, "Slavery, Race, and Equality: Jefferson and the Pathos of the Enlightenment," *American Quarterly* 28 (Summer 1976): 206–28; John Hope Franklin, *Racial Equality in America* (Chicago: University of Chicago Press, 1976), 12–34; William W. Freehling, "The Founding Fathers and Slavery," *AHR* 76 (Feb. 1972): 81–93; Winthrop D. Jordan, *White over Black,* 429–81; Robert McColley, *Slavery and Jeffersonian Virginia,* 2d ed. (Urbana: University of Illinois Press, 1973), 114–40, 163–81; John Chester Miller, *Wolf by the*

Ears; Noonan, *Persons and Masks of the Law,* 29–64; Donald L. Robinson, *Slavery in the Structure of American Politics, 1765–1820* (New York: Harcourt Brace Jovanovich, 1971), 81–97; Robert E. Shalhope, "Thomas Jefferson's Republicanism and Antebellum Southern Thought," *JSH* 42 (Nov. 1976): 529–56.

The most recent discussions of Jefferson's attitudes concerning slavery are William W. Freehling, *The Road to Disunion,* vol. 1, *Secessionists at Bay, 1776–1854* (New York: Oxford University Press, 1990), 121–31, 140–42, 154–57, 167–69; Finkelman, "Jefferson and Slavery," 181–221; and idem, "Thomas Jefferson and Antislavery: The Myth Goes On," *VMHB* 102 (April 1994): 193–228. See also Jon Kukla, "On the Irrelevance of Saints George and Thomas," *VMHB* 102 (April 1994): 261–70.

6. See, e.g., James A. Bear Jr., "The Hemings Family at Monticello," *Virginia Cavalcade* 29 (Autumn 1979): 78–87; and idem, "The Hemings File," in *Report of the Curator to the Board of Trustees of the Thomas Jefferson Memorial Foundation for the Year 1978* (Monticello, Va.: Thomas Jefferson Memorial Foundation, 1978), 19–30; Mary Beth Norton, Herbert G. Gutman, and Ira Berlin, "The Afro-American Family in the Age of Revolution," in *Slavery and Freedom in the Age of the American Revolution,* edited by Ira Berlin and Ronald Hoffman (Charlottesville: University Press of Virginia, 1983), 175–91; Jack McLaughlin, *Jefferson and Monticello: The Biography of a Builder* (New York: Henry Holt, 1988), 94–145; Elizabeth Langhorne, *Monticello: A Family Story* (Chapel Hill, N.C.: Algonquin Books, 1987); Judith P. Justus, *Down from the Mountain: The Oral History of the Hemings Family* (Perrysburg, Ohio: Jeskurtara, 1990). Lucia C. Stanton, director of research at the Thomas Jefferson Memorial Foundation (hereinafter Jefferson Foundation), and others are engaged in ongoing research concerning African Americans at Monticello and Poplar Forest. See Stanton, "'Those Who Labor for My Happiness': Thomas Jefferson and His Slaves," in *Jeffersonian Legacies,* ed. Onuf, 147–80.

7. Jefferson to Edmund Pendleton, Aug. 26, 1776, and to George Wythe, Nov. 1, 1778, draft bills, in *The Papers of Thomas Jefferson,* edited by Julian Boyd et al. (Princeton, N.J.: Princeton University Press, 1950–), 1:505, 2:229–30, 275–77, 470–73, 475–78, 492–507, 616–17, 641–50

(hereinafter cited as *PTJ*); Douglas Egerton, *Gabriel's Rebellion: The Virginia Slave Conspiracies of 1800 and 1802* (Chapel Hill: University of North Carolina Press, 1993), 151–62. See also chapter 4, below. For one more indication of Jefferson's influence on legislation concerning bondage, see Jefferson to Thomas Mann Randolph Jr., Oct. 22, Nov. 2, 22, 25, Dec. 15, 1802, Jan. 17, May 5, 1803, PTJ-LC, 27, 28.

8. Jackson Turner Main, "The One Hundred," *WMQ*, 3d ser., 11 (July 1954): 354–84.

9. See, e.g., David Brion Davis, *The Problem of Slavery in the Age of Revolution, 1770–1823* (Ithaca, N.Y.: Cornell University Press, 1975), 182–84; cf. Malone, *Sage of Monticello,* 323–24. On Jefferson's debt problems, see Steven H. Hochman, "Thomas Jefferson: a Personal Financial Biography" (Ph.D. diss., University of Virginia, 1987); Marion Louise White, "Debt Unresolved: Jefferson and Monticello" (M.A. thesis, University of Virginia, 1993); and T. H. Breen, *Tobacco Culture: The Mentality of the Great Tidewater Planters on the Eve of Revolution* (Princeton, N.J.: Princeton University Press, 1985), 144.

10. See note 5 above. In Paul Finkelman's judgment, Jefferson's "words are those of a liberty-loving man of the Enlightenment. His deeds are those of a self-indulgent and negrophobic Virginia planter" ("Jefferson and Slavery," 210).

11. See Patterson, "Unholy Trinity," 543–77.

12. "Extract of a letter from a gentleman . . . to the Editor," *(Fredericksburg) Virginia Herald,* Sept. 23, 1800.

13. Will of Thomas Jefferson (Jefferson's great-grandfather), probated Dec. 7, 1697, *VMHB* 23 (April 1915): 173; inventory of the same Thomas Jefferson's estate, Dec. 22, 1697, Henrico County Deeds, Wills, 1697–1704, 113–17; will of Thomas Jefferson (Jefferson's grandfather), March 15, 1725, probated in April 1731, Henrico County Deeds and Wills, 1725–37, 293. See also Hochman, "Thomas Jefferson," 12–38.

14. Will of Peter Jefferson, proved Oct. 16, 1757, inventory of the estate of Peter Jefferson, April 6, 1758, and will of Jane Jefferson, proved Oct. 1778, all in Albemarle County Will Book 2, 1752–85, 32, 41–47, 367; Jane Jefferson to Thomas Jefferson, deed, Sept. 29, 1773, PTJ-CC, 1 (another copy, 13). See Hochman, "Thomas Jefferson," 12–38; and James A. Bear

Jr. and Lucia C. Stanton, eds., *Jefferson's Memorandum Books: Accounts, with Legal Records and Miscellany, 1767–1826* (Princeton, N.J.: Princeton University Press, forthcoming), at date. I am indebted to Lucia Stanton for allowing me to use the proofs of this publication.

See also William Short to Jefferson, Jan. 12, 1790, Jefferson to Thomas Walker, Jan. 18, 1790, *PTJ* 16:107–8, 112–14; Jefferson to Thomas Mann Randolph, March 18, 1793, PTJ-LC, 17. Useful discussions of the nature of the inheritance of slaves include C. Ray Keim, "Primogeniture and Entail in Colonial Virginia," *WMQ*, 3d ser., 25 (Oct. 1968): 545–86; Marylynn Salmon, *Women and the Law of Property in Early America* (Chapel Hill: University of North Carolina Press, 1986), 152–56; Jean Butenhoff Lee, "Land and Labor: Parental Bequest Practices in Charles County, Maryland, 1732–1783," in *Colonial Chesapeake Society*, edited by Lois Green Carr, Philip D. Morgan, and Jean B. Russo (Chapel Hill: University of North Carolina Press, 1988), 306–41, esp. 308–9, 331–38; and Noonan, *Persons and Masks of the Law*, 29–64.

15. Bear, "Hemings Family at Monticello," 78–87; idem, "Hemings File," 19–30; Dumas Malone, *Jefferson the Virginian* (Boston: Little, Brown, 1948), 163, 390–91; idem, *Jefferson and the Ordeal of Liberty* (Boston: Little, Brown, 1962), 208–13; idem, *Jefferson the President: First Term, 1801–1805* (Boston: Little, Brown, 1970), 494–98; Virginius Dabney, *The Jefferson Scandals: A Rebuttal* (New York: Dodd, Mead, 1981); Fawn M. Brodie, *Thomas Jefferson An Intimate History* (New York: Norton, 1974), 89–93, 379–81, 630–45, 668–76; Hochman, "Thomas Jefferson," 62–67, 74–78, 82; Langhorne, *Monticello,* 10–11, 16–17, 49; McLaughlin, *Jefferson and Monticello,* 94–145; John Wayles and Martha Eppes, deed, April 29, 1746, Henrico County Deeds, 1744–48, 132–34; will of Bathurst Skelton, Sept. 30, 1768, proved Sept. 10, 1771, *Tyler's Quarterly Magazine* 6 (April 1925): 268; will of John Wayles, April 15, 1760, and codicil of Feb. 12, 1773, proved July 7, 1773, Charles City County Deeds, Wills, 1766–74, 461–63; *Thomas Jefferson's Farm Book, with Commentary and Relevant Extracts from Other Writings*, in *Memoirs of the American Philosophical Society*, vol. 35, edited by Edwin Morris Betts (Princeton, N.J.: Princeton University Press, 1953), facsimile, 7–9.

16. On the doctrine of *Partus sequitur ventrem,* see Ballagh, *History of Slavery in Virginia,* 38–39, 43–45; Warren M. Billings, "The Cases of Fernando and Elizabeth Key: A Note on the Status of Blacks in Seventeenth-Century Virginia," *WMQ,* 3d ser., 30 (July 1973): 473; idem, "The Law of Servants and Slaves in Seventeenth-Century Virginia," *VMHB* 99 (Jan. 1991): 55–58; and Thomas D. Morris, "'Villeinage . . . as it existed in England, reflects but little light on our subject': The Problem of the 'Sources' of Southern Law," *American Journal of Legal History* 32 (April 1988): 108–21.

17. Jefferson to Joel Yancey, Jan. 17, 1819, PTJ-CC, 10; Jefferson to John Wayles Eppes, June 30, 1820, PTJ-MD, 8.

18. Jefferson to Thomas Mann Randolph Sr., Feb. 4, 1790, and marriage settlement of Feb. 21, 1790, *PTJ* 16:154–55.

19. Jefferson to Francis Eppes, file draft, 1797, PTJ-MD, 4; marriage indenture of John Wayles Eppes and Maria Jefferson, in hand of Thomas Jefferson, Oct. 12, 1797, PTJ-CC, 14 (draft of same in PTJ-JC, 1). Loans of slaves to his adult children received the same legal protection as did gifts. Memorandum for Nicholas Lewis, ca. Nov. 7, 1790, *PTJ* 18:29. Such transactions—indeed, many of Jefferson's legal transactions concerning slaves—relate strongly to questions of gender. Space limitations prohibit discussion of these questions here.

20. Bear and Stanton, eds., *Jefferson's Memorandum Books.* See also Jefferson deed to Thomas Jefferson Randolph, March 26, 1813, VHS, Mss. 2 J3595 a48; Jefferson to John Jordan, Feb. 9, 1806, PTJ-CC, 5; "Negroes alienated from 1784. to 1794. inclusive," apparently page 25 of the "Farm Book," photocopy, Research Department, Jefferson Foundation; *Jefferson's Memorandum Books,* Jan. 21, 29, 1773; Jefferson to Archibald Thweatt, May 29, 1810, and Jefferson to Mr. Ladd, June 11, 1810, PTJ-LC, 44.

21. Jefferson to Jeremiah Goodman, deed, Nov. 30, 1815, Jefferson to Goodman, July 20, 1817, PTJ-LC, 48, 50.

22. Jefferson to Bowling Clarke, Sept. 21, 1792, *PTJ* 24:408–9; Jefferson power of attorney to Edmund Winston, Charles Clay, and Bowling Clarke to effect sale of Sam, Dilcey, Ambrose, Hanah, and Dinah "of one family," York, Jameboy, Judy, Amy, Will, and Frank, Sept. 21, 1792,

PTJ-CC, 2; Jefferson to James Lyle, April 15, 1793, PTJ-LC, 18; "Negroes alienated from 1784. to 1794. inclusive," apparently page 25 of the "Farm Book," photocopy, Research Department, Jefferson Foundation.

23. Jefferson to Nicholas Lewis, April 12, 1792, Jefferson to Bowling Clarke, Sept. 21, 1792, *PTJ* 23:408–9, 24:408–9; Joseph Dougherty to Jefferson, March 14, 1803, Jefferson to Craven Peyton, Nov. 27, 1815, PTJ-CC, 4, 8; Hochman, "Thomas Jefferson," 74–75, 149–50, 177–79, 197, 241, 279; Victor Dennis Golladay, "The Nicholas Family of Virginia, 1722–1820" (Ph.D. diss., University of Virginia, 1973), chap. 10. The Wilson Cary Nicholas ill-fated deed of trust of 1819 named eighty-two slaves. See Wilson Cary Nicholas and wife Mary's deed of trust to twenty-two people—among grantees are Jefferson, Thomas J. Randolph, and John Marshall—Aug. 1819, recorded in Albemarle County Court, Sept. 28, 1819 (copy, VHS). See also Hochman, "Thomas Jefferson," 278.

24. *Thomas Jefferson's Farm Book*, 23–24, 26–34. Other letters concerning the same arrangement are in PTJ-CC, 5, 6, 7, 8, 14, correspondents Edmund Bacon, William Chamberlayne, Mary Dangerfield, Dr. Everett, Patrick Gibson, Nathaniel Hooe, David C. Ker, and Thomas M. Randolph, 1806–13; PTJ-JC, 2, correspondent Edmund Bacon, 1808; PTJ-MD, 6, correspondent Edmund Bacon, 1807; VHS photocopy, Mss. 2 J3595 a11, correspondent John Minor, 1807; PTJ-LC, 46, correspondent Mr. Patrick Gibson, 1813. On hiring, see Sarah S. Hughes, "Slaves for Hire," *WMQ*, 3d ser., 35 (April 1978): 260–86; and James Sidbury, "Gabriel's World: Race Relations in Richmond, Virginia, 1750–1810" (Ph.D. diss., Johns Hopkins University, 1991), 107–27, 137–39.

25. Besides the references in note 24, see Jefferson to Andrew Ellicot, Sept. 15, 1791, PTJ-MD, 4; Jefferson to Thomas Mann Randolph Jr., Jan. 25, 1798, Jefferson to Thomas Mann Randolph, Jan. 3, 1799, Jan. 1800 [note on copy] or Jan. 1797 [note on backing sheet], Jan. 9, 1801, PTJ-LC, 21, 22; Jefferson to John Wayles Eppes, Oct. 9, 1801, and May 24, 1806, PTJ-JC, 2; William Baker power of attorney to Samuel Carr, July 15, 1802, Jefferson to George Jefferson, July 22, 1804, PTJ-CC, 3, 4. Most of Jefferson's payments and receipts for hiring are calendared in Bear and Stanton, eds., *Jefferson's Memorandum Books*.

26. On illness and death, see Jefferson to General William Chamberlayne, Aug. 17, 1810, Chamberlayne to Jefferson, Dec. 27, 1810, Jefferson to Chamberlayne, Jan. 6, 1811, and Jefferson to Dr. Everett, June 24, 1811, PTJ-CC, 7. On resistance, see Martha Jefferson Randolph to Jefferson, Nov. 30, 1804, PTJ-MD, 5.

27. Jefferson to Nicholas Lewis, Dec. 19, 1786, July 11, 1788, *PTJ* 10:614–16, 13:339–44.

28. Jefferson to Nicholas Lewis, Dec. 19, 1786, July 11, 1788, *PTJ* 10:614–16, 13:339–44; "Heads of agreemt between John H. Craven and Th. Jefferson," Aug. 22, 1800, Jefferson to John H. Craven, Aug. 22, 1800, Jefferson to John H. Craven, lease, Sept. 20, 1803, PTJ-CC, 3.

29. General William Chamberlayne to Jefferson, Dec. 27, 1810, Jefferson to Chamberlayne, Jan. 6, 1811, PTJ-CC, 7.

30. Jefferson to Joel Yancey, Jan. 17, 1819, PTJ-CC, 10. For the 1796 mortgage and other mortgages that used slaves as collateral, see Jefferson to James Lyle, May 12, 1796 [1795 on film, but mortgage is dated 1796], mortgage to Henderson and McCaul, May 12, 1796, PTJ-CC, 2; and Hochman, "Thomas Jefferson," 214.

31. Absent from all of Jefferson's efforts to defend his slave property was any special attempt to guard the slaves against personal danger. Yet Jefferson the former lawyer undoubtedly knew he could have recourse to the courts if anyone not within his "family" injured or killed one of his bondspeople. The purchase of life insurance policies on slaves would have to await a later time.

32. "Negroes alienated from 1784. to 1794. inclusive," apparently page 25 of the "Farm Book," photocopy, Research Department, Jefferson Foundation. See the discussions of the sales in Finkelman, "Jefferson and Slavery"; Stanton, "'Those Who Labor for My Happiness,'" 148, 151, 186, 192; and Finkelman, "Thomas Jefferson and Antislavery," 201, 205, 220. Hochman, in "Thomas Jefferson," also discusses some of the sales in relation to Jefferson's debts.

33. On the law of fugitive slaves, see chapter 5, below. See also Mullin, *Flight and Rebellion*, 39–47, 55–58, 107–12; Schwarz, *Twice Condemned*, 135–36, 139–40, 186–88, 225–26; and Lathan Windley, ed., *Runaway Slave Advertisements: A Documentary History from the 1730s to 1790*,

vol. 1, *Virginia and North Carolina* (Westport, Conn.: Greenwood Press, 1983). For another look at Thomas Jefferson and fugitive slaves, see Daniel E. Meaders, "Fugitive Slaves and Indentured Servants before 1800" (Ph.D. diss., Yale University, 1990), 278–83.

34. Jefferson's most difficult legal challenge in recovering runaway slaves resulted from the British attack on Virginia in 1781. See Jefferson to Edward Stevens, Sept. 15, 1780, George Wythe to Jefferson, Dec. 31, 1781, Jefferson Statement of Losses to the British at His Cumberland Plantations in 1781 (which indicates a loss of fourteen slaves), Jan. 27, 1783, and Jefferson to Alexander McCaul, London (which claims a loss of thirty slaves overall), April 19, 1786, *PTJ* 3:649, 6:144–45, 224–25, 9:388–90; *Thomas Jefferson's Farm Book* (which claims a loss of thirty), 29; and "Negroes alienated from 1784. to 1794. inclusive," apparently page 25 of the "Farm Book," photocopy, Research Department, Jefferson Foundation. On slaveholders' claims, see *PTJ* 7:47–48, 394, 497, 522–24, 9:111–12, 16:197. See also Hochman, "Thomas Jefferson," 113–15; Sylvia R. Frey, "Between Slavery and Freedom: Virginia Blacks in the American Revolution," *JSH* 49 (Aug. 1983): 375–98; idem, *Water from the Rock: Black Resistance in a Revolutionary Age* (Princeton, N.J.: Princeton University Press, 1991), 81–193; Arthur B. Darling, *Our Rising Empire, 1763–1803* (New Haven, Conn.: Yale University Press, 1940; Hamden, Conn.: Archon Books, 1962), chaps. 4–6; Frederic A. Ogg, "Jay's Treaty and the Slavery Interests of the United States," *Annual Report of the American Historical Association for 1901* (Washington, D.C.: GPO, 1902), 273–98; Charles Ritcheson, *The Aftermath of Revolution: British Policy Toward the United States, 1793–1795* (Dallas: Southern Methodist University Press, 1969), 231–36, 239; and Thomas J. Farnham, "The Virginia Amendments of 1795: An Episode in the Opposition to Jay's Treaty," *VMHB* 75 (Jan. 1967): 75–88.

35. Christopher Smith to Jefferson, Dec. 4, 1801, Jefferson to James Oldham, July 20, 1805, James Oldham to Jefferson, July 23, 1805, PTJ-CC, 3, 4. On James's age, see *Thomas Jefferson's Farm Book*, 30.

36. Daniel Bradley to Jefferson, Sept. 7, 1805, Jefferson to Bradley, Oct. 6, 1805, Bradley to Jefferson, Oct. 6, 1805, Jefferson to John Jordan, Dec. 21, 1805, Jefferson to Bradley, Jan. 19, 1806, Jefferson to Lewis

Deblois, Jan. 19, 1806, Jefferson account with Isham Chisholm, March 10–April 15, 1812, PTJ-CC, 4, 5, 7; Jefferson to Reuben Perry, April 16, 1812, Tucker-Coleman Papers, Manuscripts and Rare Books Department, Earl Gregg Swem Library, College of William and Mary; Bear and Stanton, eds., *Jefferson's Memorandum Books*, Dec. 17, 1805, Jan. 19, 1806; Jefferson deed to Reuben Perry, Sept. 3, 1812, in *Thomas Jefferson's Farm Book*, 35–36. (The *Farm Book*, 36, cites the Tucker-Coleman Papers as the source, but the staff of the Manuscripts and Rare Books Department was unable to locate the deed.)

While governor of the Commonwealth of Virginia, Jefferson had repeatedly participated in de facto transportation out of the state of slaves pardoned of capital convictions. See chapter 4, below. Hiring allowed Jefferson to discipline defiant hirees without using punishments he had administered to his own bondsmen who ran away. He only had to refuse to rehire them the following January or else do so on more agreeable terms. See Edmund Bacon to Jefferson, Dec. 21, 1808, PTJ-MD, 6.

37. Joel Yancey to Jefferson, Oct. 20, 1819, Yancey to Jefferson, Oct. 26, 1819, Jefferson to Yancey, Feb. 11, 1820, Yancey to Jefferson, Feb. 27, 1820, May 22, 1821, Jefferson to Edmund Bacon, Nov. 29, 1817, Jefferson to Yancey, Jan. 11, Feb. 18, 1818, PTJ-CC, 10, 11, 14, 9. See also Meaders, "Fugitive Slaves and Indentured Servants," 277–83.

38. Jefferson to Thomas Mann Randolph Jr., Feb. 22, 1798, PTJ-LC, 21. But see Jefferson to Randolph, Dec. 4, 1798, PTJ-LC, 21; and Jefferson to Youen Carden, April 7, 1825, PTJ-CC, 12.

39. Jefferson to Thomas Mann Randolph Jr., Oct. 9, 1803, PTJ-LC, 29.

40. Bear and Stanton, eds., *Jefferson's Memorandum Books;* Jefferson to Hugh Chisholm, June 5, 1807, PTJ-CC, 5.

41. Jefferson to Thomas Mann Randolph, June 14, 1798, PTJ-LC, 21; Jefferson to Hugh Chisholm, June 5, 1807, PTJ-CC, 5. But see Malone, *Sage of Monticello*, 80; Jefferson to Edmund Bacon, Dec. 26, 1808, PTJ-JC, 2; Edmund Bacon to Jefferson, Dec. 29, 1808, PTJ-MD, 6. See also his payment of an annual "gratuity" to Burwell and John Hemings from 1812 through 1826, in Bear and Stanton, eds., *Jefferson's Memorandum Books*, March 30, May 13, 1812, July 12, 28, 1813, Oct. 26, Nov. 1, 1816, April 26, Sept. 17, 1817, March 6, 1819, Dec. 14, 1820, Oct. 13, 25, 1821,

Feb. 12, 1824, June 18, 1825, and May 6, 1826. See also July 12, 1813: "Premium to Wm. & Phil." For payments for "extra" services, see Dec. 19, 1824, and for other payments to slaves, see the *Memorandum Books*, 1812–26. On slaves' ownership of property, see Philip D. Morgan, "The Ownership of Property by Slaves in the Mid-Nineteenth-Century Low Country," *JSH* 49 (Aug. 1983): 399–420; and Loren Schweninger, *Black Property Owners in the South, 1790–1915* (Urbana: University of Illinois Press, 1990), 29–60. On the peculium, see Alan Watson, *Roman Slave Law* (Baltimore: Johns Hopkins University Press, 1987), 90–101.

42. Jefferson stated his criteria in a letter to John W. Eppes, June 30, 1820, PTJ-CC, 14. But see Stanton, "'Those Who Labor for My Happiness,'" 148 and n. 6; and Hochman, "Thomas Jefferson." Jefferson may have suppressed his memory of the many sales in the 1780s and 1790s; he may also have changed his mind about their legitimacy.

43. Jefferson to Daniel L. Hylton, Nov. 22, 1792, PTJ-CC, 2; James A. Bear, ed., *Jefferson at Monticello* (Charlottesville: University Press of Virginia, 1967), 53; *Thomas Jefferson's Farm Book*, 24; Martha Jefferson Randolph to Jefferson, Jan. 15, 1795, PTJ-CC, 14; Jefferson to Martha Jefferson Randolph, Jan. 22, 1795, PTJ-MD, 4. See Bear and Stanton, eds., *Jefferson's Memorandum Books*, Dec. 24, 1794: "Executed a deed of emancipation for Bob, by the name of Robert Hemmings. He has been valued at £60. which Stras is to advance. Inclosed to TMR. an order to recieve the £60. & to pay to" a Jefferson creditor. *Jefferson's Memorandum Books*, 1794, n. 20, explains the transaction. See also Hochman, "Thomas Jefferson," 197–98. The "special circumstances" were that Robert Hemings was related to Jefferson. See also Finkelman, "Thomas Jefferson and Antislavery," 215; and idem, "Jefferson and Slavery," 204.

44. Jefferson to Reuben Perry, April 16, 1812, Tucker-Coleman Papers, Manuscripts and Rare Books Department, Earl Gregg Swem Library, College of William and Mary; Jefferson to Craven Peyton, Nov. 27, 1815, PTJ-CC, 8. See also Bear and Stanton, eds., *Jefferson's Memorandum Books*, Dec. 24, 1794, Aug. 21, 1805, May 11, 1807; and Boynton Merrill Jr., *Jefferson's Nephews: A Frontier Tragedy* (Princeton, N.J.: Princeton University Press, 1976), 91–2.

45. Jefferson to George Jefferson, April 19, May 1, 18, June 8, 12, 1809, Jefferson to Martha Jefferson Randolph, June 14, 1807, George Jefferson to Jefferson, May 5, 1809, PTJ-CC, 6, 14.

46. J. S. Harrison to Gibson and [George] Jefferson, July 16, 1809, enclosed with George Jefferson to Jefferson, July 21, 1809, which says the other letter is enclosed, PTJ-CC, 6; Jefferson to Mr. Barnes, Aug. 3, 1809, PTJ-LC, 44; George Jefferson to Jefferson, Sept. 1, 1809, PTJ-CC, 6. Richmond City Hustings Court Order Book 8 (1808–10), 326, called court on July 25, 1809, for the trial of Ned. Ned was accused of stealing the trunk, and two slaves testified that he broke it open, so a civil action was undoubtedly deemed inappropriate.

47. Jefferson to Messrs. Gordon, Trokes and Co., July 25, 1809, PTJ-CC, 6; Jefferson to Joel Barlow, Dec. 31, 1809, PTJ-LC, 44; Jefferson to Mr. J. Darmsdatt, May 27, 1810, Jefferson to Bernard Peyton, March 8, 1816, PTJ-CC, 7, 8; Jefferson to Joseph Dougherty, Dec. 13, 1816, Jefferson to Messrs. Fitzwhylson and Potter, May 1, 1817, PTJ-LC, 49. Lawmakers shared some of Jefferson's concern about boatmen. See "An act, to amend an Act for regulating the Navigation of James River, above the Falls of the said River," passed Feb. 9, 1811, in *Acts of the General Assembly*, 1810–11 (Richmond: 1811), 56–59. See also Sidbury, "Gabriel's World," 76–79, 83–87, 188–91; and Reginald Dennin Butler, "Evolution of a Rural Free Black Community: Goochland County, Virginia, 1728–1832" (Ph.D. diss., Johns Hopkins University, 1989), 147–50, 152–55.

48. Jefferson to George Jefferson, June 19, 1808, PTJ-CC, 6. For a discussion of slaves' defense of "taking" versus stealing, see my *Twice Condemned*, 30–31, 118–20, 214.

49. Thomas Jefferson, *Notes on the State of Virginia* (Chapel Hill: University of North Carolina Press, 1955), 142.

50. Dumas Malone concluded, "In some of his comments on this irreparable loss Jefferson seemed vindictive." Malone, *Sage of Monticello*, 4–5.

51. *PTJ* 1:499–502. I am indebted to Paul Finkelman for pointing this out to me.

52. Bedford CCOB, 1774–82, 323–24. There is no entry in Bear and Stanton, eds., *Jefferson's Memorandum Books*, relating to this prosecution.

53. Bear, ed., *Jefferson at Monticello*, 97–98. Mr. (Reuben?) Grady, overseer of the nailery, did board with Edmund Bacon in early 1807, so the date of the incident may have been 1807. It would have to have occurred during one of Jefferson's visits to Monticello. Jefferson to Bacon, Jan. 11, 1807, PTJ-JC, 2.

54. See Douglas Hay, "Property, Authority, and the Criminal Law," in *Albion's Fatal Tree: Crime and Society in Eighteenth-Century England*, by Douglas Hay et al. (New York: Pantheon, 1975), 17–63; Jefferson to Jeremiah Goodman, July 26, 1813, PTJ-LC, 46.

55. Anonymous letter, undated, PTJ-LC, 25, at 1801–9, reproduced in McLaughlin, *Jefferson and Monticello*, 100.

56. Jefferson to Thomas Mann Randolph, Jan. 23, 1801, PTJ-LC, 22.

57. Jefferson to Reuben Perry, April 16, 1812, Tucker-Coleman Papers, Manuscripts and Rare Books Department, Earl Gregg Swem Library, College of William and Mary.

58. Jefferson to Bernard Peyton, Aug. 28, 1824, PTJ-CC, 12; Bedford CCOB 18 (1820–23), 318–19.

59. Jefferson to Thomas Mann Randolph, June 8, 1803, PTJ-LC, 28. Cary was sold in 1803, and in 1806 Brown was also sold, in order to unite him with his wife. Jefferson to John Jordan, Dec. 21, 1805, PTJ-CC, 4; Bear and Stanton, eds., *Jefferson's Memorandum Books*, Aug. 6, 1803, Jan. 30, 1804, Feb. 9, 1806.

60. William Radford to Jefferson, Dec. 26, 1822, Jefferson to Bernard Peyton, Aug. 28, 1824, PTJ-CC, 11, 12; Bedford CCOB 18 (1820–23), 318–19. In 1823 Virginia legislators made the offense of which Billy was convicted subject to the mandatory sentence of transportation out of the state; by 1832 the penalty for such knifings, as for all actions allegedly motivated by the intent to kill, became death without benefit of clergy. See *Supplement to the Revised Code of Virginia* (Richmond, Va.: Samuel Shepherd, 1833), 147, 234; *The Code of Virginia* (Richmond, Va.: Printed by W. F. Ritchie, 1849), 753; Schwarz, *Twice Condemned*, 27–28.

61. For variants of de facto transportation against hired slaves, see Martha Jefferson Randolph to Jefferson, Jan. 30, 1800, PTJ-CC, 14; and Martha Jefferson Randolph to Jefferson, Nov. 30, 1804, PTJ-MD, 5.

62. Jefferson to Henry Clark, Oct. 18, 1820, PTJ-CC, 10.

63. Jefferson to Nicholas Lewis, July 11, 1788, *PTJ* 13:340, 343; Jefferson to John H. Craven, Aug. 22, 1800, PTJ-CC, 3 (another copy in *PTJ* 13). See also Agreement with William MacGehee, Aug. 8, 1809, and "Memms of an agreement between Thos. Jefferson & Thomas J. Randolph for the lease of the Tufton & Lego plantations of the sd Th. Jefferson with all the negroes, stock and utensils on them," PTJ-CC, 9, at Jan. 1, 1818.

64. Jefferson to Edward Coles, Aug. 25, 1814, PTJ-LC, 47.

65. John W. Eppes to Jefferson, June 12, 1820, *Scribner's Magazine* 36 (Nov. 1904): 579–80 (checked for accuracy against copy of original, to which access is restricted, by Elizabeth Blazejewski of the Jefferson Papers); Eppes to Jefferson, July 29, 1820, PTJ-MD, 8; Jefferson to Eppes, June 30, 1820, PTJ-CC, 14; Jefferson to John Wayles Eppes, Oct. 13, 1820, draft agreement, Oct. 13, 1820, and Jefferson to Francis Eppes, May 1, 1824, PTJ-JC, 3; Bear and Stanton, eds., *Jefferson's Memorandum Books*, Oct. 18, 1820.

66. Paul Finkelman strongly criticizes earlier defenses of Jefferson's failure to free more than a very few of his slaves and sharply attacks Jefferson's self-justification. See Finkelman, "Thomas Jefferson and Antislavery," 193–228; and idem, "Jefferson and Slavery," 196–210.

67. Jefferson to Edward Bancroft, Jan. 26, 1788 [actually 1789], *PTJ* 14:492–94. For discussions of emancipation in Virginia, see Theodore Stoddard Babcock, "Manumission in Virginia, 1782–1806" (M.A. thesis, University of Virginia, 1974); David St. Clair Lowman, "Unwanted Residents: The Plight of the Emancipated Slave in Virginia, 1806–1835" (M.A. thesis, College of William and Mary, 1977); McColley, *Slavery and Jeffersonian Virginia*, 141–62; Peter Joseph Albert, "The Protean Institution: The Geography, Economy, and Ideology of Slavery in Post-Revolutionary Virginia" (Ph.D. diss., University of Maryland, 1976), 159–204; Butler, "Evolution of a Rural Free Black Community," 289–346; and Philip J. Schwarz, "Clark T. Moorman, Quaker Emancipator," *Quaker History* 69 (Spring 1980): 27–35.

68. Garry Wills, *Cincinnatus: George Washington and the Enlightenment* (Garden City, N.Y.: Doubleday, 1984), 234; Eugene E. Prussing, *The Estate of George Washington, Deceased* (Boston: Little, Brown, 1927), 154–60, 392, 447.

69. William Waller Hening, ed., *The Statutes at Large, Being a Collection of All the Laws of Virginia, from the First Session of the Legislature, in the Year 1619*, 13 vols. (Richmond, Va.: R. and W. and G. Bartow for the Editor, 1809–23), 11:39. The law was modified several times after 1782. See *The Revised Code of the Laws of Virginia*, vol. 1 (Richmond, Va.: Thomas Ritchie, 1819), 433–34; *The Code of Virginia*, 2d ed. (Richmond: Ritchie, Dunnavant and Co., 1860).

70. Samuel Shepherd, ed., *The Statutes at Large of Virginia, from October Session 1792, to December Session 1806, Inclusive*, 3 vols. (Richmond: Samuel Shepherd, 1835–36), 3:251, in effect May 1, 1806; *Acts of the General Assembly*, 1815–16, 51–52, passed Jan. 24, 1816, to take effect upon passage; *Revised Code*, 1819 ed., 436; *Acts of the General Assembly*, 1836–37, 47–49.

71. Jefferson deed of emancipation of Robert Hemings, Albemarle, Dec. 24, 1794, PTJ-CC, 2 (reproduced in Dabney, *Jefferson Scandals*, facing p. 28). See also Jefferson to Martha Jefferson Randolph, Jan. 22, 1795, PTJ-MD, 4. Jefferson deed of emancipation of James Hemings, Feb. 5, 1796, Albemarle Deeds 12 (1795–98), 83; Bear and Stanton, eds., *Jefferson's Memorandum Books*, Feb. 26, 1796; Jefferson, will, in his own hand, March 16–17, 1826, PTJ-MD, 10; inventory of Albemarle property, Oct. 4, 1826, Albemarle County Will Book 8 (1824–26), 281–82.

72. For the month and year of each emancipated person's birth, see *Thomas Jefferson's Farm Book*, 128. John Hemings, however, was born on April 24, 1776, rather than in 1775, as listed in the *Farm Book*. See "Births and Deaths in 1776," apparently page 26 of the "Farm Book," photocopy, Research Department, Jefferson Foundation.

73. Jefferson, will, in his own hand, March 16–17, 1826, PTJ-MD, 10; reprinted in Bear, ed., *Jefferson at Monticello*, 118–22. Other printed versions are slightly unreliable with respect to the text of the manumission clauses. On the skills of the various Hemings men and of Joe Fosset, see *Thomas Jefferson's Farm Book*.

74. Thomas J. Randolph, executor of Jefferson, for fifty dollars paid by Francis Eppes, another Jefferson grandson, deed of emancipation, Jan. 20, 1827, Albemarle County Deeds 32 (1834–35), 412.

75. Shepherd, ed., *Statutes at Large* 3:252. Later legislation terminated sales for the benefit of the poor.

76. Jefferson to Edward Coles, Aug. 25, 1814, PTJ-LC, 47. On Coles, see Elihu Benjamin Washburne, *Sketch of Edward Coles, Second Governor of Illinois, and of the Slavery Struggle of 1823–4* (Chicago: Jansen, McClurg, 1882), reprinted in *Governor Edward Coles,* edited by Clarence W. Alvord (Springfield, Ill.: Trustees of the Illinois State Historical Society, 1920), 3–201; and Drew McCoy, *The Last of the Fathers: James Madison and the Republican Legacy* (Cambridge: Cambridge University Press, 1989), 308–22. Elsewhere I discuss one expedient solution to this terrible dilemma: see Philip J. Schwarz, "Emancipators, Protectors, and Anomalies: Free Black Slaveowners in Virginia," *VMHB* 95 (July 1987): 317–38.

77. *Acts of the General Assembly,* 1815–16, 51–52. Even this privilege contained a trap. Should any person who benefited from this act be convicted of a crime, the courts could revoke the privilege, sell the person, and give the proceeds of such a sale to the overseers of the poor. Moreover, the residency granted by any court was only in the county or corporation whose court granted it. A law passed in 1823 and in effect until 1828 empowered the transportation and sale into slavery of free blacks convicted of crimes otherwise punishable by two or more years in the Virginia Penitentiary. See *Acts of the General Assembly,* 1822–23, 36, and 1827–28, 29. At about the same time that the threat of sale and transportation was lifted from free black convicts, the legislature also made the state's Literary Fund, rather than the poor, the beneficiary of the sales of freed people. See *Acts of the General Assembly,* 1827–28, 25.

78. Jefferson, will, in his own hand, March 16–17, 1826, PTJ-MD, 10. Madison and Eston Hemings first appear in the Albemarle Personal Property Taxes, 1832B.

79. *Acts of the General Assembly,* 1826–27, 127. On the unconfirmed emancipation of Wormley Hemings, see Henry Stephens Randall, *The Life of Thomas Jefferson,* 3 vols. (New York: Derby and Jackson, 1858), 3:562; on two emancipations, of Harriet Hemings and of Beverley Hemings, in accordance with customary law, see Bear, ed., *Jefferson at Monticello,* between 24 and 25, 102, 136n11; *Thomas Jefferson's Farm Book,* 130; Brodie, *Thomas Jefferson,* 220, 474–76.

The preemptive refusal of the Virginia legislature of 1816 to allow the continued residence in the state of about 350 slaves emancipated by

Samuel Gist in his will leads me to believe that even if Jefferson had freed all of his bondspeople in 1826, neither the legislature nor a county court would have been eager to allow Jefferson's former property to remain in the Old Dominion. See *Acts of the General Assembly*, 1815–16, 240–43. Another fate could befall slaves emancipated by a will. Debt suits against the emancipator's estate could delay freedom, and if successful, such suits could result in slaves' being taken in payment of a judgment, nullifying their emancipation.

80. On Jefferson as trustee, see, e.g., Jefferson as trustee for sale of slaves, 1771, *PTJ* 1:59–60, 64–65; and Wilson Cary Nicholas and wife Mary's deed of trust to twenty-two people—among grantees are Jefferson, Thomas J. Randolph, and John Marshall—Aug. 1819, recorded in Albemarle County Court, Sept. 28, 1819 (copy, VHS). Jefferson was surety for a debt to the Bank of the United States.

As agent: Thaddeus Kosciuszko power of attorney to Jefferson, April 30, 1798, Thaddeus Kosciuszko request to Jefferson, Oct. 2, 1798, PTJ-CC, 3; Jefferson to Mr. F. X. Zeltner, July 23, 1818, PTJ-JC, 3; Jefferson to William Wirt, June 27, 1819, PTJ-LC, 51; John Chester Miller, *Wolf by the Ears*, 256; Virginia Writers' Project, Works Projects Administration in the State of Virginia, comp., *The Negro in Virginia* (New York: Hastings House, 1940), 25; Jefferson memorandum (unendorsed), Jan. 1, 1804, Jefferson to James Walker, March 1, 1807, Jefferson to Mr. Peyton, Dec. 6, 1810, Jefferson to Benjamin Morgan, June 11, 1811, PTJ-CC, 4, 5, 7; Jefferson to Joseph C. Cabell, Dec. 23, 1815, PTJ-LC, 48.

As legal adviser: Jefferson to Lucy Ludwell Paradise, Sept. 11, 1792, PTJ-CC, 2; Peter Carr to Jefferson, March 28, 1793, PTJ-MD, 4; Jefferson to Peter Carr, April 14, 1793, Jefferson to Thomas Mann Randolph Jr., Dec. 26, 27, 1794, PTJ-LC, 18, 20; Margaret Page to Jefferson, Sept. 30, 1808, PTJ-CC, 6; Jefferson to Mrs. Andrews, Sept. 15, 1815, PTJ-LC, 48; Francis Wayles Eppes to Jefferson, April 23, 1824, PTJ-MD, 9; Jefferson to Francis Wayles Eppes, May 6, 1824, PTJ-JC, 3.

As lawyer: Jefferson to Thomas Burke, Dec. 6, 1771, Jefferson's memoranda for a legal opinion, Jan. 13, 1782, *PTJ* 1:85–86, 6:145; Commonplace Book, Legal Notes, PTJ-LC, 59, fol. 82; "Record of Cases Tried in Virginia Courts, 1768–69," PTJ-LC, 59, ser. 7, vol. 1; arguments in *Archibald Bolling vs. Robert Bolling*, PTJ-JC, 1; Thomas Jefferson, *Re-*

ports of Cases Determined in the General Court of Virginia: From 1730 to 1740; and From 1768 to 1772 (Charlottesville, Va.: F. Carr, 1829), 1. The first case reported by Jefferson dealt with slave property, as did numerous other cases. Neither Frank L. Dewey nor Edward Dumbauld offers much discussion of cases in which Jefferson had to deal with the law of slavery. See Dewey, *Thomas Jefferson, Lawyer* (Charlottesville: University Press of Virginia, 1986); and Dumbauld, *Thomas Jefferson and the Law* (Norman: University of Oklahoma Press, 1978).

81. *PTJ* 1:129–30, 314–15, 317–18, 320–23, 426; Jefferson, *Notes on the State of Virginia*, 162–63; William James Van Schreeven, comp., *Revolutionary Virginia: The Road to Independence*, edited by Robert L. Scribner, 7 vols. (Charlottesville: University Press of Virginia, 1973–83), 7:454n16; Malone, *Sage of Monticello*, 318–20.

82. Kosciuszko asked Jefferson to use money from his estate to buy slaves in order to educate and free them. Jefferson refused. See John Chester Miller, *Wolf by the Ears*, 205–8, 256; Malone, *Sage of Monticello*, 320–26; McCoy, *Last of the Fathers*, 310–17; Thaddeus Kosciuszko request to Jefferson, Oct. 2, 1798, PTJ-CC, 3; Jefferson to William Wirt, June 27, 1819, PTJ-LC, 51; Virginia Writers' Project, Works Projects Administration, comp., *Negro in Virginia*, 25; Helen T. Catterall, ed., *Judicial Cases Concerning American Slavery and the Negro*, 5 vols. (Washington, D.C.: Carnegie Institution of Washington, 1926–37), 1:204–6; Frank Mathias, "Notes and Documents: John Randolph's Freemen; The Thwarting of a Will," *JSH* 39 (Aug. 1973): 263–72; Leonard U. Hill, "John Randolph's Freed Slaves Settle in Ohio," *Cincinnati Historical Bulletin* 23 (July 1954): 179–87.

83. David Brion Davis, *Was Thomas Jefferson an Authentic Enemy of Slavery?* (Oxford: Clarendon Press, 1970). Much of this lecture is incorporated into Davis, *Problem of Slavery*.

84. Garry Wills's discussion of the way that Washington ensured the emancipation of his slaves is instructive. See Wills, *Cincinnatus*, 96–97. For more light on Washington's manumission of his slaves, see the essays by Edna Greene Medford and Philip J. Schwarz in the forthcoming volume based on the Conference on Slavery in the Age of Washington, Mount Vernon, Virginia, November 1994.

85. On the execution of more than two dozen men convicted only of planning a slave revolt, see Egerton, *Gabriel's Rebellion*, 80–115; Mullin, *Flight and Rebellion*, 140–63; and Schwarz, *Twice Condemned*, 165–90, 255–79.

86. "Extract of a letter from a gentleman . . . to the Editor," *(Fredericksburg) Virginia Herald*, Sept. 23, 1800.

87. The figure of 97 percent is based on a rounded estimate of 200 for the number of slaves in Jefferson's estate. Seven slaves were emancipated, if one includes Critty, who was freed by Jefferson's executor, and Wormley, who was emancipated as well, according to Randall. See Randall, *Life* 3:562. The number of owners who made purchases at the two sales of Jefferson's bondspeople in 1827 and 1829 is an estimate based on sales slips, photocopies of which are in the Research Department at the Jefferson Foundation, and on "An acct. of sales of negroes of the Est. of Thomas Jefferson 1st Jan. 1829," photocopy, Research Department, Jefferson Foundation.

CHAPTER 3: SLAVES AND CAPITAL PUNISHMENT IN VIRGINIA

This chapter is based on a paper delivered at the annual meeting of the Southern Historical Association, Houston, 1985.

1. A reproduction of Blake's famous print appears in Robert N. Essick, *William Blake, Printmaker* (Princeton, N.J.: Princeton University Press, 1980), pl. 39. For some particularly dramatic examples of executions of slaves, see Eugene D. Genovese, *From Rebellion to Revolution: Afro-American Slave Revolts in the Making of the New World* (Baton Rouge: Louisiana State University Press, 1979), 105–8. Some descriptions of more typical executions of slaves are in John Edwards, "Slave Justice in Four Middle Georgia Counties," *Georgia Historical Review* 27 (Summer 1973): 266–68; Michael Wayne, "An Old South Morality Play: Reconsidering the Social Underpinnings of the Proslavery Ideology," *JAH* 77 (Dec. 1990): 858–60; and Benjamin Henry Latrobe, *The Virginia Journals of Benjamin Henry Latrobe*, edited by Edward C. Carter II, 3 vols. (New Haven, Conn.: Yale University Press, 1977–80), 2:191–93.

2. Besides the works of historians cited in note 1, see, e.g., Willie Lee Rose, ed., *A Documentary History of Slavery in North America* (New York: Oxford University Press, 1976), 239–41.

3. Helpful discussions of criminal justice systems as applied to slaves are in Douglas Greenberg, *Crime and Law Enforcement in the Colony of New York, 1691–1776* (Ithaca, N.Y.: Cornell University Press, 1976), 72–76; and Hindus, *Prison and Plantation.* Hindus includes comprehensive data on executions of bondspeople in South Carolina. See also Daniel J. Flanigan, "The Criminal Law of Slavery and Freedom, 1800–1868" (Ph.D. diss., Rice University, 1973); and Ulrich B. Phillips, "Slave Crime in Virginia," *AHR* 20 (Jan. 1915): 336–40.

Useful discussions of the history of capital punishment in England and America are Sir Leon Radzinowicz, *A History of English Criminal Law and Its Administration from 1750,* 5 vols. (London: Stevens, 1948–86), 1:165ff.; Kathryn Preyer, "Penal Measures in the American Colonies: An Overview," *American Journal of Legal History* 26 (Oct. 1982): 326–53; Hugo Adam Bedau, introduction to *The Death Penalty in America: An Anthology,* edited by Hugo Adam Bedau, rev. ed. (Garden City, N.Y.: Doubleday, 1967), 1–32; and Eliza Husband, "A Geographical Perspective on U.S. Capital Punishment, 1801–1960" (Ph.D. diss., Louisiana State University, 1990).

4. Eugene D. Genovese discusses issues of control in slave societies in *Roll, Jordan, Roll,* 25–49. See also Norrece T. Jones Jr., *Born a Child of Freedom, Yet a Slave;* and Philip J. Schwarz, "Forging the Shackles: The Development of Virginia's Criminal Code for Slaves," in *Ambivalent Legacy,* ed. Bodenhamer and Ely, 125–46. Prosecution of legally "will-less" slaves created the central paradox of the slave code. Many a commentator on the law of slavery has discovered that when white authorities found it necessary to treat slaves as persons and not property, or at least as people-as-property, they did so. See, for example, Genovese, *Roll, Jordan, Roll,* 28–31; Tushnet, *American Law of Slavery,* 158–69; Patterson, *Slavery and Social Death,* 22–23, 196–200; and Flanigan, "Criminal Law of Slavery and Freedom," 1–11.

5. Weighed against Kenneth M. Stampp's reasonable tests for the historical accuracy of the kind of "white source" represented by trials of

slaves, the trials stand up fairly well. They reflect the pressure for accurate *description* more than for distortion, they often contain firsthand testimony, and they were recorded soon after the event. See Stampp, "Slavery: The Historian's Burden," in *Perspectives and Irony in American Slavery,* edited by Harry P. Owens (Jackson: University Press of Mississippi, 1976), 169.

6. In contrast to the documentation for the 1780s through 1865, there is no systematic, comprehensive source concerning executions of slaves before the 1780s. Hence, the pre-1780s verifications are random. It is therefore probable that many more executions were unrecorded in local records than were recorded. The Condemned Slaves records (CS) at the Library of Virginia verified some of the 1780s executions. Other means were Legislative Petitions (Library of Virginia); unusually detailed itemized annual levies in county court order books; clerks' notes on trial records; official correspondence (Library of Virginia); the *Virginia Gazette;* H. R. McIlwaine et al. eds., *Executive Journals of the Council of Colonial Virginia,* 6 vols. (Richmond: Virginia State Library, 1925–66); H. R. McIlwaine, ed., *Legislative Journals of the Council of Virginia,* 3 vols. (Richmond: Virginia State Library, 1918–19), esp. 3:1598–1600; and miscellaneous other sources. I am also indebted to Watt Espy of the Capital Punishment Research Project for sharing his findings with me concerning executed slaves and the seventy known executions of free Virginians between 1706 and 1784. Figures given in table 3.1 for the numbers of slaves sentenced to hang in the period 1706–84 differ slightly from those in my book *Twice Condemned* because of evidence discovered after publication.

7. In addition to CS, used by Phillips and Flanigan, I used county court records, VEPLR, which are arranged by date; and Virginia Treasury Office, Cash Disbursements Journals (hereafter referred to as Cash Journal). I have also relied on the files of the Capital Punishment Research Project: M. Watt Espy and John Ortiz Smykla, *Executions in the United States, 1608–1987: The Espy File,* a machine-readable data file (Tuscaloosa, Ala., 1987; Ann Arbor, Mich.: Inter-University Consortium for Political and Social Research, 1987). (I am indebted to Mr. Espy for his correspondence concerning this project. I am also indebted to Neil W.

Henry and Neil J. Glock of Virginia Commonwealth University for accessing and analyzing this file for me.) I have thus been able to locate almost all of the missing cases for 1855–65 and also to identify many charges and other aspects in cases that Flanigan had to label as unspecified. Because of missing or poorly kept court records, some information about these cases is still incomplete. See Flanigan, "Criminal Law of Slavery and Freedom," 404; and Phillips, "Slave Crime in Virginia," 336–40.

There are several lists of slaves condemned for capital crimes in James Hugo Johnston, *Race Relations in Virginia and Miscegenation in the South, 1776–1860* (Amherst: University of Massachusetts Press, 1970). Johnston, however, who worked before the availability of numerous Virginia records on microfilm (the dissertation upon which the book was based was completed in 1937), had to rely mostly on VEPLR, so his lists should by no means be considered complete. Indeed, they are sometimes inaccurate.

8. The Capital Punishment Research Project has found fifty executions of free people in Virginia between 1785 and 1864. Data concerning capital sentencing of free African Americans are regrettably too meager to use for this analysis. Free black Virginians never comprised more than 4.7 percent of the total population of the state.

9. Besides the sources given for tables 3.1, 3.2, and 3.3, these figures are based on data from the Capital Punishment Research Project and on Hindus, *Prison and Plantation*, 103, 157. For a perspective on this type of comparison, see A. E. Keir Nash, "Reason of Slavery," 61–63. See also Husband, "Geographical Perspective."

10. Hening, ed., *Statutes at Large* 2:270, 3:86–88, 102–3, 4:126, 5:104–5; Shepherd, ed., *Statutes at Large* 2:5–14; *Supplement to the Revised Code*, 247, 280–81; *Acts of the General Assembly*, 1836–37, 49; *Peter v. the Commonwealth*, 2 Va. Cases (4 Va.) 330 (1823); Elvira, a slave, 16 Grattan 57 (Va.), 561 (1865).

11. See, e.g., trial of Sam, Sept. 22, 1809, Montgomery County, CS (also in VEPLR); trial of Jim, Jan. 14, 1808, Campbell County, CS, box 2 (also in VEPLR). European American servants may have received similar treatment in the criminal courts, but they were a minority of the

population by the 1700s. Convict servants, who could labor under similar disabilities, were not sufficiently prevalent in eighteenth-century Virginia to make for a useful comparison.

Daniel J. Flanigan's conclusion in "The Criminal Law of Slavery and Freedom" that "the surviving records of slave crime reveal that whites other than owners and overseers were the most frequent victims of slave violence" (404) is incorrect because his figures are incomplete (see note 7 above). In fact, the opposite is true. Of the 239 whites who were killed by slaves between 1785 and 1864, at least 91 were owners or overseers. Many of the 148 other whites killed by slaves in the same period might have been overseers. Among the 142 white victims of slaves convicted of assault with intent to kill during 1785–1864, 25 of the victims were owners or other authorities, but I did not investigate the status of many of the victims who were named in the records but not otherwise described. I strongly suspect from the circumstances of many such cases that the victim was often a hirer, overseer, or other authority.

12. The notion of a common law of slavery appears in Great Britain, Commissioner of Inquiry into the Administration of Civil and Criminal Justice in the West Indies, "First Report . . . Barbados, Tobago, Grenada," *British Parliamentary Papers, Colonies: West Indies,* vol. 3 (London, 1825), 65. The best description of Virginia's oyer and terminer court system is in Peter Charles Hoffer, introduction to *Criminal Proceedings in Colonial Virginia,* edited by Peter Charles Hoffer and William B. Scott (Athens: University of Georgia Press, 1984), xliv–lii. Thad W. Tate, *The Negro in Eighteenth-Century Williamsburg* (Williamsburg, Va.: Colonial Williamsburg Foundation, 1965), 93–96, offers another excellent description of the judicial system for slaves. From 1692 to 1786, designated white Virginians, usually justices of the peace, heard capital trials of slaves under commissions of oyer and terminer, which the governor issued on a case-by-case basis until 1765 and as open-ended authorizations after then. The same system, controlled now exclusively by county justices, covered all felony trials of slaves from 1786 to 1865. For a discussion of the development of the slave code and courts in the Old Dominion, see Schwarz, "Forging the Shackles," 125–46.

13. Radzinowicz, *History of English Criminal Law* 1:165–227. Albert Hartshorne, in *Hanging in Chains* (London, 1891), 110, asserts that 1834 was the last year in which a condemned person was hanged in chains in England. One of Bacon's followers was hanged in chains after the 1676 uprising, and two servants met similar fates in 1678 and 1679, but except for four pirates, I have found no evidence of the use of this punishment against other than slave convicts in Virginia thereafter. See Arthur P. Scott, *Criminal Law in Colonial Virginia* (Chicago: University of Chicago Press, 1930), 158–59, 195; Marcus Rediker, "'Under the Banner of King Death': The Social World of Anglo-American Pirates, 1716 to 1726," *WMQ*, 3d ser., 38 (April 1981): 219.

There is also one verified case of an enslaved woman suffering death by burning after conviction of murder in 1737, and another woman died in the same fashion in 1746 because she was found guilty of fatally poisoning her master. In a variation on this punishment, the Surry County court in 1755 ordered the burning of the remainder of the corpse of an enslaved man whose head was to be displayed. See *Virginia Gazette*, Feb. 18, 1737; Orange CCOB, 1743–46, 454–55, and 1746–47, 99, 103; Surry County Criminal Proceedings, 1742–1822, 39–41. Michael M. Craton argues that such decapitations and displays of heads in the Caribbean islands "played on the belief common among Africans that such dismemberment deprived them of the longed-for chance of a return in the spirit world to the African heartland." He adds that such a practice "probably unbeknownst to the planters—duplicated the practice of Akan and other African warriors, who made much of the display of the heads of defeated enemies." See Craton, *Testing the Chains: Resistance to Slavery in the West Indies* (Ithaca, N.Y.: Cornell University Press, 1982), 100.

There could be no doubt about reservation of the worst forms of executions for slaves in such episodes as Antigua's slave rebellion in 1736. David Barry Gaspar determined that "5 slaves were broken on the wheel, 6 gibbeted alive, and 77 burned: 88 executions in less than four months." See Gaspar, *Bondmen and Rebels: A Study of Master-Slave Relations in Antigua, with Implications for Colonial British America* (Baltimore: Johns Hopkins University Press, 1985), 29–37. Europeans ordered the quartering of the corpses of executed people in the context of the Christian belief in the resurrection of the soul *and* the body.

14. "Punitive death by other means than execution" refers to delegated powers to kill outlawed slaves—that is, runaways identified by court order as living secretly and off the land for long periods—lashings beyond the usual number of thirty-nine, inadequate "dieting" or clothing of jailed slaves, bungled castrations, the laws that exonerated owners from prosecution when they killed slaves who were being "corrected," the shock of being transported out of Virginia, or various other forms of deprivation. See Hening, ed., *Statutes at Large* 2:270, 3:86, 210–11, 460–61, 4:32, 132–33, 6:110–11, 8:358, 522–23, 12:86–88; Mullin, *Flight and Rebellion*, 56–58; and chapter 4, below. Trials and convictions of whites for murdering slaves occurred regularly but not frequently.

15. Foucault, *Discipline and Punish;* David J. Rothman, *The Discovery of the Asylum: Social Order and Disorder in the New Republic* (Boston: Little, Brown, 1971); Kathryn Preyer, "Crime, the Criminal Law, and Reform in Post-Revolutionary Virginia," *Law and History Review* 1 (Spring 1983): 53–85; Edward L. Ayers, *Vengeance and Justice: Crime and Punishment in the Nineteenth-Century American South* (New York: Oxford University Press, 1984); Hindus, *Prison and Plantation*, 99–124; William J. Bowers, *Executions in America* (Lexington, Mass.: Lexington Books, 1974), published in a later edition as Bowers et al., *Legal Homicide: Death as Punishment in America, 1864–1982* (Boston: Northeastern University Press, 1984); Raymond T. Bye, "Capital Punishment in the United States" (Ph.D. diss., University of Pennsylvania, 1919); Bedau, introduction to *Death Penalty in America*, 1–32; David Brion Davis, "The Movement to Abolish Capital Punishment in America, 1787–1861," *AHR* 63 (Oct. 1957): 23–46; Paul W. Keve, *The History of Corrections in Virginia* (Charlottesville: University Press of Virginia, 1986), 28–64; David D. Cooper, *The Lesson of the Scaffold: The Public Execution Controversy in Victorian England* (Athens: Ohio University Press, 1974); Philip English Mackey, *Hanging in the Balance: The Anti–Capital Punishment Movement in New York State, 1776–1861* (New York: Garland, 1982); Louis P. Masur, *Rites of Execution: Capital Punishment and the Transformation of American Culture, 1776–1865* (New York: Oxford University Press, 1989); Edward Schriver, "Reluctant Hangman: The State of Maine and Capital Punishment, 1820–1887," *New England Quarterly* 63 (June 1990): 271–87.

There continued to be widespread support for capital punishment of some free convicts, however. See Daniel A. Cohen, "In Defense of the Gallows: Justifications of Capital Punishment in New England Execution Sermons, 1674–1825," *American Quarterly* 40 (June 1988): 147–64; Randall McGowen, "The Body and Punishment in Eighteenth-Century England," *Journal of Modern History* 59 (Dec. 1987): 651–79; and Negley K. Teeters, ". . . *Hang by the Neck* . . .": *The Legal Use of Scaffold and Noose, Gibbet, Stake, and Firing Squad from Colonial Times to the Present* (Springfield, Ill.: C. C. Thomas, 1967). See also Adam Jay Hirsch, *The Rise of the Penitentiary: Prisons and Punishment in Early America* (New Haven, Conn.: Yale University Press, 1992); Hindus, *Prison and Plantation*, 185–214; and Husband, "Geographical Perspective," 47–69, 163–95.

16. Masur, *Rites of Execution*, 53–54, 59, 71–73, 86–87; "Capital Punishment in Virginia," *Virginia Law Review* 18 (Jan. 1972): 97–142; Shepherd, ed., *Statutes at Large* 2:5–14, 77 (aiding or conspiring, 1798), 405–6 (treason, 1803), 3:119 (arson of dwellings, especially in towns, 1805).

17. June Purcell Guild, *Black Laws of Virginia* (Richmond, Va.: Whittet and Johnson, 1936), 94–122.

18. *Acts of the General Assembly*, 1847–48, 125; *Code of Virginia*, 1849 ed., 753. George M. Stroud listed sixty-eight capital offenses for slaves, only one of which, first-degree murder, was a capital crime for whites. Stroud's detailed table thus left out the other three capital offenses for whites: treason, conspiring with a slave rebellion, and arson of occupied dwellings. See Stroud, *A Sketch of the Laws Relating to Slavery in the Several States of the United States of America* (Philadelphia: H. Longstreth, 1856; New York: Negro Universities Press, 1968), 77–80.

19. Trial of Jack, July 26, 1745, Richmond County "Fines, Examination of Criminals, Trials of Slaves, etc., from March 1710"; trial of Ned, Sept. 18, 1761, Spotsylvania CCOB, 1755–65, 234; trial of Braxton, Hanover County, Aug. 2, 1792, CS, 1; trial of Albert, Sept. 15, 1828, CS, 5; Richmond City Hustings Court Minute Book, 1828–31, 112. See also the trial of Jim, Aug. 16, 1858, CS, 9; and Prince Edward CCOB, 1853–62, 281, 283, 288.

20. H. R. McIlwaine et al., eds., *Journals of the Council of the State of Virginia*, 4 vols. to date (Richmond: Virginia State Library, 1931-), 1:488; trial of Pierce, June 6, 1774, Southampton CCOB, 1772-77, 370-71.

21. Record of trial of Randolph, Patrick County, Nov. 17, 1825, CS, 5; trial of Will, Dec. 21, 1785, Henrico CCOB, 1784-87, 380.

22. Hay, "Property, Authority, and the Criminal Law," 17-63, esp. 55. John H. Langbein takes issue with most of Hay's argument. See Langbein, "Albion's Fatal Flaws," *Past and Present* 98 (Feb. 1983): 96-120.

23. A. G. Roeber, *Faithful Magistrates and Republican Lawyers: Creators of Virginia Legal Culture, 1680-1810* (Chapel Hill: University of North Carolina Press, 1981), 160-230.

24. Schwarz, *Twice Condemned*, 39. Langbein, in "Albion's Fatal Flaws," 104, discusses "down-valuing" in English courts.

25. These counties are (Tidewater) Essex and Southampton, (Piedmont) Spotsylvania, and (Southside) Henry. The respective figures for executions are four, thirteen, nine, and seven. Measured against the average slave population from 1790 to 1860, the ranking is Henry (3.3 executions per thousand slaves), Southampton (2.5), Spotsylvania (1.5), and Essex (0.8). Aggregate statistics show the reduction of per capita executions over time. The figures from these representative counties only indicate the manner in which judges and the state executive were able to effect that decrease.

26. It is even possible that slaves' hostile reaction to hanging judges could have a restraining effect. The aftermath of John Brown's Raid suggests this possibility. Whites assumed that slaves had set the many fires that burned near Harpers Ferry after Brown's raid. Three of the jurors in Brown's trial were thought to be arson victims. See Jean Libby, *Black Voices from Harpers Ferry: Osborne Anderson and the John Brown Raid* (Palo Alto, Calif.: Libby, 1979), 175-77; Stephen B. Oates, *To Purge This Land with Blood: A Biography of John Brown* (New York: Harper and Row, 1970), 322, 342; and Benjamin Quarles, *Allies for Freedom: Blacks and John Brown* (New York: Oxford University Press, 1974), 107-8.

27. In *Southern Honor*, Bertram Wyatt-Brown occasionally discusses the dishonored status of slaves, but the most extensive treatment of this

subject is Patterson, *Slavery and Social Death,* 77–101. Alan Watson analyzes the extent to which laws of slavery resulted from legal traditions that had a life of their own, unconnected with the dictates of bondage. See Watson, *Slave Law in the Americas.*

28. Harrison M. Ethridge, "The Jordan Hatcher Affair of 1852: Cold Justice and Warm Compassion," *VMHB* 84 (Oct. 1976): 446–63; Green, "Urban Industry, Black Resistance, and Racial Restriction," 576–605.

29. I discuss these issues at length in *Twice Condemned.*

30. Between 1740 and 1784 oyer and terminer courts in counties whose records have survived handled more trials of slaves for poisoning than for any other offense except theft.

Statistics concerning slaves executed or transported for alleged insurrection, murder, or attempted murder support the judgment that these crimes were the most dangerous forms of slave resistance or aggression between the 1790s and 1831. Seventy-six Virginian slaves were hanged and another 46 were transported for insurrection, 155 went to the gallows and 161 were exported for murder, and 12 suffered death and 23 were sold out of the United States for attempted murder between 1790 and 1831.

Arson convictions resulted in 11 executions and 97 deportations of slaves between 1830 and 1865. Capital convictions for theft and murder were more numerous, but those for attempted murder were the same as before this period.

31. The transportation of 110 and execution of 9 slaves for theft between 1815 and 1829, higher figures than for any other fifteen-year period and occurring in a well-known time of economic problems for Virginia, constitute a correlation that does not prove causation. Yet the number of hangings and the character of the offenses of which the executed slaves were found guilty suggest a connection. The 9 slaves were about one-third of all slaves hanged for offenses against property, excluding arson, between 1801, the year in which transportation began, and 1865 (9 of 26). Seven of the hanged slaves were convicted of burglary, two instances of which involved violence and two other instances of which included the theft of particularly large amounts of goods. The other two slaves were convicted of violent robbery.

32. "Insurrection anxiety" seemed to be more pronounced during war years. See Herbert Aptheker, *American Negro Slave Revolts*, new ed. (New York: International Publishers, 1943), 18–52; and Armstead L. Robinson, "In the Shadow of Old John Brown: Insurrection Anxiety and Confederate Mobilization, 1861–1863," *JNH* 55 (Fall 1980): 279–97.

Even concern about "normal" offenses could increase. For example, the percentages of slaves tried for capital crimes who were sentenced to death in 1780 and 1781, the years in which Virginia experienced invasion, were 30.3 (23 of 76) and 27.6 (8 of 29), respectively, and the percentage dropped to 20.4 (11 of 54) in 1782. During the Civil War the same pattern appeared. Only three slaves went to the gallows after being found guilty of assault on a white person with intent to kill during the 1850s, but another three did so in the two years 1862 and 1863.

33. One hundred seventy-nine known trials of slaves for poisoning occurred between 1740 and 1784. The 118 convictions in these trials, however, were mostly for illegal administration of medicine, an offense closely connected with poisoning. Slaves could plead for benefit of clergy upon conviction of this offense. Sometimes judges reduced the offense to a misdemeanor. Between 1785 and 1865, 35 slaves were executed and 49 transported for the same offenses. During the same period the slave court judges of Essex, Henry, Southampton, and Spotsylvania Counties convicted only 8 slaves of the 34 tried for these crimes, yielding a very low conviction rate of 23.5 percent.

34. Aptheker, in *American Negro Slave Revolts*, 94–95, cites a report of the execution of seventeen free and enslaved African Americans in Culpeper County in 1863, but there is no record of any executed or transported slaves from Culpeper in 1862 or 1863 in CS or in Cash Journal, 1861–62 or 1862–64. It is, of course, possible that these executions occurred without being recorded.

35. Trials of Dick, Jack, Franck, Robin, and George, Aug. 26, 1706, Westmoreland CCOB, 1705–21, 32ab, 37a, 150; McIlwaine et al., eds., *Executive Journals of the Council of Colonial Virginia* 3:128.

36. On lynchings of individual slaves, see affidavit of John Wilson, Feb. 19, 1819, George E. Howard to Governor Henry A. Wise, Sept. 10, 1856, deposition of Agnes J. Sanford attached to petition of Spotsylvania

NOTES TO PAGE 84

residents, Nov. 3, 1856, P. F. Howard to Governor Wise, received Aug. 29, 1859, VEPLR; and Virginia Council Minutes, 1838–39, 221. A seventeen-year-old slave on trial for rape of a white woman was knifed in court by the woman's husband. Documentation appears in the *Richmond Enquirer*, Sept. 24, 28, 1858; Prince Edward CCOB, 1853–62, 281, 283, 288, 292; and Herbert Clarence Bradshaw, *History of Prince Edward County, Virginia* (Richmond, Va.: Dietz Press, 1955), 285. The slave survived and was transported; the husband was indicted for assault with intent to kill, but the charge was quickly dropped for lack of "probable cause."

On the lynchings that followed Turner's Revolt, see Henry Box Brown, *Narrative of the Life of Henry Box Brown, Written by Himself* (Boston: Brown and Stearns, 1849), 37–38; and Stephen B. Oates, *The Fires of Jubilee: Nat Turner's Fierce Rebellion* (New York: Harper and Row, 1975), 113–14.

See also the petition of inhabitants of Petersburg, etc., 1784, in William Palmer et al., eds., *Calendar of Virginia State Papers and Other Manuscripts, 1652–1869, Preserved at the Capitol in Richmond*, 11 vols. (Richmond: Secretary of the Commonwealth and State Librarian, 1875–93), 3:577, 632; and petition of inhabitants of Cumberland County, received Feb. 12, 1817, VEPLR. Perhaps the best example of how public opinion could pressure even a governor to mandate execution of a slave whose offense did not often result in hanging is the example of Julius, a Charlotte County man convicted of second-degree murder of another bondsman in 1856. He was hanged after Governor Wise received a "word to the *Wise*" from a political ally. See trial of Julius, Feb. 4, 1856, Charlotte CCOB, 1852–57, 304, 309, 316–17; transcription of trial record and Robert B. Foster to Governor Wise, April 21, 1856, VEPLR. Documentation of the execution is not in CS but is in Cash Journal, 1855–56. See also Edmund Ruffin, *Diary of Edmund Ruffin*, edited by William K. Scarborough, 3 vols. (Baton Rouge: Louisiana State University Press, 1972–89), 2:207–9; Wyatt-Brown, *Southern Honor*, 402–34; and George McIntosh to Governor Henry A. Wise, Dec. 22, 1856, VEPLR.

37. See the fifty-three-page record of trials of March 20, 1827, and Richard J. Cradle to Governor William B. Giles, April 2, 1827, VEPLR; CS, 5.

38. Between 1785 and 1865 six slaves went to the gallows, and nine were transported or sent to the public works, after conviction of murdering free blacks. Also, twenty-one slaves were executed and twenty-two were transported for murdering unidentified people.

39. Indictment of William, Loudoun County Court Minute Book, 1856–58, 314, 332 (the charge was dropped); trial of John, Dec. 2, 1850, Spotsylvania CCOB, 1849–58, 78. John was found guilty and recommended for transportation. There is no record of the final disposition of his case.

40. Hening, ed., *Statutes at Large* 3:269; *Code of Virginia*, 1860 ed., 120–21.

41. A nineteenth-century report of compensation paid for both executed and transported slaves between 1820 and 1831 appears conveniently in Henry Irving Tragle, ed., *The Southampton Slave Revolt of 1831: A Compilation of Source Material* (New York: University of Massachusetts Press, 1971), 445–54. For analyses of the economic aspects of compensation, see Robert William Fogel and Stanley L. Engerman, *Time on the Cross: The Economics of American Negro Slavery* (Boston: Little, Brown, 1974), 55; and Marvin L. Michael Kay and Lorin Lee Cary, "'The Planters Suffer Little or Nothing': North Carolina Compensations for Executed Slaves," *Science and Society* 40 (Fall 1976): 288–306.

An important modification of the compensation system occurred in 1840 in recognition of the "undervaluing" that resulted from knowledge of the circumstances of slave convicts. Thereafter, judges were to estimate the value of condemned slaves, explicitly recognizing the impact of condemnation on the slaves' market value. See *Acts of the General Assembly*, 1839–40, 51–52.

42. Hening, ed, *Statutes at Large* 8:522, 12:345; Landon Carter, *The Diary of Landon Carter of Sabine Hall*, edited by Jack P. Greene, 2 vols. (Charlottesville: University Press of Virginia, 1965), 2:676, May 6, 1772.

43. For a good breakdown of such expenses, see trials of Senner, May 30, 1754, Sussex County Court of Oyer and Terminer record; Sussex County Accounts, 1754, Sussex County Court Papers, 1754–55. The trials of Senner for murder of a slave, which resulted in a not-guilty verdict, and for poisoning another slave, which resulted in a guilty verdict with a

grant of benefit and a whipping, cost the county 2,134 pounds of tobacco plus 11*s* 9*d* for miscellaneous equipment. State records of the 1804 hanging of Daniel in Lancaster County show that someone earned $8.00 for making the gallows, and the sheriff received $5.25 for the execution. Trial of Daniel, Lancaster County, May 14, 1804, CS, 2; Criminal Charges, Box 3, 1804–6, 1804 folder, Auditor's Item 147.

44. *Journal of the Senate*, 1800 (Richmond, Va., 1800), 55; Tragle, ed., *Southampton Slave Revolt*, 453.

45. Hening, ed., *Statutes at Large* 4:126. Interestingly, the statutes excluded those convicted of rebellion and conspiracy to rebel or to commit murder from benefit of clergy, even though the legislature did not clarify the application of benefit to slaves until 1732. See Hening, ed., *Statutes at Large* 4:325–27.

46. Had the option of transportation not been available when the state abolished benefit for slaves in 1848, the number of hangings might have risen dramatically. See *Acts of the General Assembly*, 1847–48, 124. Exactly that condition almost prevailed because of careless revision of the criminal code. See Revisors of the Code of Virginia, *Report . . . Made to the General Assembly in July 1849, Being Their Final Report, and Relating to the Criminal Code* (Richmond, Va., 1849), 990.

47. Archibald Campbell to Henry Tucker, May 12, 1763, James Monroe to Joseph Carrington Cabell, Feb. 8, 1828, VHS; Miles King to William Wirt, Sept. 23, 1809, with record of six trials of King's slaves for murder of their overseer, June 15, 1809, CS, 2 (also VEPLR); record of trial of York, Rockbridge County, Dec. 1, 1786, CS, 1. A certification of April 4, 1787, of the execution of York accompanies the trial record.

48. Caroline T. Sparrow, "Notes Concerning the Case of the Slave Girl Virginia," unpublished typescript, VHS; Lucy H. Govan to William M. Waller, March 21, June 17, 1843, and Archibald Govan to William M. Waller, June 18, 1843, William M. Waller Papers, VHS. On the successful intervention of an Episcopalian minister on behalf of two slaves condemned to death in 1865 after conviction for burglarizing his house and stealing large amounts of food, see trials of Oliver and George, Richmond, Feb. 14, 1865, the Reverend Dr. Charles Minnigerode to Governor

William Smith, March 14, 1865, and B. R. Wellford Jr. to Governor Smith, March 14, 1865, VEPLR, Pardons, Jan.–April 1865.

49. Hay, "Property, Authority, and the Criminal Law," 23; petition of Augusta County residents to the governor and Council, Sept. 1829, VEPLR.

50. Gooch to the Bishop of London, May 31, 1731, Fulham Palace Papers, 15, in correspondence of the Bishop of London, no. 111, Virginia Colonial Records Project microfilm, VHS; Landon C. Bell, "Benefit of Clergy," 1931 typescript, Library of Virginia; Jeffrey K. Sawyer, "'Benefit of Clergy' in Maryland and Virginia," *American Journal of Legal History* 33 (Jan. 1990): 49–68. On evangelical Christianity's ambivalent relationship with slave-owning planters, see Raboteau, *Slave Religion,* 152–77; Blassingame, *Slave Community,* 268–71; and James Oakes, *The Ruling Race: A History of American Slaveholders* (New York: Knopf, 1982), 96–122.

51. The various papers in Berlin and Hoffman, eds., *Slavery and Freedom in the Age of the American Revolution,* admirably summarize and extend knowledge of this result of the American Revolution. See also Mullin, *Flight and Rebellion;* Duncan J. MacLeod, *Slavery, Race and the American Revolution* (London: Cambridge University Press, 1974); and David Brion Davis, *Problem of Slavery.* On the nineteenth century, see Genovese, *Roll, Jordan, Roll,* 3–112; Willie Lee Rose, *Slavery and Freedom* (New York: Oxford University Press, 1982), 18–36; Barbara L. Bellows, *Benevolence Among Slaveholders: Assisting the Poor in Charleston, 1670–1860* (Baton Rouge: Louisiana State University Press, 1993), 98–119; and Oakes, *Ruling Race,* 135–38. Oakes disputes claims that the conditions of slavery improved in the late antebellum period.

52. *PTJ* 2:504; Malone, *Jefferson the President,* 252–53; John Chester Miller, *Wolf by the Ears,* 126–28. Jefferson hoped that whites could eventually guarantee their safety by deporting all blacks. See Winthrop D. Jordan, *White over Black,* 542–69; Egerton, *Gabriel's Rebellion,* 92–93, 151–62; Finkelman, "Jefferson and Slavery," 181–221; and idem, "Thomas Jefferson and Antislavery," 193–228.

53. John Caruthers to Governor William H. Cabell, June 10, 1806, VEPLR.

54. Revisors of the Code of Virginia, *Report*, 990; Virginia Assembly, *Amendments Made by the Joint Committee of Revision to the Reports of the Revisors*, in *Assembly Reports*, vol. 2 (Richmond, Va., 1849), section concerning p. 990 of the Revisors' *Report*.

55. Record of trial of Jim Gooch, Rockbridge County, Oct. 31, 1853, CS, 8; Samuel McDowell Reid to Samuel McDowell Reid Jr., Feb. 10, 1854, Ulrich B. Phillips Collection, Yale University Library; trials of Richard, Harry, and Dow, Henry County Court Minute Book, 1859–64, 9–11, and Cash Journal. An Amherst County incident of 1863 shows official fears of the presence of slaves at hangings. The justices ordered the county sheriff to keep six slaves under sentence of death for murder of their master at a "suitable place outside of the village of the Court House" and also ordered him to "summon a sufficient guard for the purposes of preserving order and preventing a large assemblage of slaves at the place of execution." See Amherst CCOB, 1859–64, at May 18, 1863. The executions did take place; see Cash Journal. On the general "privatization of hangings" in the mid–nineteenth century, see Husband, "Geographical Perspective," 56–69; and Masur, *Rites of Execution*, 6–7, 93–116.

56. Robert Tinsley to Governor John Tyler and the Council, June 22, 1826, VEPLR. For perspectives on the limited antislavery component of this sort of petition, see Patricia E. P. Hickin, "Antislavery in Virginia, 1831–1861" (Ph.D. diss., University of Virginia, 1968); and Alison G. Freehling, *Drift Toward Dissolution: The Virginia Slavery Debate of 1831–1832* (Baton Rouge: Louisiana State University Press, 1982).

57. Palmer et al., eds., *Calendar of Virginia State Papers* 9:156, 294; James Monroe to Thomas Newton, Oct. 5, 1800, in *The Writings of James Monroe*, edited by Stanislaus Murray Hamilton, 7 vols. (New York: G. P. Putnam's Sons, 1898–1903), 2:213–14; Tragle, ed., *Southampton Slave Revolt*, 306–19; Robert Sutcliff, *Travels in Some Parts of America, in the Years 1804, 1805, and 1806* (York, Eng.: Printed by C. Peacock for W. Alexander, 1811), 50; Aptheker, *American Negro Slave Revolts*, 223.

58. *Richmond Enquirer*, Jan. 28, 1830, Dec. 14, 1847; Latrobe, *Virginia Journals* 2:191–93.

59. James T. Callender to Thomas Jefferson, postscript, Sept. 13, 1800, PTJ-MD; *Richmond Enquirer*, Dec. 14, 1847; Ronald A. Bosco, "Lectures

at the Pillory: The Early American Execution Sermon," *American Quarterly* 30 (Summer 1978): 156–76. I have found surprisingly little evidence of slaves' scaffold speeches in Virginia.

60. On "taking" versus stealing, see, e.g., *Minutes of the Baptist Association, in the District of Goshen . . . 1816* (Fredericksburg, Va.: William F. Gray, 1816), 7–8.

61. Record of trials of Landon, Barnaba, Sarah, Robert, Randolph, Ralph, Harry, and Thomas for murdering their master, May 25, 1818, Frederick County, CS, 4, and VEPLR; petition of Preston County residents, May 22, 1836, VEPLR; Charles L. Perdue Jr. et al., eds., *Weevils in the Wheat: Interviews with Virginia Ex-Slaves* (Charlottesville: University Press of Virginia, 1976), 80, 346–47.

62. We can also acknowledge that newly imported Africans might have brought with them the legal values, customs, and sometimes even writings of the societies from which they came, against which they could measure the slave code and courts and find them wanting. See chapter 1.

63. Hindus, *Prison and Plantation*, 125–61. It is a truism that the capital punishment of slaves was partly a method of social control. Given its particular application, however, it was a very special method.

64. As a basis for comparison, New York executed more people (in absolute numbers) between 1890 and 1963 (695). During the same years Virginia executed 300 African Americans. On a per capita basis, however, neither state ranked in the top five for those years. See Bowers, *Executions in America*, 296; Bye, "Capital Punishment in the United States," 57–58. (These are extrapolated figures. Problems of dating may have led to errors of a very small statistical magnitude, perhaps errors of two to five for Virginia from 1890 to 1963.)

65. Hay, "Property, Authority, and the Criminal Law," 17–63.

CHAPTER 4: THE TRANSPORTATION OF SLAVES
FROM VIRGINIA, 1800–1865

This chapter is based on a paper delivered at the annual meeting of the Organization of American Historians, Minneapolis, 1985. A slightly different version appeared in *Slavery and Abolition* 7 (Dec. 1986): 215–40.

1. Trial of Nov. 20, 1838, cited in CS, box 6, and described in Virginia Council Minutes, 1838–39, 182, 214–15, 218–19.

2. Trial citation and note of remittance, CS, box 6; "A List of Slaves and Free persons of color received into the Penitentiary of Virginia for sale and transportation from the 25th June 1816 to the 1st February 1842" (hereinafter referred to as "List," 1816–42), "Slaves transported and Executed—paid for—1 Octr. 37 to 30 Sept. 38" through "1 Octr. '41 to 30 Sept. '42," CS, box 10; "A Table Shewing the number of Slaves, Free negroes and Mullatoes brought to the Penitentiary for Transportation, and those remaining on the 30th November 1845," with general penitentiary report, 1845, VEPLR, Dec. 1–14, 1845, folder; "Bonds for Transportation of Condemned Slaves, 1840–1849," CS, box 10; Virginia Council Minutes, 1838–39, 182, 214–15, 218–19, 221; Virginia Executive Letter Book, 1839–44, 121, 127–28; William H. Williams to Governor John Rutherfoord, New Orleans, July 3, 1841, with copies of affidavits from the office of the mayor of New Orleans, VEPLR; *Niles' Register* 60, May 22, 1841, 189; *The State of Louisiana v. William H. Williams*, 7 Rob. 252, La., 1844, excerpted in Catterall, ed., *Judicial Cases* 3:558–59; and file of the case in Louisiana State Supreme Court dockets, 1818–94, docket 4671, Archives and Manuscripts Department, Earl K. Long Library, University of New Orleans. I am indebted to Warren M. Billings of the Department of History, University of New Orleans, and to Marie E. Windell of the Archives and Manuscripts Department, Long Library, for securing photocopies of this file, especially because only the manuscript papers give the names of the convict slaves.

3. See note 2 above; and *Gil v. Williams and Davis*, 12 La. An. 219, 1857, excerpted in Catterall, ed., *Judicial Cases* 3:653. On an 1845 federal investigation concerning what was perhaps the same brig *Uncas*, see U.S. Senate, *Executive Documents*, 28th Cong., 2d sess., vol. 9, no. 150, 106–14. Kenneth M. Stampp briefly discusses Williams's case in *Peculiar Institution*, 258.

4. On the domestic slave trade, see Fogel and Engerman, *Time on the Cross: The Economics of American Negro Slavery*, 44–52; Robert

William Fogel and Stanley L. Engerman, *Time on the Cross: Evidence and Methods—A Supplement* (Boston: Little, Brown, 1974), 43–54; Richard Sutch, "The Breeding of Slaves for Sale and the Westward Expansion of Slavery, 1850–1860," in *Race and Slavery in the Western Hemisphere: Quantitative Studies*, edited by Stanley L. Engerman and Eugene D. Genovese (Princeton, N.J.: Princeton University Press, 1975), 173–210; Herbert G. Gutman and Richard Sutch, "The Slave Family: Protected Agent of Capitalist Masters or Victim of the Slave Trade?" in *Reckoning with Slavery: A Critical Study in the Quantitative Study of American Slavery and the Negro*, by Paul A. David et al. (New York: Oxford University Press, 1976), 100–103; Herbert G. Gutman, *Slavery and the Numbers Game: A Critique of Time on the Cross* (Urbana: University of Illinois Press, 1975), 102–4; and Michael Tadman, *Speculators and Slaves: Masters, Traders, and Slaves in the Old South* (Madison: University of Wisconsin Press, 1989).

Citations of the numerous treatments of the law of slavery that have appeared in the last three decades appear throughout this book.

On the nature of slavery in different societies, see Rubin and Tuden, eds., *Comparative Perspectives on Slavery in New World Plantation Societies.*

On the transportation of convict servants from Britain, see Richard B. Morris, *Government and Labor in Early America* (New York: Columbia University Press, 1946), 323–37; Abbot Emerson Smith, *Colonists in Bondage: White Servitude and Convict Labor in America, 1607–1776* (Chapel Hill: University of North Carolina Press, 1947), 89–147, 311–12, 325–28, 330–31, 337; A. Roger Ekirch, "Bound for America: A Profile of British Convicts Transported to the Colonies, 1718–1775," *WMQ*, 3d ser., 42 (April 1985): 184–200; Kenneth Morgan, "The Organization of the Convict Trade to Maryland: Stevenson, Randolph, and Cheston, 1768–1775," *WMQ*, 3d ser., 42 (April 1985): 201–27; A. Roger Ekirch, "The Transportation of Scottish Criminals to America During the Eighteenth Century," *Journal of British Studies* 24 (July 1985): 366–74; idem, *Bound for America: The Transportation of British Convicts to the Colonies, 1718–1775* (Oxford: Clarendon Press, 1987); Fairfax Harrison, "When the Convicts Came," *VMHB* 30 (April 1922): 250–60; and Marion Dargan,

"Crime and the Virginia Gazette, 1736–1775," *University of New Mexico Bulletin, Sociological Series* 2, no. 1 (1934): 55. On these and other precedents for transportation, see Nicholson, "Legal Borrowing and the Origins of Slave Law," 47–48.

5. Shepherd, ed., *Statutes at Large* 2:279. By December 1801 the legislature had to make it clear that the state would pay compensation to owners just as soon as the executive decided in favor of transportation. See Shepherd, ed., *Statutes at Large* 2:314. There was, of course, nothing new about transportation of convicts as such. It was the government's transportation of slaves convicted of capital crimes that was an innovation. It might appear that transportation of slaves out of the United States was in direct violation of the U.S. statute of 1794, "An Act to prohibit the carrying on the Slave Trade from the United States to any foreign place or country." The case law on this statute, however, never claims this coverage for it. It is reasonable to assume that, as in *Groves v. Slaughter* (15 Peters [U.S.] 449 [1841]), federal judges would have viewed transportation as a protected exercise of a state's police power. See *Statutes at Large of the United States of America, 1789–1873*, 17 vols. (Boston: Little, Brown, 1850–73), 1:347–49, with commentary; and William M. McKinney and Peter Kemper Jr., eds., *The Federal Statutes Annotated*, 10 vols. (Northport, N.Y.: Edward Thompson Co., 1903–6), 7:100, including citations. The best cases are *The Caroline*, 5 Fed. Case no. 2418, *Tryphenia v. Harrison*, 24 Fed. Case no. 14209, *U.S. v. Libby*, 26 Fed. Case no. 15597, and *U.S. v. Naylor*, 27 Fed. Case no. 15858.

6. *PTJ* 2:504; Malone, *Jefferson the President*, 252–53; Egerton, *Gabriel's Rebellion*, 92–93, 151–62.

7. Trial of John, Feb. 22, 1808, Brunswick County, John Wyche to Governor William H. Cabell, Feb. 24, March 22, 29, 1808, petition of Brunswick citizens, March 5, 1808, VEPLR; CS, box 2; David Brion Davis, "Movement to Abolish Capital Punishment," 23–46.

8. Wyche to Cabell and petition of March 5, 1808, VEPLR; CS, box 2.

9. See, e.g., Robert Tinsley to Governor John Tyler, June 22, 1826, petition of Staunton citizens to Governor William B. Giles, Sept. 1829, VEPLR. Not all such petitions were successful. See, e.g., full record of trial and execution of Billy, alias Bill Williams, property of James

Williamson, for murder of a free black man, Norfolk city, Sept. 12, 1807, CS, box 2; petition of Norfolk citizens, Oct. 1807, Arthur Lee to Governor William H. Cabell, Oct. 11, 1807, William Sharp to Governor Cabell, Oct. 29, 1807, VEPLR. On the other hand, because of the prevailing prejudice and proslavery attitude, whites did not even conceive of terms in the penitentiary as an option for slaves. Indeed, in the 1820s and late 1850s legislators even prohibited penitentiary sentences for free black convicts, relegating them either to transportation and sale into slavery or to hard labor on the public works. On the sale and transportation as well as the sentencing to hard labor of free black Virginians, see Ira Berlin, *Slaves Without Masters: The Free Negro in the Antebellum South* (New York: Oxford University Press, 1974), 83, 323–24; and John H. Russell, *The Free Negro in Virginia, 1619–1865* (Baltimore: Johns Hopkins Press, 1913), 105–6.

10. Washington to Capt. Josiah Thompson, Mount Vernon, July 2, 1766, in John C. Fitzpatrick, ed., *The Writings of George Washington from the Original Manuscript Sources, 1745–1799*, 39 vols. (Washington, D.C.: GPO, 1931–44), 2:437.

11. Petition for Ned, received May 22, 1836, VEPLR. For a handful of examples from the many available ones of punitive, private sales, see John W. Blassingame, ed., *Slave Testimony: Letters, Speeches, Interviews, and Autobiographies, 1736–1938* (Baton Rouge: Louisiana State University Press, 1977), 163; George Bourne, *Picture of Slavery in the United States of America* (Middletown, Conn.: E. Hunt, 1834), 114–15; Moncure D. Conway, *Autobiography*, 2 vols. (Boston: Houghton, Mifflin, 1904), 1:12–13, 28; John Davis, *Personal Adventures and Travels of Four Years and a Half in the United States of America* (London: For J. Davis, 1817), 89–92; Perdue et al. eds., *Weevils in the Wheat*, 103; Alexander Smyth to Governor Cabell, Wythe County, Sept. 14, 1807, VEPLR; George Carter to Thomas Maund, Sept. 25, 1817, George Carter of Oatlands Letterbook, 1807–19, VHS, 100–102; *Chapman v. Campbell*, 13 Grattan 105 (Va.), 106, excerpted in Catterall, ed., *Judicial Cases* 1:239; Mary Beth Norton, *Liberty's Daughters: The Revolutionary Experience of American Women, 1750–1800* (Boston: Little, Brown, 1980), 70; and Norton, Gutman, and Berlin, "Afro-American Family," 184–85.

12. McIlwaine et al., eds., *Executive Journals of the Council of Colonial Virginia* 3:118, 4:243; Virginia General Court, judgment in *King v. Sam,* Nov. 2, 1722, and order of April 26, 1723, "Value of Negro's by the Commtee May the 20th, 1723," copies in Virginia General Assembly, Committee of Propositions and Grievances, Papers, 1711–30, VHS, sec. 14; H. R. McIlwaine and Wilmer L. Hall, eds., *Journals of the House of Burgesses,* 13 vols. (Richmond: Virginia State Library, 1905–15), 1712–26, 368, 371, 373, 375; McIlwaine, ed., *Legislative Journals of the Council of Virginia* 2:690–91; Waverly K. Winfree, ed., *The Laws of Virginia, Being a Supplement to Hening's Statutes at Large, 1700–1750* (Richmond: Virginia State Library, 1971), 257–59; York CCOB, 1732–40, 189; Elizabeth City CCOB, 1731–47, 121; Caroline CCOB, 1741–46, 288–90, 1751 57, 177–78; Hening, ed., *Statutes at Large* 9:106; Frey, "Between Slavery and Freedom," 384–85; Northampton CCOB, 1777–83, 334–35.

Like other slave colonies and states, Virginia had taken several measures to prevent slave convicts from being traded to its citizens from the West Indies. See Darold D. Wax, "Preferences for Slaves in Colonial America," *JNH* 58 (Oct. 1973): 377–89. For the offer by the Elizabeth City County slave court to George Ware of the choice of giving five hundred pounds of security for Jack's good behavior or else transporting him out of Virginia, see Elizabeth City County Order Book, 1731–47, 265 (Jan. 7, 1742). Among other British West Indian colonies, Antigua had banished convicted slaves, especially the nearly fifty convicted rebels after the revolt of 1736. See Gaspar, *Bondmen and Rebels,* 29, 35–37.

13. Latrobe, *Virginia Journals* 2:192; McIlwaine et al., eds., *Journals of the Council of the State of Virginia,* vols. 1–5, esp. vol. 3. Volume 3 shows forty-one pardons of condemned slaves between 1782 and 1786.

14. Latrobe, *Virginia Journals* 2:192–93; *Richmond Enquirer,* Jan. 28, 1830, Dec. 14, 1847.

15. Mullin, *Flight and Rebellion,* 130–36; Frey, "Between Slavery and Freedom," 375–98; Benjamin Quarles, "Lord Dunmore as Liberator," *WMQ,* 3d ser., 15 (Oct. 1958): 494–507; Tommy L. Bogger, "Slave Resistance in Virginia During the Haitian Revolution, 1791–1804," *Hampton Institute Journal of Ethnic Studies* 5 (April 1978): 86–100; Donald R. Hickey, "America's Response to the Slave Revolt in Haiti, 1791–1806,"

Journal of the Early Republic 2 (Winter 1982): 361–79; Schwarz, *Twice Condemned,* 193–254; idem, "Gabriel's Challenge," 283–309.

16. In reaction to increased convictions of slaves for murder of whites in the 1820s as well as to the Turner Revolt of 1831, the Old Dominion's lawmakers did stipulate in 1832 that death would be the penalty for slaves who were found guilty of assault on a white person with intent to kill. Slaves would not be allowed to plead benefit of clergy upon conviction of this offense. Yet between 1832 and the revision of the transportation law in 1848, 78 percent of slaves (25 of 32) convicted of assault with intent to kill a white person were transported, not hanged. See *Supplement to the Revised Code,* 247.

17. Owners of condemned slaves had been receiving compensation since 1705. See Hening, ed., *Statutes at Large* 3:269. A nineteenth-century report of compensation paid for both executed and transported slaves appears in Tragle, ed., *Southampton Slave Revolt,* 445–54. For analyses of the economic aspects of compensation, see Fogel and Engerman, *Time on the Cross: The Economics of American Negro Slavery,* 55; and Kay and Cary, "'Planters Suffer Little or Nothing,'" 288–306.

18. Shepherd, ed., *Statutes at Large* 2:279–80. The case of John and the other slaves illegally transported to New Orleans in 1840 illustrates the difference that frequently existed between the valuations of condemned slaves and the price that traders paid for them. The price could be the same, however. See note 19, below.

19. "The person or persons, at the time of making such a purchase, shall enter into bond, with sufficient security, in the penalty of five hundred dollars for each slave, payable to the governor and his successors, for the use of the commonwealth, with condition that he or they will carry out of the United States all the slaves by him or them purchased, who are now, or who thereafter may be under sentence of death." Shepherd, ed., *Statutes at Large* 2:279.

South Carolinians had expressed fears of insurrection caused by slaves imported from the Chesapeake in the 1790s. See Philip D. Morgan, "Black Society in the Lowcountry, 1760–1810," in *Slavery and Freedom in the Age of Revolution,* ed. Berlin and Hoffman, 84n3, 140. But when some slave states passed laws against the importation of bondspeople who had been convicted of major crimes, it became a matter of inter-state comity for Virginia to give "full faith and credit" to such laws. See note 30, below.

20. William Morris and John G. Brown to Governor James Monroe, Richmond, Jan. 20, 1801, VEPLR; citation of trial and record of payment of compensation, CS, box 2; "A List of Slaves Reprieved for Transportation and Sold by the Commonwealth," March 8, 1806 (hereinafter referred to as "List," 1806), VEPLR; Henrico CCOB, 1799–1801, 399, 408–9, 445; Richmond City Hustings Court Order Book, 1797–1801, 474; Virginia Executive Council Journal, 1799–1801, 340–42; "Negroes Condemned by the County Court of Caroline, for conspiracy in the year 1800 and their valuation," attached to penitentiary receipt for transported slave, July 15, 1809, VEPLR.

21. William Fulcher to Governor James Monroe, July 1802, George Goosley to Monroe, June 5, 24, 1802, Thomas Newton to Monroe, Aug. 28, Sept. 8, 1802, and memorandum of Martin Mims, keeper of the penitentiary, Oct. 12, 1802, VEPLR; citation of trials and records of payment of compensation, CS, box 2; "List," 1806; Henrico CCOB, 1801–3, 328. See also Egerton, *Gabriel's Rebellion*, 151–62.

22. Henrico CCOB, 1799–1801, 408–9: sentence of hanging, Oct. 29, 1800; Virginia Executive Council Journal, 1799–1801, 322, 339–40: reprieves of Bowler, Dec. 23, 1800, until fourth Friday in Jan., and Jan. 22, 1801, until fourth Friday in March, and acceptance of offer for Jack Bowler and other reprieved slaves, Jan. 23, 1801, CS, box 2; citation of trial and record of payment of compensation, CS, box 2; "List," 1806; "Negroes Condemned by the County Court of Caroline, for conspiracy in the year 1800 and their valuation," attached to penitentiary receipt for transported slave, July 15, 1809, VEPLR. Bowler's name is written below the names of the Caroline County men.

23. Morris and Brown to Monroe, Jan. 20, 1801, VEPLR; U.S. Census Office, *Return of the Whole Number of Persons Within the Several Districts of the United States . . . Second Census* (Washington, D.C., 1801); Joy J. Jackson, "New Orleans, La.," in *Encyclopedia of Southern History*, edited by David C. Roller and Robert W. Twyman (Baton Rouge: Louisiana State University Press, 1979), 900; George Goosley to Monroe,

June 5, 1802, VEPLR; Paul F. LaChance, "The Politics of Fear: French Louisianians and the Slave Trade, 1786–1809," *Plantation Society in the Americas* 1 (June 1979): 162–97; Malone, *Jefferson the President*, 252–53; Egerton, *Gabriel's Rebellion*, 151–62. In 1801 the suggestion of Haiti as a destination presupposed some means of emancipating the transported people.

24. William Fulcher Memorial, 1806, VEPLR, folder for Dec. 1806; miscellaneous papers related to the purchase of six condemned slaves by William Fowles and John Dyson of South Carolina, July 1810, including Sam, the property of John G. Periner, who was convicted of conspiring to rebel on June 6, 1810, in Isle of Wight County (Isle of Wight CCOB, 1810–13, 51; trial record in VEPLR; citation of trial and record of payment of compensation, CS, box 3); citation of trials of Robin and Barnabas, Frederick County, May 25, 1818, and record of payment of compensation, CS, box 4; miscellaneous papers of May and June 1818, on Robin and Barnabas, VEPLR; R. E. Griffith Sr., "Notes on Rock Hill," *Proceedings of the Clarke County Historical Association* 3 (1943): 47; Stephen Z. Starr, *Colonel Grenfell's Wars: The Life of a Soldier of Fortune* (Baton Rouge: Louisiana State University Press, 1971), 273–79. After ratification of the Adams-Onis Treaty of 1819, the Dry Tortugas islands were transferred to the United States in 1821. A search of George P. Rawick, ed., *The American Slave: A Composite Autobiography*, 41 vols. (Westport, Conn.: Greenwood Press, 1972–79), and other sources produced no evidence concerning the destination of any other slaves transported from Virginia.

25. "Statement Showing the Amount Paid Out of the Treasury in Each Year for Convict Slaves, from 1800 to 1850, Inclusive," in *Documents Containing Statistics of Virginia, Ordered to Be Printed by the State Convention* (Richmond, Va.: W. Culley, 1851).

26. Trials of Bob, Dec. 23, 1803, and May 21, 1805, Henrico CCOB, 1803–5, 251–52, and 1805–7, 52–53; citation of trial and record of payment of compensation, CS, box 4, folder for "1819, Executed," which also helps to clarify the complicated chain of title to Bob Tucker over the years; bond of Ellis Puryear and others, Feb. 25, 1804, bond of William Fulcher and William Bell, Dec. 5, 1806, CS, box 10; Virginia Council Jour-

nal, 1803–6, 313, 321, 327, 340, 358, 372, 410, 427, 499, 503; Virginia Executive Letter Book, 1803–7, 192, 253, 255–57, 268–69, 281, 367, 403; John St. Clair to Governor John Milledge of Georgia, Goochland, July 5, 1805, Milledge to Governor John Page of Virginia, July 29, 1805, Milledge to George Jefferson, Augusta, March 31, 1806, John Ingles to Governor William H. Cabell, March 20, 1807, VEPLR. Harriet Milledge Salley, ed., *The Correspondence of John Milledge, Governor of Georgia* (Columbia, S.C.: State Commercial Print Company, 1949), 112, 153, reveals that Milledge had other business dealings with George Jefferson but contains no references to Bob Tucker. The confusion involved in this case may have encouraged passage of the 1806 law that forbade compensation to non-Virginian owners of slaves condemned while illegally in or passing through the Old Dominion. See Shepherd, ed., *Statutes at Large* 3:252.

27. Richard Terrell to Governor William H. Cabell, Knoxville, Sept. 10, 1808, H. J. Gambill to Dr. Charles Evereat, Harrisonburg, Jan. 15, 1815, VEPLR; Virginia Council Journal, 1820–21, 179, Nov. 26, 1821.

28. Richard J. Cralle to Governor William B. Giles, Nottoway Court House, April 2, 1827, VEPLR. Cralle, the counsel for seven slaves condemned for murdering their master, reported that in spite of the evidence that two were only accessories after the fact, "the people of the county . . . are, in general, strongly opposed to the transportation of any." See also petition of the people of Cumberland County, received Feb. 12, 1817, VEPLR. There, angry whites declared that the executive had shown leniency in granting transportation over the years but should now make examples of several slaves convicted of poisoning by hanging them. Two of the slaves were still transported, but one, ninety-eight years of age, died in the penitentiary seven days after being taken there. See "List," 1816–42.

29. Unknown to Governor George W. Smith, Sept. 20, 1811, VEPLR, cited in Johnston, *Race Relations in Virginia*, 87. This unknown correspondent asserted that "transportation from this part of the country produces almost as strong an impression on the other slaves as hanging." I was unable to locate this letter in VEPLR. See *Richmond Enquirer*, July 30, 1852, 2.

30. D. M. Gehee to Governor James P. Preston, Cambridge, S.C., Jan. 31, 1817, VEPLR; *The State of Louisiana v. William H. Williams*, 7 Rob. 252 (La.), 1844, excerpted in Catterall, ed., *Judicial Cases* 3:558–59; case file in Louisiana State Supreme Court dockets, 1818–94, docket 4671, Archives and Manuscripts Department, Earl K. Long Library, University of New Orleans; John Codman Hurd, *The Law of Freedom and Bondage in the United States*, 2 vols. (Boston: Little, Brown, 1858–62), 2:20–23; Judith Kelleher Schafer, "The Immediate Impact of Nat Turner's Insurrection on New Orleans," *Louisiana History* 21 (Fall 1980): 367–8; Stampp, *Peculiar Institution*, 254; Joe Gray Taylor, *Negro Slavery in Louisiana* (Baton Rouge: Louisiana State University Press, 1963), 37, 41–45, 266–67; Clement Eaton, *Freedom-of-Thought Struggle in the Old South*, rev. and enlarged ed. (New York: Harper and Row, 1964), 94; Norrece T. Jones Jr., *Born a Child of Freedom, Yet a Slave*, 37–42; Chase C. Mooney, *Slavery in Tennessee* (Bloomington: Indiana University Press, 1957), 19; James Benson Sellers, *Slavery in Alabama* (University: University of Alabama Press, 1950), 174–91, esp. 180; Charles S. Sydnor, *Slavery in Mississippi* (New York: D. Appleton, 1933), 162–71; Tadman, *Speculators and Slaves*, 84–93; *Deans v. McLendon*, 30 Mississippi 343, 1855, *Glidewell v. Hite*, 5 How. Mississippi 110, 1840, both excerpted in Catterall, ed., *Judicial Cases* 3:289–90, 340.

Herbert Aptheker describes the Boxley Plot in *American Negro Slave Revolts*, 255–57; see also Schwarz, *Twice Condemned*, 270–72, 329–30. Florida was notorious as an area in which laws concerning the international slave trade were evaded. See Frances J. Stafford, "Illegal Importations: Enforcement of the Slave Trade Laws Along the Florida Coast, 1810–1828," *Florida Historical Quarterly* 46 (April 1967): 124–33. For an interpretation of interregional transfer of slaves that diverges from Tadman, see Edward James Kilsdonk, "The Economic Development of the Greater Chesapeake, 1800–1860: A Series of Conjectural Estimates" (M.A. thesis, University of Virginia, 1993), 178–212.

31. *Groves v. Slaughter*, 15 Peters 449 (U.S.), 1841, excerpted in Catterall, ed., *Judicial Cases* 3:533–37; David Brion Davis, *Problem of Slavery*, 23–36.

32. James A. Grant to Governor James P. Preston, Richmond, Dec. 29, 1817, Williams and Price to Governor John Tyler, March 1, 1826, Lewis

Collier to Governor William B. Giles, March 19, 1829 (Collier commented on the "Blemishes" of the transported slaves), James Goodwyn to Governor John Floyd, April 7, 1832, VEPLR. The transaction concerning a condemned slave whom Governor William Smith and the Council pardoned and allowed to remain a slave within Virginia in return for fifty dollars is recorded in Virginia Council Journals, 1846–47, 80, Sept. 1846. See "Slaves transported and executed . . . from 1 Octr. 44 to 1 Octr. 1845," citation of trial of Nov. 12, 1844, for attempted rape, and record of remittance of $150 to the owners, CS, box 10 and box 7.

33. *Acts of the General Assembly,* 1829–30, 23, and 1839–40, 51–42; Joe Gray Taylor, *Negro Slavery in Louisiana,* 40; "Statement Shewing the Number and Cost to the Commonwealth of Executed and Transported Slaves, for the Twenty Years Which Ended the 31st December 1840," Virginia House of Delegates, *Journal,* 1841–42, *Documents,* no. 43.

34. Virginia House of Delegates, *Journal,* 1841–42, 87–88; *Acts of the General Assembly,* 1847–48, 125–26, 162–64; Catterall, ed., *Judicial Cases* 3:565; Edward D. Jervey and C. Harold Huber, "The *Creole* Affair," *JNH* 65 (Summer 1980): 196–211; Howard Jones, "The Peculiar Institution and National Honor: The Case of the Creole Slave Revolt," *CWH* 21 (March 1975): 28–50.

35. Virginia House of Delegates, *Journal,* 1848–49, 24; citation of trial and execution of William, Aug. 1, 1848, Gloucester County, and record of remittance of $420 to owner, CS, box 8; Revisors of the Code of Virginia, *Report,* 990; *Code of Virginia,* 1849 ed., 753. An incomplete listing of capital crimes in Virginia appears in Stroud, *Sketch of the Laws Relating to Slavery,* 77–80. Stroud missed the laws making capital crimes of treason, certain kinds of arson, and conspiracy by a "free person" with a slave to commit murder or rebel, the last of which first appeared in 1798. See Shepherd, ed., *Statutes at Large* 2:77, 405–6, 3:119; *Code of Virginia,* 1860 ed., 783.

36. See table 4.1. The ratios are 1845–49, 1.93 to 1; 1850–54, 3.25 to 1; 1855–59, 4.4 to 1; 1860–64, 2.4 to 1. The pertinent part of the constitution of 1850 appears in Francis N. Thorpe, ed., *The Federal and State Constitutions, Colonial Charters, and Other Organic Laws . . . ,* 7 vols. (Washington, D.C.: GPO, 1909), 7:3844. See also Ethridge, "Jordan

Hatcher Affair of 1852," 446–63; Green, "Urban Industry, Black Resistance, and Racial Restriction," 576–605; "The Cheapness of Slave Labor Belonging to Companies in Constructing Improvements, Compared to the System of Contracts," *DeBow's Review* 17 (July 1854): 76–82, reprinted in *The Black Worker to 1859,* edited by Philip Foner and Ronald L. Lewis (Philadelphia: Temple University Press, 1978), 17–20; *Governor's Biennial Messages . . . December 7, 1857* (Richmond, Va.: John Warrock, 1857), 150–51. In *Slaves Without Masters,* 323–24, Ira Berlin correctly points out Governor Henry A. Wise's additional objection to black and white prisoners' being in the penitentiary together. Thus the 1858 law fell on free black convicts as well.

37. *Acts of the General Assembly,* 1857–58, 39–40; representative lists and contracts, VEPLR, Dec. 1859, Nov. and Dec. 1860, and July 1, 1863, the last being for two reprieved slaves hired to the Tredegar Iron Works. On the use of slave labor on Confederate fortifications, see James H. Brewer, *The Confederate Negro: Virginia's Craftsmen and Military Laborers* (Durham, N.C.: Duke University Press, 1969); and Ervin L. Jordan Jr., *Black Confederates and Afro-Yankees in Civil War Virginia* (Charlottesville: University Press of Virginia, 1995), 49–68.

38. *Daily Richmond Examiner,* Sept. 18, 1862, 1; Legislative Petitions, Bath County, Feb. 15, 1863; *Acts of the General Assembly,* 1861–62, 103. The U.S. law of 1862 said that no slaves escaping from a disloyal owner into another state would be returned except those who had escaped after committing a crime. See *Statutes at Large of the United States* 12:354, 589.

39. *Acts of the General Assembly,* 1863, 54, passed Feb. 10, 1864; Virginia House of Delegates *Journal,* 1863–64, 59, 106; Virginia Senate *Journal,* 1863–64, 22–23, 111, 121, 124, 131; *Daily Richmond Examiner,* Jan. 11, Feb. 11, 1864.

40. "List," 1816–42; citations of trials and records of payments, 1815–44, CS, boxes 3–7. Boxes 7–9 show that the trend continued through 1864, because just over 7 percent (10 of 140) of slaves' names included their family names. On the importance of slave naming practices, see Genovese, *Roll, Jordan, Roll,* 443–50; Herbert G. Gutman, *The Black Family in Slavery and Freedom, 1750–1925* (New York: Pantheon, 1976),

185–201; Cheryll Ann Cody, "Naming, Kinship, and Estate Dispersal: Notes on Slave Family Life on a South Carolina Plantation, 1786 to 1833," *WMQ*, 3d ser., 39 (Jan. 1982): 192–211; and John C. Inscoe, "Carolina Slave Names: An Index to Acculturation," *JSH* 49 (Nov. 1983): 527–54.

    41. These are rough data, of course, because of the problems indicated concerning the ages of transportees and because U.S. Census statistics on slaves are not totally trustworthy, especially when demographers use them in order to figure survival rates as a basis for determining how many slaves were carried or sold in the interstate slave trade. See "List," 1816–42. Tadman, in *Speculators and Slaves*, 25–31, documents and analyzes the age structure of the marketed slaves.

    For estimates of the interstate trade and forced migration of slaves out of Virginia, see William J. Ernst, "Changes in the Slave Population of the Virginia Tidewater and Piedmont, 1830–1860: A Stable Population Analysis," University of Virginia, Corcoran Department of History, *Essays in History* 19 (1975): 75–83; Allan Kulikoff, "Uprooted Peoples: Black Migrants in the Age of the American Revolution, 1790–1820," in *Slavery and Freedom in the Age of the American Revolution*, ed. Berlin and Hoffman, 143–71; and Donald Sweig, "Reassessing the Human Dimension of the Interstate Slave Trade," *Prologue* 12 (Spring 1980): 5–21. For general estimates of the slave trade and forced migration from the Upper South to the Lower South, see, in addition to the references in note 4 above, citations in Philip S. Foner, *History of Black Americans from the Emergence of the Cotton Kingdom to the Eve of the Compromise of 1850* (Westport, Conn.: Greenwood Press, 1983), 562–64; Frederic Bancroft, *Slave-Trading in the Old South* (Baltimore: J. H. Furst, 1931), 384–86; William Calderhead, "How Extensive Was the Border State Slave Trade? A New Look," *CWH* 18 (March 1972): 42–55; F. V. Carstensen and S. E. Goodman, "Trouble on the Auction Block: Interregional Slave Sales and the Reliability of a Linear Equation," *Journal of Interdisciplinary History* 8 (Autumn 1977): 315–18; W. H. Collins, *The Domestic Slave Trade of the United States* (New York: Broadway Publishing Co., 1904), 61–67; Robert Evans Jr., "Some Economic Aspects of the Domestic Slave Trade, 1830–1860," *Southern Economic Journal* 27 (April

1961): 329–37; Laurence J. Kotlikoff and Sebastian Pinera, "The Old South's Stake in the Inter-Regional Movement of Slaves, 1850–1860," *Journal of Economic History* 37 (June 1977): 434–50; Richard G. Lowe and Randolph B. Campbell, "The Slave-Breeding Hypothesis: A Demographic Comment on the 'Buying' and 'Selling' States," *JSH* 42 (Aug. 1976): 401–12; Peter D. McClelland and Richard J. Zeckhauser, *Demographic Dimensions of the New Republic: American Interregional Migration, Vital Statistics, and Manumissions, 1800–1860* (Cambridge: Cambridge University Press, 1983), esp. 52–53, 159–64; William L. Miller, "A Note on the Importance of the Interstate Slave Trade of the Ante Bellum South," *Journal of Political Economy* 73 (April 1965): 181–87; Jonathan B. Pritchett and Herman Freudenberger, "A Peculiar Sample: The Selection of Slaves for the New Orleans Market," *Journal of Economic History* 52 (March 1992): 109–27; Michael Tadman, "Slave Trading in the Ante-Bellum South: An Estimate of the Extent of the Inter-Regional Trade," *Journal of American Studies* 13 (Aug. 1979): 195–220; Alrutheus A. Taylor, "The Movement of Negroes from the East to the Gulf States from 1830 to 1850," *JNH* 8 (Oct. 1923): 367–83; and Kilsdonk, "Economic Development of the Greater Chesapeake."

42. Although I argue in *Twice Condemned* that slaves convicted of crimes had predominantly been engaged in individual or group resistance to aspects of slavery, if not to slavery itself, there obviously were exceptions. It remains true that resistance was the driving force behind white leaders' definitions of major crime. Thus Langbein's objections to Hay's argument concerning crime in England cannot significantly help the analysis of most slave convicts. See Langbein, "Albion's Fatal Flaws," 96–120; and Hay, "Property, Authority, and the Criminal Law," 17–63.

43. Between 1785 and 1831 at least 142 Virginian slaves were convicted of insurrectionary plotting or action. Forty-six of them were transported; 76 went to the gallows; 13 were pardoned; 4 received corporal punishment; 1 escaped or died in prison; and the punishment of 2 is unknown. In contrast, at least 15 slaves were found guilty of plotting or attempting to start an insurrection between 1832 and 1865—5 in 1840; 2 in 1843; 1 each in 1857, 1859, 1860, and 1861; and 2 each in 1864 and 1865. Five of them were hanged—2 in 1840, 2 in 1864, and 1 in 1865—and the other

10 were transported or sent to labor on the public works. See Schwarz, *Twice Condemned*, 248, 255–79, 308–11, 323–35.

44. Aptheker, *American Negro Slave Revolts*, 34–39, 49–52, 325–67; Genovese, *From Rebellion to Revolution*, 106–17; Ulrich B. Phillips, *American Negro Slavery: A Survey of the Supply, Employment, and Control of Negro Labor as Determined by the Plantation Regime* (New York: D. Appleton, 1918), 482–88; Wyatt-Brown, *Southern Honor*, 405–7. In *"Been in the Storm So Long": The Aftermath of Slavery* (New York: Knopf, 1979), 138, Leon Litwack suggests that slaves brought to Louisiana and Mississippi from "the more 'benign' slaveholding states" may account for the higher level of slave disaffection there during the Civil War. The most recent discussion of disagreements concerning slavery within the South is William W. Freehling, *The Road to Disunion: Secessionists at Bay, 1776–1854*. One of the most intriguing hints of possible transmission of a tradition of resistance from Virginia to the Deep South appears in an interview of an African American man in the 1970s. He reported that his father in Louisiana "named me Gabr'l for one of them slavery-time prophets, and you better believe there is some power in that name." See John Langston Gwaltney, *Drylongso: A Self-Portrait of Black America* (New York: Random House, 1980), 127.

45. John W. Blassingame and Mary Frances Berry, *Long Memory: The Black Experience in America* (New York: Oxford University Press, 1982), 233; Sellin, *Slavery and the Penal System*, esp. 145. Sellin argues that the convict-lease system was simply an extension of slavery beyond 1865. See also William Cohen, "Negro Involuntary Servitude in the South, 1865–1940: A Preliminary Analysis," *JSH* 42 (Feb. 1976): 31–60; and Jack Temple Kirby, *Westmoreland Davis: Virginia Planter-Politician, 1859–1942* (Charlottesville: University Press of Virginia, 1948), 98–103. Virginia also made extensive use of its penitentiary. See, e.g., Virginia Department of Corrections, Register of Convicts, Penitentiary, 1865–84, Library of Virginia; Virginia Penitentiary, Board of Directors, *Annual Report*, 1878, 26–27, 1879, 24–25, 1880, 31, 1881, 33. See also Ayers, *Vengeance and Justice*, 67, 185–222.

46. Patterson, *Slavery and Social Death*, esp. 5.

47. Other states or colonies transported condemned slaves to various jurisdictions. The experience of the Old Dominion provides an excellent

introduction to the study of other slave societies' reliance on that penal practice. There are, for example, indications that authorities in both Jamaica and Louisiana shipped convict slaves to Spanish Florida. See *Payne ads. Robinson,* Harper 279 (Florida), Jan. 1824, and *Navigation Co. v. Mayor, etc. of New Orleans,* 1 Mart. La. 269, Spring 1811, both excerpted in Catterall, ed., *Judicial Cases* 2:327–28, 3:448. See also Michael M. Craton, *Searching for the Invisible Man: Slaves and Plantation Life in Jamaica* (Cambridge, Mass.: Harvard University Press, 1978), 253; David Lowenthal and Colin G. Clarke, "Slave-Breeding in Barbuda: The Past of a Negro Myth," in *Comparative Perspectives on Slavery in New World Plantation Societies,* ed. Rubin and Tuden, 521; and Phillips, *American Negro Slavery,* 456.

CHAPTER 5: "THE FULL AND PERFECT ENFORCEMENT OF OUR RIGHTS"

1. William Still, *The Underground Railroad* (Philadelphia: Porter and Coates, 1872), 235–40; Journal C of Station no. 2 of the Underground Railroad (Philadelphia, Agent William Still), 1852–1857, PASP, reel 32, at Nov. 13, 1854. The journal contains almost all of the same material as Still's book, but it also specifies the date of Gilbert's arrival in Philadelphia. See also Julie Winch, "Philadelphia and the Other Underground Railroad," *Pennsylvania Magazine of History and Biography* 111 (Jan. 1987): 3–25.

2. Trial of Lott Mundy, City of Richmond Hustings Court, Aug. 12, 1856, VEPLR. Part of the declining population of free African American seamen, Mundy probably expected little or no protection from the white hands. See W. Jeffrey Bolster, "'To Feel Like a Man': Black Seamen in the Northern States, 1800–1860," *JAH* 76 (March 1990): 1173–99.

3. Paul Singleton, "The Keziah Affair" (M.A. thesis, Virginia State University, 1963).

4. Stanley Campbell, *The Slave Catchers: Enforcement of the Fugitive Slave Law, 1850–1860* (Chapel Hill: University of North Carolina Press, 1970); Larry Gara, *The Liberty Line: The Legend of the Underground Railroad* (Lexington: University Press of Kentucky, 1961); Paul Finkelman, ed., *Slavery in the Courtroom: An Annotated Bibliography of*

American Cases (Washington, D.C.: Library of Congress, 1985), 58–137; Paul Finkelman, ed., *Fugitive Slaves, Articles on American Slavery,* vol. 6 (New York: Garland, 1989); Paul Finkelman, *An Imperfect Union: Slavery, Federalism, and Comity* (Chapel Hill: University of North Carolina Press, 1981); Thomas D. Morris, *Free Men All: The Personal Liberty Laws of the North, 1780–1861* (Baltimore: Johns Hopkins University Press, 1974); Robert M. Cover, *Justice Accused: Antislavery and the Judicial Process* (New Haven, Conn.: Yale University Press, 1975), 87–93, 175–93.

5. Larry Gara has argued that the Fugitive Slave Act of 1850 was a southern "concession to nationalism, and a recognition by the South that when problems exceeded the ability of the states to solve them the power of the national government should be brought into play." See Gara, "The Fugitive Slave Law: A Double Paradox," *CWH* 10 (Sept. 1964): 229–40. For a general discussion of fugitive slaves in Virginia, see Green, "Urban Industry, Black Resistance, and Racial Restriction," 471–500, 504–26, 710–13; Hickin, "Antislavery in Virginia," 71–106; and Ervin L. Jordan Jr., *Black Confederates,* 69–90.

6. Mullin, *Flight and Rebellion;* Windley, ed., *Runaway Slave Advertisements,* vol. 1. See also Meaders, "Fugitive Slaves and Indentured Servants," 56–120, 208–25. The work in progress by Philip D. Morgan and Michael L. Nicholls, titled "Runaway Slaves in Eighteenth-Century Virginia: A New World Perspective," promises to yield rich insights.

7. Wood, *Black Majority;* Windley, ed., *Runaway Slave Advertisements,* vol. 1. On slaves fleeing from Albany City and County, New York, to the French enemy in Canada, see Hurd, *Law of Freedom and Bondage* 1:280–81.

8. Mullin, *Flight and Rebellion,* 130–36; Benjamin Quarles, *The Negro in the American Revolution* (Chapel Hill: University of North Carolina Press, 1961), 19–32, 111–33; Frey, *Water from the Rock,* 45–171.

9. Shane White, *Somewhat More Independent: The End of Slavery in New York City, 1770–1810* (Athens: University of Georgia Press, 1991); Gary B. Nash, *Race and Revolution* (Madison, Wis.: Madison House, 1990); Gary B. Nash and Jean R. Soderlund, *Freedom by Degrees: Emancipation in Pennsylvania and Its Aftermath* (New York: Oxford University

Press, 1991); Arthur Zilversmit, *The First Emancipation: The Abolition of Slavery in the North* (Chicago: University of Chicago Press, 1967).

10. See Gara, *Liberty Line*.

11. Edmund S. Morgan, *American Slavery, American Freedom*, 216–17; Mullin, *Flight and Rebellion*, 107, 109, 111. For laws, see Hening, ed., *Statutes at Large* 1:253–55, 483, 517–18, 2:26, 187–88, 239, 266, 273–74, 277–79, 395, 3:270–75, 447–62, 5:547–58, 6:356–69, 8:135–37, 358–61, 12:192–93; and Shepherd, ed., *Statutes at Large* 1:179–82.

12. T. H. Breen and Stephen Innes, *"Myne Owne Ground": Race and Freedom on Virginia's Eastern Shore, 1640–1676* (New York: Oxford University Press, 1980), 28–29, 65–67, 106–7.

13. Hening, ed., *Statutes at Large* 2:26, 35, 117, 277–79, 299–300, 3:86–88, 455–61, 4:126–34, 168–75, 5:552–57, 6:109–10, 363–67, 8:135–37, 358–61, 522, 12:182–83, 192–93; Shepherd, ed., *Statutes at Large* 2:78; *Acts of the General Assembly*, 1814–15, 53.

14. Hening, ed., *Statutes at Large* 3:455–58 (1705). These returned slaves were supposed to be whipped only before a justice of the peace.

15. Hening, ed., *Statutes at Large* 5:552–57, 555 (1748), and as repassed in 1753, 6:363–67.

16. Ibid., 3:86–88; see also 8:358–61.

17. Ibid., 7:363–67; Van Schreeven, comp., *Revolutionary Virginia* 5:64n20.

18. Shepherd, ed., *Statutes at Large* 1:363–65. It was this law that required suits in *forma pauperis* for recovery of freedom. See also statement of Archibald McLean, Alexandria Society for Promoting the Abolition of Slavery, Feb. 15, 1796, and George Drinker to Joseph Bringhurst[?], Alexandria, Dec. 10, 1804, PASP, ser. 2, reel 12.

19. Shepherd, ed., *Statutes at Large* 2:77–78; McColley, *Slavery and Jeffersonian Virginia*, 91–101; Berlin, *Slaves Without Masters*, 82–83. Contemporary testimony from the Pennsylvania Abolition Society reveals the weakness of the tangible threat. Adopted address to the American [Anti-Slavery] Convention, General Meeting, Minute Book, vol. 2, 1800–24, p. 25, 6 Mo. 30th, 1817, PASP, reel 1. The section on free people conspiring with slaves is one of the laws under which John Brown would be tried in 1859.

20. Shepherd, ed., *Statutes at Large* 3:123–24.

21. "A List of Prisoners in the Penitentiary on 1st July 1810," VEPLR, no. 74, Isaac Austin, admitted April 1, 1809, for a five-year term for slave stealing, and no. 76, Joseph Liggan, admitted April 21, 1809, for a four-and-one-half-year term for a second offense of "abetting the stealing of a slave." Sentences of more than four years suggest that Austin and Liggan were charged with the older variety of slave stealing.

22. The two acts appear in Shepherd, ed., *Statutes at Large* 3:290, Jan. 12, 1807; and in *Acts of the General Assembly,* 1807–8, 23, Feb. 1, 1808.

23. *Acts of the General Assembly,* 1813–14, 34–35, Jan. 10, 1814; *Acts of the General Assembly,* 1814–15, 53–54, Jan. 6, 1815.

24. *Acts of the General Assembly,* 1816–17, 36–38, Feb. 22, 1817.

25. Isaac A. Walton Jr. to Robert Walton, mayor of Philadelphia, Poplar Tree, Greensville County, Va., March 25, 1816; To Whom It May Concern from ?, Philadelphia, April 9, 1816; James Harris to "My dear Wife," Phoebe Harris, Sussex Courthouse, Va., June 5, 1816; Mayor John Hinton of Petersburg to Mayor Wharton of Philadelphia, July 1, 1816; Thomas Shipley to Mayor John Hinton, Philadelphia, July 13, 1816; James Harris to Robert Walton, Mathews Courthouse, Virginia, Aug. 11, 1816; Mayor John Hinton to ?, Petersburg, Sept. 18, 1816, all in PASP, ser. 2, reel 12. The law requiring sale after one year was passed on February 1, 1808. See *Acts of the General Assembly,* 1807–8, 23–24. The process of executing such sales was modified by a law of February 5, 1822. See *Acts of the General Assembly,* 1821–22, 23–24. On kidnapping, see Carol Wilson, "'The Thought of Slavery Is Death to a Free Man': Abolitionists' Response to the Kidnapping of Free Blacks," *Mid-America* 74 (April–July 1992): 105–24.

26. *Acts of the General Assembly,* 1816–17, 36–38, Feb. 22, 1817; *Acts of the General Assembly,* 1822–23, 37–38, Feb. 17, 1823.

27. *Acts of the General Assembly,* 1835–36, 49–50, March 21, 1836; 64–66, March 23, 1836; 1839, 47, March 11, 1839.

28. See *Acts of the General Assembly,* 1846–47, 75–77, March 18, 1847; 1847–48, 102 (revision of the Criminal Code). Some slave owners worried about stagecoaches as well. A Fairfax County resident complained to Governor William B. Giles in 1827 that black hack drivers drove by his

residence and enticed slaves to run away. With the drivers' aid, fugitives could reach Philadelphia before being missed. A stage could leave Alexandria on Saturday night and arrive at Baltimore on Sunday night, in time for the evening steamboat to Philadelphia. See William Moss to Governor William B. Giles, May 9, 1827, VEPLR.

29. *Acts of the General Assembly*, 1836–37, 101, March 25, 1837.

30. David Walker, *David Walker's Appeal, in Four Articles, Together with a Preamble, to the Coloured Citizens of the World, But in Particular, and Very Expressly, to Those of the United States of America*, edited by Charles M. Wiltse (New York: Hill and Wang, 1965); Alison G. Freehling, *Drift Toward Dissolution*.

31. On assaults by slaves, see Schwarz, *Twice Condemned*, 246–49, 255–79.

32. Ibid., 282, 306–12.

33. Brown, *Narrative of the Life of Henry Box Brown*, 37–38.

34. Upshur to Floyd, Oct. 4, 1832, VEPLR. On the incident in question, see deposition of Peter Bowdoin, Oct. 4, 1832, William S. Floyd to Governor John Floyd, Northampton, Oct. 4, 1832, VEPLR; Virginia Council Journal, April 3, 1832–March 30, 1833, 156, 169–70. On similar incidents in neighboring Accomack County, see Colonel Joynes and others to Governor William B. Giles, Aug. 13, 1829, VEPLR; and Virginia Council Journals, March 31, 1836–March 30, 1837, 143, 184, 195–96. There had definitely been earlier incidents in Northampton: see John Eyre to Governor Giles, Aug. 27, 1829, Eastville Resolution, Aug. 26, 1829, VEPLR.

35. *Acts of the General Assembly*, 1833–34, 77–81, March 11, 1834; 1834–35, 161–65, 149, March 10, 1835.

36. Society for the Prevention of the Absconding and Abduction of Slaves, Richmond, Va., Minutes, 1833–49, VHS, photocopy of original, which is at the New York Historical Society; resolutions of meeting of Aug. 3, 1835, Library of Virginia, acc. no. 26728. One year later a Virginia government official sought information from U.S. Secretary of State John Forsyth concerning possible agreements with Great Britain concerning the return of fugitive slaves from Canada. There were no such agreements then, and any agreements later negotiated were interpreted by British officials in favor of some, but not all, fugitives. See

Alexander L. Murray, "The Extradition of Fugitive Slaves from Canada: A Re-evaluation," *Canadian Historical Review* 43 (Dec. 1962): 298–314.

37. For thorough discussions of the context, circumstances, and significance of this episode, see Paul Finkelman, "The Protection of Black Rights in Seward's New York," *CWH* 34 (Sept. 1988): 211–34; and idem, "States' Rights, Federalism, and Criminal Extradition in Antebellum America: The New York–Virginia Controversy, 1839–1846," in *German and American Constitutional Thought: Contexts, Interaction, and Historical Realities*, edited by Hermann Wellenreuther et al. (Oxford, Eng.: Berg Publishers, 1990), 293–327. See also *Acts of the General Assembly*, 1839–40, 155–69, Resolution no. 1, March 17, 1840; 1840–41, 79–82, March 13, 1841; 1840–41, 157, Resolution no. 1, March 16, 1841; 1840–41, 157, Resolution no. 2, March 20, 1841; 1842–43, 60, March 27, 1843; 1844–45, 61–62, Feb. 18, 1845; 1845–46, 67–68, March 5, 1846. See Virginia Executive Letterbook, 1839–44. For a smaller-scale, yet similar case in 1806 and 1807, see indictment of Sarah, slave of James Pindall, for stealing his horse, Aug. 9, 1808; note of Virginia Council action, Dec. 15, 1809; governor of Pennsylvania to Fayette County sheriff, Feb. 3, 1810; governor of Pennsylvania to Governor John Tyler of Virginia, Feb. 3, 1810; Council Note, Feb. 1810; governor of Ohio to Governor Tyler, March 22, 1810; Jacob Beeson to Tyler, April 7, June 11, 1810, Jan. 10, 1811; Council Note, May 21–31, 1810; Joseph Tomlinson release of claim to Jane, June 11, 1810, all in VEPLR. (The Beeson letter of 1811 is inexplicably in the folder dated Jan. 1–15, 1818.)

38. Reports of increasing escapes from the Martinsburg area of Virginia to Pennsylvania increased at this time. See Merton L. Dillon, *Slavery Attacked: Southern Slaves and Their Allies, 1619–1865* (Baton Rouge: Louisiana State University Press, 1990), 232.

39. *Acts of the General Assembly*, 1840–41, 82, Feb. 10, 1841; 82–84, March 13, 1841.

40. The state records do not differentiate between stealing slaves for profit and stealing to help runaways.

41. E.g., affidavit of Dr. Thomas J. L. Nottingham, Dec. 15, 1845, VEPLR, Jan. 1846 folder; *The Latimer Case* (which involved a fugitive slave from Norfolk, Va.), 5 Month L. Rep. 481 (Mass. Cir. Ct. 1842);

Finkelman, *Slavery in the Courtroom*, 64–68; Paul Finkelman, ed., *Fugitive Slaves and American Courts: The Pamphlet Literature*, Slavery and the American Legal System, 1700–1872, 16 vols. (New York: Garland, 1988), ser. 2, 1:157–230; Cover, *Justice Accused*, 169–71; Thomas D. Morris, *Free Men All*, 109–12; Campbell, *Slave Catchers*, 13–14; Leonard W. Levy, *The Law of the Commonwealth and Chief Justice Shaw: The Evolution of American Law, 1830–1860* (Cambridge: Harvard University Press, 1957), 78–85.

42. *Prigg v. Pennsylvania*, 16 Peters 539 (1842); *Jones v. Van Zandt*, 5 Howard 215 (1847). For discussions of *Prigg*, see Paul Finkelman, "*Prigg v. Pennsylvania* and Northern State Courts: Anti-Slavery Use of a Pro-Slavery Decision," *CWH* 24 (March 1979): 5–35, reprinted in *Fugitive Slaves (Articles on American Slavery)*, ed. Finkelman, 6:107–37; idem, "Sorting Out *Prigg v. Pennsylvania*," *Rutgers Law Journal* 24 (Spring 1993): 605–65; Barbara Holden-Smith, "Lords of the Lash, Loom, and Law: Justice Story, Slavery, and *Prigg v. Pennsylvania*," *Cornell Law Review* 78 (July 1993): 1086–1151.

43. "Preamble and Resolutions relative to the legislation of congress upon the subject of fugitive slaves, and suggesting additional legislation thereon," *Acts of the General Assembly*, 1849–50, 240–54, Feb. 7, 1849. This was also printed as *Report of a Select Committee Appointed under a Resolution of the House to Enquire into the Existing Legislation of Congress upon the Subject of Fugitive Slaves, and to Suggest such Additional Legislation as May Be Proper*, Virginia General Assembly, 1848–49 (House of Delegates), Document no. 50 (Richmond, Va., 1848). For "frontier" cases, see Alexander Laidly to acting governor Wyndham Robertson, Aug. 8, 10, 1836, deposition of Laidly, Aug. 11, 1836, Philip R. Thompson to Robertson, Aug. 1836, and Sherrard Clemens to Governor William Smith, Nov. 12, 1847, VEPLR.

44. "Preamble and Resolutions," 253.

45. Campbell, *Slave Catchers*, 15; William W. Freehling, *Road to Disunion* 1:502–5; James L. Bugg, "The Political Career of James Murray Mason" (Ph.D. diss., University of Virginia, 1950), 362–63; Marion Gleason McDougall, *Fugitive Slaves, 1619–1865* (Boston: Ginn and Co., 1891), 110–14; *Congressional Globe*, 1849–50, vol. 21, pt. 1, p. 233.

46. Bugg, "Political Career of James Murray Mason," 362–63; *Congressional Globe*, 1849–50, vol. 21, pt. 1, p. 233. There are enough similarities between the federal statute and the provisions recommended by the Virginia Assembly to raise the question of the degree of Virginia's influence on the Fugitive Slave Act of 1850. When some of Sheridan's troops burned Mason's home and papers, however, they probably destroyed evidence relevant to this question. See Frank Lawrence Owsley, *Dictionary of American Biography*, s.v. "Mason, James Murray"; *Statutes at Large of the United States*, 31st Cong., 1st sess., 9:462–65. Lurking behind the appeal of Virginians to federal aid was a real dilemma. Slaveholding states feared a strong federal government, which they nevertheless needed in order to suppress "slave stealing."

47. *Acts of the General Assembly*, 1850–51, 37, March 31, 1851.

48. Campbell, *Slave Catchers;* Finkelman, *Slavery in the Courtroom*, 85–119; Finkelman, ed., *Fugitive Slaves and American Courts*, ser. 2, 2:343–490, 3:1–330; Levy, *Law of the Commonwealth*, 87–91, 105–6. Burns had escaped Virginia by secreting himself on a northern ship at Richmond's docks. See Jane H. Pease and William H. Pease, *The Fugitive Slave Law and Anthony Burns: A Problem in Law Enforcement* (Philadelphia: Lippincott, 1975); John D'Entremont, *Southern Emancipator: Moncure Conway, the American Years* (New York: Oxford University Press, 1987), 82–84. On the antebellum judicial experience of a Deep South state with fugitive slave cases, see Judith Kelleher Schafer, *Slavery, the Civil Law, and the Supreme Court of Louisiana* (Baton Rouge: Louisiana State University Press, 1994), 90–126.

49. Virginia, General Assembly, House of Delegates, *Journal of the House of Delegates*, 1855–56, 39–40, 73, 89–90. On guarded use of the proposed exception during the Civil War, see Ervin L. Jordan Jr., *Black Confederates*, 73.

50. *Richmond Daily Dispatch*, Feb. 14, 26, March 18, 1856; *Acts of the General Assembly*, 1855–56, 45, March 5, 1856.

51. *Richmond Daily Dispatch*, March 18, 1856; *Acts of the General Assembly*, 1855–56, 38–44, March 17, 1856.

52. Commission of an inspector, March 26, 1856, VEPLR, April 1856 folder. On flaws that Wise attempted to correct, see D. Tunsten[?] to Gov-

ernor Henry A. Wise, Alexandria, April 17, 1856; T. B. Robertson to Governor Wise, Alexandria, July 30, 1856; application of Thomas Cropper to Governor Wise for post of chief inspector, Norfolk, April 1858, May 1858; Addison Hall to Wise, Kilmarnock, June 1, 1858; James Luffsey to Wise, Petersburg, June 2, 1858; John F. D. Robinson to Wise, Urbanna, Aug. 19, 1858, VEPLR.

53. J. J. Simkins report to Governor Henry A. Wise for the fourth quarter of 1856, Jan. 12, 1857, VEPLR.

54. In the Slave Schedules of the 1850 and 1860 U.S. Census, enumerators were supposed to indicate those slaves who were "Fugitives from the State" in the sixth column of their printed forms. The uselessness of these forms for statistical aggregation or comparison is obvious upon inspection. For example, the 1850 schedules for Accomack County on the Eastern Shore, one of the most vulnerable counties in the state, contain only one check mark for a fugitive, and that mark may very well be a smudge or stray line. Yet the schedules for 1860 show 145 slaves gone from the county and out of the state. Only 13 slaves are singled out as fugitives in the 1850 schedules for the entire city of Richmond and the surrounding county of Henrico, and only 17 in the 1860 schedules. A similarly inconsistent and implausible pattern exists in the slave schedules for other counties.

55. Local officials in Maryland were willing to cooperate with Virginia officials. See sheriff of Washington County, Maryland, to George W. Munford, Secretary of the Commonwealth, Oct. 23, 1858, VEPLR.

56. Trial of Lott Mundy, City of Richmond Hustings Court, Aug. 12, 1856, VEPLR; Still, *Underground Railroad*, 235–40; Journal C of Station no. 2 of the Underground Railroad (Philadelphia, Agent William Still), 1852–57, PASP, reel 32, at Nov. 13, 1854.

57. Business associates to Governor Henry A. Wise, Jan. 8, 1856; petition of Lambdin's business associates, May 21, 1856; Edward T. Taylor to Wise, May 26, 1856; Mary Emma (Mrs. William) Lambdin to Wise, May 12, 1858; B. T. Cox to Wise, May 15, 1858; Thomas Young, mayor of Wilmington, Delaware, to Wise, Oct. 27, 1858; petition of Delaware citizens, received Dec. 7, 1858; William Lambdin to Wise, June 18, 1856, Dec. 1858, VEPLR. The building fear is apparent in a letter of January 2,

1857, from James Roy Micou of Essex County to Governor Henry A. Wise (in VEPLR), in which Micou complained of a white peddler who had recently passed through Tappahannock and who had been heard talking with slaves and asking if they wished to be free. All peddlers in Virginia should thereafter report to county justices, Micou angrily urged.

58. *Richmond Whig and Public Advertiser,* June 2, 1858; petition of Willett Mott, Richmond, Aug. 24, 1858, with accompanying materials, VEPLR, Sept. 1858; Singleton, "Keziah Affair."

59. *Richmond Daily Dispatch,* June 2, 1858.

60. *Richmond Daily Dispatch,* June 11, 1858; Singleton, "Keziah Affair," 65–67. Bayliss's case would be pleaded to the state chief executive in a manner similar to the petitions for Lambdin. Although some secondary sources state that federal soldiers freed Bayliss in April 1865, Governor William Smith pardoned Bayliss because of age and illness in January 1865. William Storrs to President Jefferson Davis, Nov. 12, 17, 1864, VEPLR; Singleton, "Keziah Affair," 80–81; Virginia Writers' Project, Works Projects Administration, comp., *Negro in Virginia,* 138; Governor William Smith's endorsement of the pardon of Bayliss, Jan. 17, 1865, VEPLR, Jan.–April 1865, pardons; Executive Department, Governor's Office, Secretary of the Commonwealth, Executive Journal, Nov. 2, 1863–April 1, 1865, 492–93. Smith commented that Bayliss was "one of that pestilent class which have been the main cause of our present trouble."

61. *Richmond Daily Dispatch,* June 11, 1858; Singleton, "Keziah Affair," 80–96; Hickin, "Antislavery in Virginia," 74–76. See table 5.3.

62. Edmund Ruffin, *Two Great Evils of Virginia, and Their One Common Remedy,* 2d ed. (Richmond, Va., 1859). The pamphlet is addressed "To the Members elect of the General Assembly of Virginia." See Ruffin, *Diary* 1:152, 205, 207, 328, 340–42, 346–48, 355.

63. Clay quoted in Bugg, "Political Career of James Murray Mason," 381. For a thorough discussion of wartime and postwar disruptions to the slave economy of the tobacco-belt counties, see Lynda J. Morgan, *Emancipation in Virginia's Tobacco Belt, 1850–1870* (Athens: University of Georgia Press, 1992), 87–123. The first volume of *Freedom* also contains ample evidence of the same kinds of disruption. See Ira Berlin, ed.,

The Destruction of Slavery, vol. 1 of *Freedom: A Documentary History of Emancipation, 1861–1867*, ser. 1 (New York: Cambridge University Press, 1985).

64. *Acts of the General Assembly*, 1861, appendix, "Ordinances Adopted by the Convention of Virginia in Secret Session," 35–36, May 1, 1861, Ordinance no. 43.

65. *Acts of the General Assembly*, 1861–62, 104, chap. 86, "An Act to prevent the Escape of Slaves in Tide Water Counties"; *Acts of the General Assembly*, 1862 (called session), 6–8, chap. 2, Oct. 3, 1862, "An Act to further provide for the Public Defence." The latter act provided for the calling up of slaves for support of the war effort, yet promised payment of compensation to owners whose slaves absconded while in such service. For a discussion of these and similar measures, see Ervin L. Jordan Jr., *Black Confederates*, 72–73, 76–77.

66. *Acts of the General Assembly*, 1862 (called session), 12–15, chap. 6, Oct. 3, 1862, "An Act to protect and indemnify Citizens of Virginia." Section 5 provided that anyone who aided in carrying out the confiscation and emancipation laws of the United States was liable to owners for double the value of the "property" plus 6 percent per annum plus penalties.

67. See Virginia Senate *Journal*, Dec, 7, 1863, Governor's Message, 22–23. Governor John Letcher said that several convict "negroes" hired to J. R. Anderson and Company had absconded within the previous year and probably had gone to the enemy lines. Convicts hired at furnaces near war lines are "hard to restrain and keep in proper subjection," Letcher continued, "and are therefore much more likely to effect their escape." See also certificate of Oct. 17, 1863, Powhatan County, VEPLR; Ervin L. Jordan Jr., *Black Confederates*, 50–52; and Berlin, ed., *Destruction of Slavery*, 782–84, 807–8.

68. Runaway and Escaped Slaves, Receipts and Reports, 1806–59, 1863, Auditor's Office, Library of Virginia. The 1863 sections are county and city reports of slaves escaped to the enemy from the beginning of the war to February 1, 1863, and later. Several separate returns were filed for some counties; no returns were filed for others. See Ervin L. Jordan Jr., *Black Confederates*, 72, 342.

69. *Acts of the General Assembly,* 1863 (adjourned session), 122–23, Resolution no. 4, Jan. 27, 1863, "Resolution to authorize the Governor to suspend the law of the 3rd Oct. 1862 to further provide for the Public Defence, so far as it applies to those Counties whose loss of Slaves has been so great as to interfere with the Agricultural Products of said Counties"; *Acts of the General Assembly,* 1863 (adjourned session), 42–46, chap. 6, March 13, 1863, "An Act to amend and re-enact an act further to provide for the Public Defence, passed October 3, 1862"; *Acts of the General Assembly,* 1863 (called session), 4–6, chap. 5, Oct. 10, 1863, "An Act to amend and re-enact the 1st and 3d sections of an act passed March 13th, 1863, entitled an act to amend and re-enact an act further to provide for the Public Defence, passed October 3, 1862." The law that required lists of escaped slaves is in *Acts of the General Assembly,* 1863 (adjourned session), 33–34, chap. 1, March 28, 1863.

70. The hesitation of the Union concerning emancipation as a war measure before January 1863 is apparent in a federal law passed in July 1862, which declared that no slave escaping from one state into another would be returned, *except for a crime,* to a *dis*loyal owner. See *Statutes at Large of the United States* 12:354, 589, July 17, 1862.

71. The *Creole* affair involved Virginian fugitives as well, but in the completely unique context of the high seas. See Cover, *Justice Accused,* 109–16; Howard Jones, "Peculiar Institution and National Honor," 28–50; Hickin, "Antislavery in Virginia," 89–93.

CONCLUSION

1. Henry County Court Minute Books, 1783–1900, Library of Virginia; Virginia Department of Corrections, Register of Convicts, Penitentiary, 1865–84, 32, 80, 85, 90, 107, 110–11, 121, 133–35, 165, 169, 186, 188, 194, 208–9.

2. Elizabeth Seawell Hairston, *The Hairstons and Penns and Their Relations* (Roanoke, Va., 1940); Virginia D. Pedigo and Lewis G. Pedigo, *History of Patrick and Henry Counties, Virginia* (Roanoke, Va.: Stone Printing, 1933), 147–57; Judith Parks America Hill, *History of Henry County, Virginia* (Martinsville, Va.: J. P. A. Hill, 1925), 80–82, 188–94; *Notes on*

Virginia, no. 20 (1980): 14, no. 26 (1985): 18; *Florida Sentinel*, June 20, 1854, quoted in Julia Floyd Smith, *Slavery and Plantation Growth in Antebellum Florida, 1821–1860* (Gainesville: University of Florida Press, 1973), 32n17; *Richmond Whig and Public Advertiser*, Feb. 7, 1851, quoted in Joseph Clarke Robert, *The Tobacco Kingdom: Plantation, Market, and Factory in Virginia and North Carolina, 1800–1860* (Durham, N.C.: Duke University Press, 1938), 19.

I attempted to check the slaveholdings of Samuel Hairston. I was unable to make a final reckoning, but his holdings were clearly quite large. See U.S. Census, 1850, Slave Schedules, Henry County, 705, 713, 715, 723–25; U.S. Census, 1860, Slave Schedules, Henry County, 4, 6–11, 25, 28–29, 54–63; Virginia Bureau of Vital Statistics, (WPA) Index to Births of Slaves, 1853–66, esp. 352–53; Agnes J. P. Hairston Journal, Feb. 1864–Dec. 1879, Wilson and Hairston Papers, Southern Historical Collection, University of North Carolina, microfilm, reel 69, vol. 169.

3. Ethel L. Williams, *Biographical Directory of Negro Ministers*, 3d. ed. (Boston: G. K. Hall, 1975), 201–2, Rev. Samuel Henry Hairston, born in Henry County; *Who's Who Among Black Americans*, vol. 1, *1975–1976* (Northbrook, Ill.: Who's Who Among Black Americans Publishing Co., 1976), 256, Joseph Henry Hairston, born in Henry County; Robert E. Tomasson, "1,400 Hairstons Honor Kinship Born of Slavery," *New York Times*, Sept. 10, 1989, sec. 1, p. 26. I do not know whether professional football player Carl Hairston is from the Virginia, the North Carolina, or the Mississippi branch of the African American Hairstons.

4. Fernald to Brown, June 30, 1867, Records of the Freedmen's Bureau in Virginia, National Archives and Records Service, microfilm, reel 60.

5. 109 U.S. 3 (1883).

6. 163 U.S. 537 (1896).

7. Charles Black, in a panel discussion of *Brown v. Board of Education,* 347 U.S. 483 (1954), at the annual meeting of the American Society for Legal History, Williamsburg, Va., Nov. 1984.

8. *Code of Virginia*, 1860 ed., 783; *Code of Virginia* (Richmond, Va.: James E. Goode, 1873), 1188; *The Code of Virginia, 1950* (Charlottesville, Va.: Michie Co., 1950–), sec. 18.2–485.

INDEX

Boxley Plot, 110
Branigan, Nicholas, 108–9
Braxton (slave), 76
Brazil, 115
British soldiers: aid fugitive slaves, 128, 148
Brown (slave), 52
Brown, Henry Box, 132
Brown, John, 7
Brown, John G., 106–7
Brown, Mr., 51
Brown, Oliver, 151
Buckingham County, 45, 47
Burglary: 7; slaves accused of, 49
Burns, Anthony: returned to owner by federal government, 138–39

Cabell, William H., 91, 100–101, 107
Campbell, Archibald, 89
Campbell, Stanley, 148
Canada, 131; fugitive slaves in, 233 (n. 36)
Capital punishment: 7, 10, 63–96 passim; African, 22, 25–26; extreme methods of, African, 26; as more severe for slaves than for whites, 64, 72–75; decreased use of, against slaves, 64, 73, 75, 78, 81–82; of free people, 65; of slaves, South Carolina, 69; of free people, Massachusetts, 71; of free people, Pennsylvania, 71; extreme methods of, 72, 73, 89; of slaves, in relation to number of free people executed, 72, 74–75, 94; extreme methods of,

72–73; of free people, in relation to slave executions, 72–74; of free people, Great Britain, 73; of slaves, supported in individual cases, 74, 80, 84; of slaves, supported, 74, 80, 84, 86–87, 89, 109, 204; of slaves, opposed, 74, 80, 84, 86–87, 90–91, 100–101; of slaves, opposed in individual cases, 74, 80, 84, 93, 100–101; as deterrent, 82, 90, 93, 103; of slaves, sentencing procedures, 86–87; of slaves, frequency, 89, 95, 104; public, revulsion against, 92; public, slaves' scaffold speeches at, 94; as support of slavery, 95–96; of slaves condemned to death, cost of, 106; reluctance of judges to order, 112
Capital Punishment Research Project, 199
Carter, Landon, 86
Caruthers, John, 91
Cary (slave), 52
Cary, Mr.: attacked by slave (1706), 102
Catherine the Great, 36
Charlottesville, 45
Civil Rights Act of 1875, 152
Civil Rights Cases of 1883, 152
Civil War, 81, 100, 114–15, 132, 146, 149, 151
Clark, Henry, 52
Clay, Henry, 146
Clements, Benjamin, 76
Coles, Edward: slaves of, manumitted by, 57, 59

Mason, James Murray, 138–39
Masur, Louis, 35
McDowell, James, 90
Milledge, John, 109
Mississippi, 101, 107, 110
Monroe, James, 91, 100, 104, 106
Monticello, 35, 37–38, 43–47,
 50–53, 55; African Americans
 at, 37
Morgan, Edmund S., 3
Morris, Thomas D., 6
Morris, William, 106–7
Mott, Willard, 143–44
Mudd, Samuel, 108
Mullin, Gerald W., 123
Mundy, Lott, 120–21, 142–43

Nash, A. E. Keir, 6
Native Americans, 16
Nat Turner's Revolt, 10
Ned (slave), 47–49, 75, 91
New Jersey, 129, 133, 143
New Orleans, 51, 98, 107, 111, 130
Newton, John, 27
New York, 120–21, 129–30, 133,
 135, 142; refuses to extradite
 African Americans accused of
 aiding fugitive slaves, 135
Nicholas, Wilson Cary, 41
Norfolk, 89, 120, 132, 138, 140,
 142–44
Northampton County, 102, 133,
 136
North Carolina, 90, 109, 122, 124,
 130
Northerners: accused of aiding
 fugitive slaves, 127, 134; aid of
 fugitive slaves by, 131
Nullification crisis, 132

Ohio, 107, 114, 129, 131, 135, 145
Old Point Comfort, 120
Orange County, 46
Overseers, 45, 51, 53, 89, 95

Pardons, 9; of slaves condemned to
 death, 71, 93; governors
 required to publish reasons for,
 113
Partus sequitur ventrem, 40
Paternalism, 9
Patrick County, 150
Patterson, Orlando, 3, 39, 119
Patton, John M., 112
Peculium, 46, 58
Penal conditions: for free African
 Americans, 74; for free people,
 in Virginia, 74–75
Penal reform, United States, 74,
 100
Personal Liberty Laws, 136
Petersburg, 8, 121, 130, 143–44
Philadelphia, 46, 120–21, 130
Pierce (slave), 76
Pittsylvania County, 150
Plessy v. Ferguson, 152
Poisoning, 7
Poplar Forest, 42, 45, 47, 49, 51, 55
Prigg v. Pennsylvania, 136
Prince Edward County, 109
Punishment, 9
Puryear, Ellis, 109

Randolph (slave), 76
Randolph, A. Philip, 1
Randolph, John, of Roanoke, 59
Randolph, Thomas Jefferson, 56
Randolph, Thomas Mann, 46,
 51–52

Randolph, Thomas Mann, Jr.,
40, 46
Reid, Samuel McDowell, 92
Reprieves, 9; of slaves condemned
to death, 71; governors required
to publish reasons for, 113
Republicanism and slavery, 35
Resistance, slave, 2–3, 16, 31–32,
44, 47, 60, 64, 80, 83, 94–95,
110, 117, 156; African, 21
Reuther, Walter, 1
Richmond, 11, 44, 75–76, 80, 88,
90, 99, 106–7, 110, 113, 120,
128–29, 132, 134, 138, 142, 144,
150, 155
Richmond Common Council:
regulations of, concerning
fugitive slaves, 138
River pilots. *See* Inspectors
Robin (slave), 108
Robinson, Conway, 112
Roediger, David, 168 (n. 3)
Ruffin, Edmund, 145–46
Rutherfoord, John, 98, 111–12

Sellin, Thorsten, 119
Seward, William H., 135
Shadrack. *See* Wilkins, Frederick
Skelton, Martha Wayles, 40
Slave code, 112; residual effects of,
151; in relation to post–Civil
War white supremacist laws,
152
Slave convicts, 119; sent to hard
labor, 113–14, 118–19; escapes
of, 114; resented by white
citizens, 114; sent to hard labor
on public works, 114;

threatened with mob action,
114; and attitude toward labor
on the public works, 114, 119;
female, 115; female, auctioned
off, 115; names of, 116; attitude
toward transportation of, 119;
sent to hard labor on
fortifications, 119
Slave owners: legal relationship of,
to slaves, 60; subject to slave
laws, 60; rights of, 79;
compensated for executed
slaves, 87, 97, 99; compensated
for transported slaves, 88–89,
97, 99, 108; attempt to retrieve
fugitive slaves, 123, 139, 141;
suspicious of Northerners, 127;
unable to capture fugitive slaves
in the North, 136; exempted
from supplying slaves to the
Confederacy, 147
Slavery, 30; cultural interaction
involved in, xiii–xiv, 34;
political interaction involved in,
xiii–xiv, 34; African, 21; support
of, 80
Slaves: customary laws of, 8;
disputes among, 8; inheritance
of, 8, 40–41; hired, 11, 42, 45,
60; laws of, customary, 32–33;
legal relationship of, with
whites, 37; settlement on
children of, 40–41; purchases
of, 41; as security for debts,
41–43; as collateral, 42; hired,
liability for, 42; sales of, 43, 46;
control of, 43–44, 60, 64, 79, 95,
102, 114, 117; jailed, 45;

whipping of, 45, 48, 52, 59,
92–93; as agents of owners, 46;
overwork by, 46; paid for goods,
46; paid for services, 46; threat
of sale of, 46, 52; *peculium* of,
46, 58; preferences of, for
owners, 47; accused of theft,
47–50; executions of, 48, 63;
laws of, 48, 94; executions of,
extreme methods, 63, 72–73,
89; executions of, public, 63–64;
executions of, eighteenth
century, 65; executions of,
nineteenth century, 65;
executions of, number
compared to number of free
people executed, 65, 69;
reprieved from execution, 71;
pardoned, 71, 76, 78, 102–3;
criminal convictions of,
appealed, 72; attitudes of,
towards slave courts, 77, 87, 93;
trials of, "not guilty" verdicts
in, 78–79; as defendants in
capital cases, 79; rights of, 79,
93–95; influence of, on slave
court judges, 80–81; sentenced
to hard labor, 81; convicted of
murdering slaves, 84; convicted
of murdering whites, 84;
executions of, government
compensation to owners for, 86;
killing of other slaves by, 87;
attitudes of, toward capital
punishment, 93–94;
transported, sales of, 97;
punitive sales of, 101–3;
scaffold speeches of, 103;

private punishments of, 111;
names of, 115; ages of, 115–16;
traded from Virginia, 116;
aiding of fugitive slaves by, 123;
accused of aiding fugitive
slaves, 147. *See also* Benefit of
clergy; Capital punishment;
Fugitive slaves; Insurrection;
Lynching; Resistance, slave;
Slave convicts; Transported
slaves
Slave stealing, 127; abolitionists
accused of, 127; accusations of,
127
Slave trade, 20, 21, 106–7;
domestic, 98–99
Slave traders, 106–8, 110;
convicted of illegal importation
of transported slaves, 98. *See
also* Transportation
Smith, Venture, 13–14
Sobel, Mechal, 4
Society for the Prevention of the
Absconding and Abduction of
Slaves, 134
Southampton County, 76
South Carolina, 109
Spanish West Indies, 107
Stafford County, 76
Stagecoaches: as means of escape
by fugitive slaves, 232–33
(n. 28)
Staunton, Va., 107
St. Croix, 107
Steamboats, 143, 144; as means of
escape for fugitive slaves, 121,
134
Still, William, 144